ANARCHY AND ORDER

ANARCHY AND ORDER

Essays in Politics

by

HERBERT READ

INTRODUCTION BY HOWARD ZINN

Beacon Press   Boston

Introduction copyright © 1971 by Howard Zinn
First published in 1954 by Faber and Faber Limited
Printed by special arrangement with the Herbert Read
    Discretionary Trust
All rights reserved
Library of Congress catalog card number: 76-141875
International Standard Book Number: 0-8070-4393-1

Beacon Press books are published under the auspices of the
    Unitarian Universalist Association
Published simultaneously in Canada by Saunders of Toronto, Ltd.
Printed in the United States of America

CONTENTS

PREFACE

This volume assembles all the various essays that I have written specifically on the subject of Anarchism. There is no categorical separation, however, between what I have written on this subject and what I have written on social problems generally (*The Politics of the Unpolitical*) or on the social aspects of art (*Art and Society* and *The Grass Roots of Art*) or on the social aspects of education (*Education Through Art* and *Education for Peace*). The same philosophy reappears in my literary criticism and in my poetry.

The first essay is now published for the first time. The rest have been revised, sometimes drastically, but though I may here and there have removed a rash or ambiguous phrase, I have not attempted to give an air of caution to the impetuous voice of youth. Indeed, I now envy those generous occasions.

Poetry and Anarchism was first published by Messrs. Faber and Faber in 1938 as a separate volume, but it already included writings of an earlier date. *The Philosophy of Anarchism* was first published by the Freedom Press in 1940; *Existentialism, Marxism, and Anarchism* by the same press in 1949. 'The Paradox of Anarchism' has already appeared in *A Coat of Many Colours* (Routledge, 1945); and *Chains of Freedom* contains aphorisms and paragraphs from fugitive writings in a wide range of periodicals, the details of which would be tedious to enumerate.

H.R.

INTRODUCTION BY HOWARD ZINN
THE ART OF REVOLUTION

The word *anarchy* unsettles most people in the Western world; it suggests disorder, violence, uncertainty. We have good reason for fearing those conditions, because we have been living with them for a long time, not in anarchist societies (there have never been any) but in exactly those societies most fearful of anarchy—the powerful nation-states of modern times.

At no time in human history has there been such social chaos. Fifty million dead in the Second World War. More than a million dead in Korea, a million in Vietnam, half a million in Indonesia, hundreds of thousands dead in Nigeria, and in Mozambique. A hundred violent political struggles all over the world in the twenty years following the second war to end all wars. Millions starving, or in prisons, or in mental institutions. Inner turmoil to the point of large-scale alienation, confusion, unhappiness. Outer turmoil symbolized by huge armies, stores of nerve gas, and stockpiles of hydrogen bombs. Wherever men, women, and children are even a bit conscious of the world outside their local borders, they have been living with the ultimate uncertainty: whether or not the human race itself will survive into the next generation.

It is these conditions that the anarchists have wanted to end; to bring a kind of order to the world for the first time. We have never listened to them carefully, except through the hearing aids supplied by the guardians of disorder—the national government leaders, whether capitalist or socialist.

The order desired by anarchists is different from the order ("*Ordnung*," the Germans called it; "*law and order*," say the American politicians) of national governments. They want a voluntary forming of human relations, arising out of the needs

ix

of people. Such an order comes from within, and so is natural. People flow into easy arrangements, rather than being pushed and forced. It is like the form given by the artist, a form congenial, often pleasing, sometimes beautiful. It has the grace of a voluntary, confident act. Thus there is nothing surprising in Herbert Read, poet and philosopher of art, being an anarchist.

Read came to philosophical anarchism out of his special set of experiences: growing up in Yorkshire as the son of an English farmer, spending several years as a clerk in the industrial city of Leeds, going to the University there, writing poetry, entranced by art and literature—and then enduring the sounds and smells of war as a British Army Captain in World War I. For a while he was captivated, as were so many, by the Bolshevik Revolution, but the party dictatorship turned him firmly toward anarchism, which also seemed to fit more comfortably his wide-ranging interest in the arts: pottery, poetry, Wordsworth and Coleridge, art criticism, the philosophy of art.

He had written over forty books before he died in 1968, mostly on art and literature. In *Anarchy and Order*, published in England in 1954, he put together various essays he had written on anarchism, from his slim volume of 1938, *Poetry and Anarchism*, to his essay "Revolution and Reason," of 1953. This important book was never published in the United States, perhaps because America in the Fifties was not hospitable to anarchism, or to serious dissent of any kind. As we start the Seventies, the mood is different. Read offers us something that this generation seems to want and need: an aesthetic approach to politics.

The order of politics, as we have known it in the world, is an order imposed on society, neither desired by most people, nor directed to their needs. It is therefore chaotic and destructive. Politics grates on our sensibilities. It violates the elementary requirement of aesthetics—it is devoid of beauty. It is coercive, as if sound were forced into our ears at a decibel level such as to make us scream, and those responsible called this music. The "order" of modern life is a cacophony which has made us almost deaf to the gentler sounds of the universe.

It is fitting that in modern times, around the time of the French and American Revolutions, exactly when man became most proud of his achievements, the ideas of anarchism arose to challenge that pride. Western civilization has never been modest in describing its qualities as an enormous advance in human history: the larger unity of national states replacing tribe and manor; parliamentary government replacing the divine right of kings; steam and electricity substituting for manual labor; education and science dispelling ignorance and superstition; due process of law canceling arbitrary justice. Anarchism arose in the most splendid days of Western "civilization" because the promises of that civilization were almost immediately broken.

Nationalism, promising freedom from outside tyranny, and security from internal disorder, vastly magnified both the stimulus and the possibility for worldwide empires over subjected people, and bloody conflicts among such empires: imperialism and war were intensified to the edge of global suicide exactly in the period of the national state. Parliamentary government, promising popular participation in important decisions, became a facade (differently constructed in one-party and two-party states) for rule by elites of wealth and power in the midst of almost-frenzied scurrying to polls and plebiscites. Mass production did not end poverty and exploitation; indeed it made the persistence of want more unpardonable. The production and distribution of goods became more rational technically, more irrational morally. Education and literacy did not end the deception of the many by the few; they enabled deception to be replaced by self-deception, mystification to be internalized, and social control to be even more effective than ever before, because now it had a large measure of *self*-control. Due process did not bring justice; it replaced the arbitrary, identifiable dispenser of injustice with the unidentifiable and impersonal. The "rule of law," replacing the "rule of men," was just a change in rulers.

In the midst of the American Revolution, Tom Paine, while calling for the establishment of an independent American government, had no illusions about even a new revolutionary government when he wrote, in *Common Sense:* "Society in every state is a blessing, but government even in its best state is but a necessary evil."

Anarchists almost immediately recognized that the fall of kings, and the rise of committees, assemblies, parliaments, did not bring democracy; that revolutions had the potential for liberation, but also for another form of despotism. Thus, Jacques Roux, a country priest in the French Revolution concerned with the lives of the peasants in his district, and then with the workingmen in the Gravilliers quarter of Paris, spoke in 1792 against "senatorial despotism," saying it was "as terrible as the scepter of kings" because it chains the people without their knowing it and brutalizes and subjugates them by laws they themselves are supposed to have made. In Peter Weiss's play, *Marat-Sade*, Roux, straitjacketed, breaks through the censorship of the play within the play and cries out:

> Who controls the markets
> Who locks up the granaries
> Who got the loot from the palaces
> Who sits tight on the estates
> that were going to be divided between the poor

before he is quieted.

A friend of Roux, Jean Varlet, in an early anarchist manifesto of the French Revolution called *Explosion*, wrote:

> What a social monstrosity, what a masterpiece of Machiavellianism, this revolutionary government is in fact. For any reasoning being, Government and Revolution are incompatible, at least unless the people wishes to constitute the organs of power in permanent insurrection against themselves, which is too absurd to believe.

But it is exactly that which is "too absurd to believe" which the anarchists believe, because only an "absurd" perspective is revolutionary enough to see through the limits of revolution itself. Herbert Read, in a book with an appropriately absurd title, *To Hell With Culture* (he was seventy; this was 1963, five years before his death), wrote:

> What has been worth while in human history—the great achievements of physics and astronomy, of geographical

discovery and of human healing, of philosophy and of art—
has been the work of extremists—of those who believed in
the absurd, dared the impossible . . .

The Russian Revolution promised even more—to eliminate
that injustice carried into modern times by the American and
French Revolutions. Anarchist criticism of that Revolution was
summed up by Emma Goldman (*My Further Disillusionment
in Russia*) as follows:

> It is at once the great failure and the great tragedy of the
> Russian Revolution that it attempted . . . to change only
> institutions and conditions while ignoring entirely the
> human and social values involved in the Revolution. . . .
> No revolution can ever succeed as a factor of liberation
> unless the *means* used to further it be identical in spirit
> and tendency with the *purposes* to be achieved. Revolution
> is the negation of the existing, a violent protest against
> man's inhumanity to man with all the thousand and one
> slaveries it involves. It is the destroyer of dominant values
> upon which a complex system of injustice, oppression, and
> wrong has been built up by ignorance and brutality. It is
> the herald of *new values*, ushering in a transformation of the
> basic relations of man to man, and of man to society.

The institution of capitalism, anarchists believe, is destructive,
irrational, inhumane. It feeds ravenously on the immense
resources of the earth, and then churns out (this is its achievement—it is an immense stupid churn) huge quantities of
products. Those products have only an accidental relationship
to what is most needed by people, because the organizers and
distributors of goods care not about human need; they are
great business enterprises motivated only by profit. Therefore,
bombs, guns, office buildings, and deodorants take priority over
food, homes, and recreation areas. Is there anything closer to
"anarchy" (in the common use of the word, meaning confusion)
than the incredibly wild and wasteful economic system in
America?
Anarchists believe the riches of the earth belong equally to all,

and should be distributed according to need, not through the intricate, inhuman system of money and contracts which have so far channeled most of these riches into a small group of wealthy people, and into a few countries. (The United States, with six percent of the population, owns, produces, and consumes fifty percent of the world's production.) They would agree with the Story Teller in Bertholt Brecht's *The Caucasian Chalk Circle*, in the final words of the play:

> Take note what men of old concluded:
> That what there is shall go to those who are good for it
> Thus: the children to the motherly, that they prosper
> The carts to good drivers, that they are well driven
> And the valley to the waterers, that it bring forth fruit.

It was on this principle that Gerard Winstanley, leader of the Diggers in 17th century England, ignored the law of private ownership and led his followers to plant grain on unused land. Winstanley wrote about his hope for the future:

> When this universal law of equity rises up in every man and woman, then none shall lay claim to any creature and say, This is mine, and that is yours, This is my work, that is yours. But every one shall put to their hands to till the earth and bring up cattle, and the blessing of the earth shall be common to all; when a man hath need of any corn or cattle, take from the next storehouse he meets with. There shall be no buying and selling, no fairs or markets, but the whole earth shall be a common treasury for every man, for the earth is the Lord's. . . .

Our problem is to make use of the magnificent technology of our time, for human needs, without being victimized by a bureaucratic mechanism. The Soviet Union did show that national economic planning for common goals, replacing the profit-driven chaos of capitalist production, could produce remarkable results. It failed, however, to do what Herbert Read and other recent anarchists have suggested: to do away with the bureaucracy of large-scale industry, characteristic of both capitalism and socialism, and the consequent unhappiness of the workers who do not feel at ease with their work, with the products, with their fellow workers, with nature, with themselves. This problem could be solved, Read has suggested, by *workers' control* of their own jobs, without sacrificing the benefits of planning and coordination for the larger social good.

"Property is theft," Proudhon wrote in the mid-19th century (he was the first to call himself an anarchist). Whether the resources of the earth and the energies of men are controlled by capitalist corporations or bureaucracies calling themselves "socialist," a great theft of men's life-work has occurred, as a kind of original sin which has led in human history to all sorts of trouble: exploitation, war, the establishment of colonies, the subjugation of women, attacks on property called "crime," and the cruel system of punishments which all "civilized societies" have erected, known as "justice."

Both the capitalist and the socialist bureaucracies of our time fail, anarchists say, on their greatest promise: to bring democracy. The essence of democracy is that people should control their own lives, by ones or twos or hundreds, depending on whether the decision being made affects one or two or a hundred. Instead, our lives are directed by a political-military-industrial complex in the United States, and a party hierarchy in the Soviet Union. In both situations there is the pretense of popular participation, by an elaborate scheme of voting for representatives who do not have real power (the difference between a one-party state and a two-party state being no more than one party—and that a smudged carbon copy of the other). The *vote* in modern societies is the currency of politics as *money* is the currency of economics; both mystify what is really taking place—control of the many by the few.

Anarchists believe the phrase "law *and* order" is one of the great deceptions of our age. Law does not bring order, certainly not the harmonious order of a cooperative society, which is the best meaning of that word. It brings, if anything, the order of the totalitarian state, or the prison, or the army, where fear and threat keep people in their assigned places. All law can do is artificially restrain people who are moved to acts of violence or theft or disobedience by a bad society. And the order brought by law is unstable, always on the brink of a fall, because coercion invites rebellion. Laws cannot, by their nature, create a good society; that will come from great numbers of people arranging resources and themselves voluntarily ("Mutual Aid," Kropotkin called it) so as to promote cooperation and happiness. And that will be the best order, when people do what they must, not because of law, but on their own.

What has modern civilization, with its "rule of law," its giant industrial enterprises, its "representative democracy," brought? Nuclear missiles already aimed and ready for the destruction of the world, and populations—literate, well-fed, and constantly voting—of a mind to accept this madness. Civilization has failed on two counts: it has perverted the natural resources of the earth, which have the capacity to make our lives joyful, and also the natural resources of people, which have the potential for genius and love.

Making the most of these possibilities requires the upbringing of new generations in an atmosphere of grace and art. Instead, we have been reared in politics. Herbert Read (in *Art and Alienation*) describes the stunted human being who emerges from this:

> If seeing and handling, touching and hearing and all the refinements of sensation that developed historically in the conquest of nature and the manipulation of material substances are not educed and trained from birth to maturity the result is a being that hardly deserves to be called human: a dull-eyed, bored and listless automaton whose one desire is for violence in some form or other—violent action, violent sounds, distractions of any kind that can penetrate to its deadened nerves. Its preferred distractions are: the sports stadium, the pin-table alleys, the dance-hall, the passive "viewing" of crime, farce and sadism on the television screen, gambling and drug addiction.

What a waste of the evolutionary process! It took a billion years to create human beings who could, if they chose, form the materials of the earth and themselves into arrangements congenial to man, woman, and the universe. Can we still choose to do so?

It seems that revolutionary changes are needed—in the sense

of profound transformations of our work processes, our decision-making arrangements, our sex and family relations, our thought and culture—toward a humane society. But *this* kind of revolution—changing our minds as well as our institutions—cannot be accomplished by customary methods: neither by military action to overthrow governments, as some tradition-bound radicals suggest; nor by that slow process of electoral reform, which traditional liberals urge on us. The state of the world today reflects the limitations of both those methods.

Anarchists have always been accused of a special addiction to violence as a mode of revolutionary change. The accusation comes from governments which came into being through violence, which maintain themselves in power through violence, and which use violence constantly to keep down rebellion and to bully other nations. Some anarchists—like other revolutionaries throughout history, whether American, French, Russian, or Chinese—have emphasized violent uprising. Some have advocated, and tried, assassination and terror. In this they are like other revolutionaries—of whatever epoch or ideology. What makes anarchists unique among revolutionaries, however, is that most of them see revolution as a cultural, ideological, creative process, in which violence would be as incidental as the outcries of mother and baby in childbirth. It might be unavoidable—given the natural resistance to change—but something to be kept at a minimum while more important things happen.

Alexander Berkman, who as a young man attempted to assassinate an American industrialist, expressed his more mature reflections on violence and revolution in *The ABC of Anarchism:*

What, really, is there to destroy?

The wealth of the rich? Nay, that is something we want the whole of society to enjoy.

The land, the fields, the coal mines, the railroads, factories, mills and shops? These we want not to destroy but to make useful to the entire people.

The telegraphs, telephones, the means of communication and distribution—do we want to destroy them? No, we want them to serve the needs of all.

What, then, is the social revolution to destroy? It is to *take over* things for the general benefit, not to destroy them. It is to reorganize conditions for the public welfare.

Revolution in its full sense cannot be achieved by force of arms. It must be prepared in the minds and behavior of men, even *before* institutions have radically changed. It is not an act, but a process. Berkman describes this:

> If your object is to secure liberty, you must learn to do without authority and compulsion. If you intend to live in peace and harmony with your fellow men, you and they should cultivate brotherhood and respect for each other. If you want to work together with them for your mutual benefit, you must practice co-operation. The social revolution means much more than the reorganization of conditions only: it means the establishment of new human values and social relationships, a changed attitude of man to man, as of one free and independent to his equal; it means a different spirit in individual and collective life, and that spirit cannot be born overnight. It is a spirit to be cultivated, to be nurtured and reared, as the most delicate flower is, for indeed it is the flower of a new and beautiful existence. . . . We must learn to think differently before the revolution can come. That alone can bring the revolution.

The anarchist sees revolutionary change as something immediate, something we must do now, where we are, where we live, where we work. It means starting this moment to do away with authoritarian, cruel relationships—between men and women, between parents and children, between one kind of worker and another kind. Such revolutionary action cannot be crushed like an armed uprising. It takes place in everyday life, in the tiny crannies where the powerful but clumsy hands of state power cannot easily reach. It is not centralized and isolated, so that it can be wiped out by the rich, the police, the military. It takes place in a hundred thousand places at once, in families, on streets, in neighborhoods, in places of work. It is a revolution of the whole culture. Squelched in one place, it springs up in another, until it is everywhere.

Such a revolution is an art. That is, it requires the courage not only of resistance, but of imagination. Herbert Read, after pointing out that modern democracy encourages both complacency and complicity, speaks (in *Art and Alienation*) of the role of art:

> Art, on the other hand, is eternally disturbing, permanently revolutionary. It is so because the artist, in the degree of his greatness, always confronts the unknown, and what he brings back from that confrontation is a novelty, a new symbol, a new vision of life, the outer image of inward things. His importance to society is not that he voices received opinions, or gives clear expression to the confused feelings of the masses: that is the function of the politician, the journalist, the demagogue. The artist is what the Germans call *ein Rüttler*, an upsetter of the established order.

This should not be interpreted as an arrogant distinction between the elite artist and the mass of people. It is, rather, a recognition that in modern society, as Herbert Marcuse has pointed out, there is enormous pressure to create a "one-dimensional mind" among masses of people, and this requires upsetting.

Herbert Read's attraction to both art and anarchy seems a fitting response to the 20th century, and underscores the idea that revolution must be cultural as well as political. The title of his book *To Hell With Culture* might be misinterpreted if one did not read in it:

> Today we are bound hand and foot to the past. Because property is a sacred thing and land values a source of untold wealth, our houses must be crowded together and our streets must follow their ancient illogical meanderings. . . . Because everything we buy for use must be sold for profit, and because there must always be this profitable margin between cost and price, our pots and our pans, our furniture and our clothes, have the same shoddy consistency, the same competitive cheapness. The whole of our capitalist

culture is one immense veneer: a surface of refinement hiding the cheapness and shoddiness of the heart of things.

To hell with such a culture. To the rubbish-heap and furnace with it all! Let us celebrate the democratic revolution creatively. Let us build cities that are not too big, but spacious, with traffic flowing freely through their leafy avenues, with children playing safely in their green and flowery parks, with people living happily in bright efficient houses. . . . Let us balance agriculture and industry, town and country—let us do all these sensible and elementary things and *then* let us talk about culture.

The anarchist tries to deal with the complex relationship between changing institutions and changing culture. He knows that we must revolutionize culture starting now; and yet he knows this will be limited until there is a new way of living for large numbers of people. Read writes in the same essay: "You cannot impose a culture from the top—it must come from under. It grows out of the soil, out of the people, out of their daily life and work. It is a spontaneous expression of their joy in life, of their joy in work, and if this joy does not exist, the culture will not exist."

For revolutionaries, the aesthetic element—the approach of the artist—is essential in breaking out of the past, for we have seen in history how revolutions have been cramped or diverted because the men who made them were still encumbered by tradition. The warning of Marx, in *The Eighteenth Brumaire of Louis Bonaparte*, needs to be heeded by Marxists as well as by others seeking change:

The tradition of all the dead generations weighs like a nightmare on the brain of the living. And just when they seem engaged in revolutionizing themselves and things, in creating something entirely new, precisely in such epochs of revolutionary crisis they anxiously conjure up the spirits of the past to their service and borrow from them names, battle slogans and costumes in order to present the new scene of world history in this time-honoured disguise and this borrowed language.

The art of revolution needs to go beyond what is called "reason," and what is called "science," because both reason and science are limited by the narrow experience of the past. To break those limits, to extend reason into the future, we need passion and instinct, coming out of those depths of human feeling which escape the bounds of a historical period. When Read spoke in London in 1961, before taking part in a mass act of civil disobedience in protest against Polaris nuclear submarines, he argued for breaking out of the limits of "reason" through action:

> This stalemate must be broken, but it will never be broken by rational argument. There are too many right reasons for wrong actions on both sides. It can be broken only by instinctive action. An act of disobedience is or should be collectively instinctive—a revolt of the instincts of man against the threat of mass destruction.
>
> Instincts are dangerous to play with, but that is why, in the present desperate situation, we must play with instincts. . . .
>
> We must release the imagination of the people so that they become fully conscious of the fate that is threatening them, and we can best reach their imagination by our actions, by our fearlessness, by our willingness to sacrifice our comfort, our liberty, and even our lives, to the end that mankind shall be delivered from pain and suffering and universal death.

Anarchism seeks that blend of order and spontaneity in our lives which gives us harmony with ourselves, with others, with nature. It understands the need to change our political and economic arrangements to free ourselves for the enjoyment of life. And it knows that the change must begin now, in those everyday human relations over which we have the most control. Anarchism knows the need for sober thinking, but also for that action which clarifies otherwise academic and abstract thought.

Herbert Read, in "Chains of Freedom," writes that we need a "Black Market in culture, a determination to avoid the bankrupt academic institutions, the fixed values and standardized products of current art and literature; not to trade our spiritual goods through the recognized channels of Church, or State, or Press; rather to pass them 'under the counter.'" If so, one of the first items to be passed under the counter must surely be the literature that speaks, counter to all the falsifications, about the ideas and imaginings of anarchism.

Boston
October 1970

INTRODUCTION:
REVOLUTION AND REASON

The great mission of the Utopia is to make room for the possible as opposed to a passive acquiescence in the present actual state of affairs. It is symbolic thought which overcomes the natural inertia of man and endows him with a new ability, the ability constantly to reshape his human universe.

ERNST CASSIRER: *An Essay on Man.*

INTRODUCTION:
REVOLUTION AND REASON

Many years ago I was present at a formal dinner of some kind and found myself seated next to a lady well known in the political world, a member of the Conservative party. A determined lady—she at once asked me what my politics were, and on my replying 'I am an anarchist', she cried, 'How absurd!', and did not address another word to me during the whole meal. I was not insulted by this behaviour, and reflected that after all 'the politics of the absurd' was a fairly accurate description of my beliefs.

Years later the phrase recurred to me when I read *Le Mythe de Sisyphe* by Albert Camus, for Monsieur Camus, beginning with a reflection on the act of suicide, and reasoning why he, who could find no philosophical justification for living in this world, should yet refrain from this act, came to the conclusion that however absurd existence might be, he yet had an animal faith in its continuance. He suggested a philosophy of the absurd, and his subsequent work, which I have read with consistent sympathy and growing admiration, has been an affirmation of 'absurdism' in politics and ethics, as well as in metaphysics.[1]

Absurdism in religion is as old as Tertullian—indeed, it might be said that all religions, in so far as they are based on a sense of the numinous, are absurd, not rooted in normal experience, closed to normal channels of perception, and resistant to normal modes of expression. The scientific mind dismisses religion because it is absurd; it cannot thereby dispose of the ever-present phenomena of religious experience. But in general we may say that the scientist now accommodates religion within a comprehensive view of the world. This does not mean that science has

[1] It is possible that the same attitude to all these subjects is expressed in the 'quichottisme' of Miguel de Unamuno, but I am not familiar enough with Unamuno's ideas to risk the comparison.

found a justification for religion, and certainly religion is not grateful for any support it may receive from the scientist—the scientific acceptance of religion as a valid state of mind is rather, as Martin Buber has shown,[1] a modern form of Gnosticism.

In the same way modern science has come to terms with anarchism, accommodated it as a type of political thought, to be listed and annotated with the rest. One of the greatest of modern sociologists, Karl Mannheim, described it as 'the purest and most genuine form' of the Chiliastic attitude,[2] which is the evidently absurd expectation of the dawn of a millenial kingdom on earth. The task of the anarchist philosopher is not to prove the imminence of a Golden Age, but to justify the value of believing in its possibility.

He might begin by a demonstration of the equivalent absurdity of what is usually contrasted with anarchism—piecemeal planning, *practical* politics. These are the policies (rarely rising from a level of opportunism to the status of *beliefs*) which are from day to day recommended by professional politicians, civil servants, diplomats, statesmen, journalists, and complacently accepted by the average citizen. They include the maintenance by armed force of a 'balance of power' (in the world and within the State), the tolerance or support of a money system originally of medieval conception and now of barbaric futility (it divides the world into mutually antagonistic standards of value, treats money as a thing-in-itself rather than as a valueless token of exchange, and creates through usury and rents debts of incalculable dimensions, debts which, directly or indirectly enslave the

---

[1] In *The Eclipse of God* (Gollancz, London, 1953).

[2] *Ideology and Utopia* (Routledge, London, 1936), p. 202. Writing to me on the first appearance of 'The Philosophy of Anarchism', Karl Mannheim said: 'I have always felt that the turning point in history is the break between Bakuninism and Marxism, and you have not only restated the super-temporaneous case of the first but revitalized it, giving it a new significance. Although I do not think that the principles of anarchism in its unhistoric form will work in a society of modern social techniques because planning without a relatively great amount of centralization seems to me to be impossible, the task of this philosophy is still to teach mankind again and again that the patterns of organization are manifold, and the organic ones should not be and need not be overridden by rigid organization. The natural forces of self-adjustment in small groups produce more wisdom than any abstract thinking and so the scope for them within the plan is even more important than we can guess.'

14

whole of mankind, and in general perpetuates systems of education, social conventions, and organizations of labour that are
destructive of all vitality and happiness). In other words, practical politics perpetuate the conditions against which reasonable
men must repeatedly revolt.

Parliamentary democracy is usually regarded as the major
achievement of such practical politics in modern times. This is a
system of government which gives absolute power (such 'checks'
as are from time to time devised are swept aside as soon as there
is any attempt to apply them) to the majority of a people. Since
such a majority, as any intelligence test will immediately reveal,
is inevitably an ignorant majority, it is a mere chance if it
places in power delegates of more than average intelligence. Intelligence, in such a system, is always suspect, and although, as
Bagehot pointed out, there is a good deal to be said for the reign
of stupidity, the situation is again evidently absurd.

The growth of authoritarian politics is due to a realization of
this absurdity: it is an attempt to replace the rule of an ignorant
majority by the rule of an intelligent élite: but unfortunately the
only judge of the élite's intelligence is the élite itself.

An élite such as Plato conceived for his Republic, made up of
highly trained political philosophers, would be a rational proposition; modern élites, which tend to be recruited from various
types of psychopaths,[1] are a final illustration of the absurdity of
practical politics. The desire to serve one's fellow-men is 'practically' of no avail against the psychopathic will-to-power.

In all this we perceive the presence of a contradiction which
is perhaps inherent in the pattern of life—of a tension which is
perhaps a psychological and therefore a biological necessity. It
is the contradiction between the life of the mind and the process
of living. The mind, though it feeds on the body, leads a life
of its own; it is a parasite that spins its own web of logic, its
own structure of thought. The biological process—in all its
physiological and economic aspects—is quite a different activity
and leads to social structures which are not logical, but pragmatic—that is to say, they are justified and retained only if they

---

[1] For a demonstration of this tendency see Dr. Alex Comfort's *Authority
and Delinquency in the Modern State: a Criminological Approach to the
Problem of Power* (Routledge & Kegan Paul, London, 1950).

15

work. Political idealists come along and try to make the social structure fit their logical structure, with consequences that are always painful and impermanent. After a confused interval, the social structure resumes its original shape; only the nomenclature of the parts has changed. 'Society' as Tolstoy said, 'resembles a crystal. No matter how you grind it, dissolve it, compress it, it will reform itself at the first opportunity into the same form. The constitution of a crystal can be changed only when chemical changes occur within it.'[1]

We will consider the possibility of chemical changes within the social crystal presently, but for the moment I wish to emphasize the separate nature of the processes of thinking and living. (A fanatic might be defined as a person who sees no difference between these processes—who tries to make the pattern of life conform strictly to the pattern of thought.) Thinking is, of course, prompted by the impact of the environment on the senses, or by drives or impulses which come from the unconscious; but to deserve the name it observes certain rules of consistency or logic. It is an architectonic structure, and it must present a façade of stability, symmetry, and order. But these qualities are self-consistent; they exist only within the structure itself. Utility is not demanded: thought is a castle in the air, without necessary function. It is the stately pleasure dome of Kubla Khan. It is arbitrarily 'decreed', and its purpose is to arouse our wonder.

Living is fundamentally an instinct—the animalistic scrounging for food and shelter, for sexual mating, for mutual aid against adversities. It is a complicated biological activity, in which tradition and custom play a decisive part. To the pure mind it can only seem monstrous and absurd—the ugly activities of eating, digesting, excreting, copulating. It is true that we can idealize these processes, or some of them, and eating and love-making have become refined arts, elaborates 'games'.[2] But only on the basis of long traditions, of social customs that are neither rational nor consistent—what could be more 'absurd' than a cocktail-party or the love-making in a Hollywood film? The

---

[1] *Diaries*. Trans. Rose Strunsky (Knopf, New York, 1917).

[2] Cf. J. F. Huizinga's *Homo Ludens* (Routledge & Kegan Paul, London, 1949) for a detailed demonstration of the 'play' element in almost all our social institutions.

political fanatic will denounce such customs as aspects of a degenerate social order, but his new social order, if he succeeds in establishing it, will soon evolve customs just as absurd, and even less elegant.

I am not attempting by casuistry to defend an attitude of complacency or compromise. The existing social order is outrageously unjust, and if we do not revolt against it, we are either morally insensitive or criminally selfish. But if all that our revolt secures is merely a reconstruction of the societal crystal along another axis, our action has been in vain. There has been no essential chemical change. We must therefore distinguish, as I do in one of these essays,[1] between revolution and insurrection; or as Albert Camus does, between revolution and rebellion. Revolutions, as has often been remarked, change nothing; or rather, they merely substitute one set of masters for another set. Social groups acquire new names, but retain their former inequality of status.

Rebellion or insurrection, on the other hand, being guided by instinct rather than reason, being passionate and spontaneous rather than cool and calculated, do act like shock therapy on the body of society, and there is a chance that they may change the chemical composition of the societal crystal. In other words, they may change human nature, in the sense of creating a new morality, or new metaphysical values. Rebellion, says Camus, 'is the refusal to be treated as an object and to be reduced to simple historical terms. It is the affirmation of a nature common to all men, which eludes the world of power.' It eludes the world of power—that is the point, for it is always power that crystallizes into a structure of injustice.

We must pause here to stress this moral imperative. Unless a society can renounce power, and the deliberate actions which arise from the desire to exercise power, there is no escape from 'the insanity of history'. A power structure is the form taken by the inhibition of creativity: the exercise of power is the denial of spontaneity. The will to power, an emotional complex in individuals, directly conflicts with the will to mutuality, which, as Kropotkin showed, is a social instinct. The will to power is an eccentric and disruptive force: the unity it would impose is

---

[1] Cf. p. 51 below.

totalitarian. Mutuality is unity itself, and is creative. When men rebel against tyranny, they are affirming, not their individuality, but the unity of their human nature; they are affirming their desire to create a unity on the basis of their common ideals (of truth or beauty). The slave is not a man without possessions (many of the Greek and Roman slaves were wealthy), but a man without qualities, a man without ideals for which he is willing to die.

To possess and to profess ideals may well be an absurdity: ideals are not facts of nature, nor are they revealed supernaturally to men today. An ideal of beauty may be discovered in nature, but nature is a limitation which has again and again in the history of art led to academicism and decadence—and to a necessary rebellion. The mind can grasp ideals beyond the natural order, and to express such ideals we need symbols that are not found 'ready-made' in nature. They require the effort of original creation, the 'formative energy' of which Goethe and Schiller used to speak.

A parallelism exists between the social and the artistic processes. Both depend on an innate creative energy, one in the mind of the artist, the other in the body politic. Both seek to give form to feeling—to symbolize feeling in an appropriate form. The symbols which the artist invents are as multiform as the feelings that motivate man, but the symbols which a society invents are limited to the expression of collective feelings—feelings of unity, of community, of aspiration to the good life; profounder feelings, too, of sacrifice and retribution. The ability to express these feelings, to create symbolic forms, always depends, in the artist and in a society, on a certain condition of freedom— on an absence of inhibition, of repression, of fear. Modern psychologists have been able to describe this process in the individual in considerable detail (it is the process known as 'individuation' or 'integration'), but we still lack social psychologists to analyse the process for the group,[1] particularly for the political group or society. We have, however, arrived at a clear differentiation between two types of society, the one 'open' or libertarian, the other 'closed' or totalitarian. The classical analysis of this distinction has been made by Dr. K. R. Popper,

[1] There are exceptions, such as Trigant Burrow and Erich Fromm.

18

in a book which has exercised a salutary influence since it was first published in 1945.[1]

Popper's main purpose was to warn us against the dangers of historicism, that pretentious school of political science which claims to have discovered laws of history that enable it to prophesy the future course of events. Popper traces the origins of this heresy as far back as Plato (or even Heraclitus), but its typical exponents are Hegel and Marx. If one believes, as these philosophers do, that a law of history can be deduced from the incomplete records of past events, it is then merely 'logical' to wish to apply this law to the present and the future. But a law must always be sanctioned by force, and so these prophets became authoritarians, ready to enforce their 'law' by the power of the State.

To this concept of totalitarian evolution, Dr. Popper opposes what he calls 'the piecemeal methods of science'. We have often heard of 'gradualism' in politics, and the Fabian Society was founded to introduce such a method into socialism. But Dr. Popper is not a socialist—he is a physicist and a logician, and has a simple longing for 'security *and* freedom', in which to pursue his scientific studies. If he is an 'ist' of any kind, he is a humanist, and he speaks of 'the task of carrying our cross, the cross of humaneness, of reason, of responsibility'. Dr. Popper is using a Christian symbol, and he believes with Christians that 'our dream of heaven cannot be realized on earth'. 'For those who have eaten of the tree of knowledge, paradise is lost.' These symbols have perhaps unduly influenced Dr. Popper's scientific methods: they have induced in him what is fundamentally a despair, a nihilism. Dismissing any hope of a perfect society, however remote, he casts his eyes to the ground and contemplates with satisfaction the piecemeal methods of the mole. He makes his little burrow, throws up a little hill to show that there is 'work in progress'. But the wide acres that stretch all around him, and which should be growing corn for the hungry multitudes—these are in danger of being destroyed by approaching storms of which he is unaware.

I do not wish to criticize the general trend of Dr. Popper's

[1] *The Open Society and Its Enemies*, 2 vols. (Routledge, London). A second revised edition was published in 1952.

argument; I, too, desire an open society and not a closed one; I, too, call myself a humanist. I think that as a scientist he misunderstands the poetic imagination of Plato, but on his scientific ground, and particularly in his criticism of Marx's method, he seems to be unanswerable. But he is not an idealist, and therefore he is not an optimist.

Ideals are admittedly vague, and that is perhaps why a scientist finds it difficult to tolerate them. But they need not be unreal or ineffective. Even if we regard them as mirages, we must remember that the mirage gives energy and direction to a man lost in the desert. But ideals do not need to remain mirage-like. They can be rendered both concrete and vital.

This concretization and vitalization of ideals is one of the main tasks of the aesthetic activity in man. It is only in so far as an ideal becomes concrete that it becomes comprehensible to the reason and subject to rational criticism. An ideal has to be 'realized' in artistic or poetic form before it can become actual enough for discussion and application. It is in this respect that I think Dr. Popper fails to appreciate the method of Plato, which is not solemnly scientific, but poetically sophistical. Plato is playing a game—the primitive game of 'let's pretend'. The whole point of the game is to pretend with conviction—and with logic. Plato twice played this game with the Ideal Society as the theme—once in the *Republic*, and, much later in his life, in the *Laws*. The games are very different. One can say that the *Laws* is a maturer game; that it comes rather nearer to Plato's realistic views on politics than the *Republic*. But there is no authority for saying that Plato ever seriously supposed that the ideal closed societies of the *Republic* or the *Laws* were the kind of societies he seriously wished to live in himself, or wished other people to live in. What happened to Plato when he was given an opportunity to intervene in politics is rather obscure, but evidently he did not succeed in establishing his 'republic' in Sicily. Plutarch tells us that on his arrival in Syracuse Plato began to teach geometry, a piecemeal method of reform which should appeal to Dr. Popper. He no doubt hoped to mould the young tyrant Dion into a philosopher king, but he had no illusions about the difficulty of such a task.

Ideals are dangerous, particularly when they are given a convincingly concrete form, but they are necessary and must be made imaginatively concrete, for the purpose of giving vitality to the social body, which so easily succumbs to apathy or *accidie*. Plato's ideal republic is not my ideal republic, and many of its features are as repugnant to me as they are to Dr. Popper. But the game Plato played was played by others who followed him— by Augustine, Thomas More, Campanella, Francis Bacon, Rabelais, Winstanley, and Morris.[1] This Utopian tradition, as we may call it, has been the inspiration of political philosophy, providing a poetic undercurrent which has kept that science intellectually vital. Even the realists, cynics like Hobbes and Machiavelli, are Utopians by reaction. The English Revolution was inspired by the Utopianism of writers like Winstanley; the French Revolution by the Utopianism of Rousseau; and the Russian Revolution by the Utopianism of Karl Marx. In each case the fact that the Utopian ideal became a totalitarian reality was due to the absence of another ideal, the ideal of measure, or moderation.[2]

It must be admitted that left to itself to imagine an ideal state of existence, the human mind betrays a distressing tendency towards authoritarianism. This is not a result, as Dr. Popper might argue, of irresponsibility, but precisely of that rationalizing faculty which he so much admires. There exists in the human mind, particularly in the mind of the scientist, an itch for tidiness, for symmetry, and formality. This leads to good results in purely mental categories, and to it we owe the achievements of logic and scientific method. But life itself is not tidy and cannot be made tidy so long as it is life. It is always spontaneous in its manifestations, unpredictable in its blind drive to the light. Most Utopians forget or ignore this fact, and as a result their ideal commonwealth can never be, or ought never to become, real. I am convinced that Plato realized this—the Guardians upon whom the whole structure of his *Republic* rests are idealized super-human types, about as remote from realizable actuality as Nietzsche's supermen. The *Republic* is a fairy-tale

[1] And many others. For a general account of Utopian writings since Plato, see Marie Louise Berneri, *Journey Through Utopia* (Routledge & Kegan Paul, London, 1950).

[2] Cf. Camus, *L'Homme révolté*, trans. *The Rebel* (Hamilton, London, 1953), passim—my own sense of 'measure' is aesthetic rather than moral.

full of beautiful fancies, and intended to teach a moral (that morality and beauty are identical). It is only in the later Utopia of the *Laws* that Plato begins to plan a society with a dangerous suggestion of realizability. But to the degree that it is more realizable, it is more 'open'. There is a golden tolerance in the Cretan air, and the Nocturnal Council of mathematical astronomers, the supreme arbiters in this ideal society, would be at home in the Abbey of Theleme. But admittedly the totalitarian spirit is still there, as it is in most of the Utopias of the Renaissance and the Enlightenment. For totalitarianism is nothing but the imposition of a rational framework on the organic freedom of life, and is more characteristic of the scientific mind than of the poetic mind. It is only in those writers who retain a sense of organic freedom—Rabelais, Diderot, and Morris—that the Utopia is in any sense libertarian. It is no strange coincidence that these are the only inspiring utopias. As we approach the era of scientific socialism, the utopias become increasingly dreary and depressing. 'There are few utopias of the nineteenth century', writes Marie Louise Berneri,[1] 'which can be read today without a feeling of utter boredom, unless they succeed in amusing us by the obvious conceit of their authors in thinking themselves the saviours of mankind. The utopias of the Renaissance contained many unattractive features yet they had a breadth of vision which commanded respect; those of the seventeenth century presented many extravagant ideas, yet they revealed searching, dissatisfied minds with which one sympathizes; but, though we are in many ways familiar with the thought of the utopias of the nineteenth century, they are nevertheless more foreign to us than those of a more distant past. In spite of the fact that these utopias were no doubt inspired by the highest motives, one cannot help "feeling bitter about the nineteenth century", like the old man in *News from Nowhere*, bitter even about the love these utopian writers lavished on humanity, for they seem like so many over-affectionate and over-anxious mothers who would kill their sons with attention and kindness rather than let them enjoy one moment of freedom.'

The most terrible utopias are the scientific utopias of the marxian socialist and the monopoly capitalist. With the same

[1] Berneri, op. cit., pp. 218–9.

rational instruments of thought that have perfected science and technology, they now advance on the spontaneous sources of life itself. They presume to plan what can only germinate, to legislate for the forms of growth, and to mould into intangible dogmas the sensitive graces of the mind. Such scientific utopias will certainly fail, for the sources of life when threatened are driven underground, to emerge in some new wilderness. But the process is long and painful, and mankind must meanwhile suffer in the flesh for the realization of a blue-print.

If the realization of a rational blue-print leads to the death of society (a process which I have described symbolically in *The Green Child*), this does not mean that the utopian mentality itself is necessarily baneful—on the contrary, utopianism, as Anatole France said, is the principle of all progress. It is the poeticization of all practicalities, the idealization of everyday activities. It is not a rational process: it is an imaginative process. The Utopia fades the moment we attempt to actualize it. But it is necessary; it is even a biological necessity, an antidote to societal lethargy. Society exists to transcend itself, and the progressive force of its evolution is the poetic imagination, the teleological instinct that moves with the organic principle of all evolution, to take possession of new forms of life, new fields of consciousness.

Freedom is the ideal polity as conceived by poetry; liberty is a political ideal and is expressed in social organization. Liberty is definitive, and from the Magna Carta onwards (in the modern world) it has been given an actuality in law. Freedom is a vaguer concept, but it is not less actual; it is personal and psychological, and is the condition in which the spirit of man achieves spontaneity and creativity. The statutes of liberty guarantee the exercise of freedom, but within this guarantee freedom functions unconsciously. It is the reaction of the mind to the restraints of matter: the attempt to transcend material conditions. Always implicit in this positive conception of freedom is, as Camus has also argued, a rebellion against reality: an affirmation of human reason, of the human perception of beauty and order, in the midst of the absurdity of our actual existence.

We affirm our superiority to mere existence because we dare to create: and by creation we do not mean construction. Construction is the skilful manipulation of given elements: creation is the extension of consciousness itself, the conquest of new areas of awareness. Creativity is the sensible extension of reality; it is the perception of what was never before perceived: the invention of new concepts and the elaboration of our conception of the universe itself (the progressive reconciliation of the unique with the universal, which was Hegel's description of the process). For freedom is meaningless without unity; without mutuality. I am free if I stand in the middle of the Sahara, but there is no use in my freedom, because I cannot communicate my consciousness of it to others, and so carry on 'the metamorphic clue'. Consciousness is social, a collective phenomenon. The human race evolves in virtue of its collectivity, as a herd. But the herd generates within itself acuter points of consciousness, which are the minds of individuals: these individuals relay to the community their creative acts of perception. There is a gradual, a very gradual, change of consciousness in the whole body.[1]

All this was first understood and brilliantly explained by Giambattista Vico. History is the work neither of Fate nor of Chance, nor of any inevitable 'law', but of a necessity which is not determination, and of a freedom which is not chance. To quote Croce's summary of Vico's philosophy of history:

'Real history is composed of actions, not of fancies and illusions: but actions are the work of individuals, not indeed in so far as they dream, but in the inspiration of genius, the divine madness of truth, the holy enthusiasm of the hero. Fate, Chance, Fortune, God—all these explanations have the same defect: they separate the individual from his product, and instead of eliminating the capricious element, the individual will in history, as they claim to do, they immensely reinforce and increase it. . . .

'The idea which transcends and corrects alike the individualistic and supra-individualistic views of history is the idea of history as rational. History is made by individuals: but individuality is nothing but the concreteness of the universal, and every individual action, simply because it is individual, is supra-

---

[1] Many anarchists are unconscious authoritarians, because they cling illogically to the notion of uniformity (they may call it equality); not realizing that the human species, like any other species in nature, develops individual variations. Uniformity must be enforced, and can be enforced only by a centralized power, i.e. by the State.

24

individual. Neither the individual nor the universal exists as a concrete thing: the real thing is the one single course of history, whose abstract aspects are individuality without universality and universality without individuality. This one course of history is coherent in all its many determinations, like a work of art which is at the same time manifold and single, in which every word is inseparable from the rest, every shade of colour related to all the others, every line connected with every other line. On this understanding alone history can be understood. Otherwise it must remain unintelligible, like a string of words without meaning or the incoherent actions of a madman.'[1]

Existence is absurd, considered as the limited life of the individual: it acquires rationality as history—as the imaginative grasp of totality in the poetic mind. Dr. Popper would no doubt argue that this is merely historicism in a new guise, and the philosopher I am now going to quote will only confirm his suspicions.

'Unity is not a fact,' says Karl Jaspers, 'but a goal. The unity of history is perhaps produced by men's ability to understand each other in the idea of the One, in the one truth, in the world of the spirit, in which all things are meaningfully related to one another and belong together, however alien to each other they may be at the outset.'[2]

The 'goal' of history? Jaspers gives us a choice of four, but 'the urge is to the most lucid consciousness', including the consciousness of freedom. Without this consciousness, growing ever more lucid, man sinks into apathy, and the tide of history turns, from flux to reflux.

The main consideration in any political philosophy should therefore be the preservation of individual freedom, to the end that consciousness may become ever more lucid. Such freedom, I argue, can only be preserved in small communities, free from a central and impersonal exercise of power, communities developing by mutual aid and with complete respect for the personality. The extent to which such communities are frustrated and eliminated by modern methods of production and social organiza-

[1] *The Philosophy of Giambattista Vico*, by Benedetto Croce. Trans. by R. G. Collingwood (Howard Latimer, London, 1913).

[2] *The Origin and Goal of History*. Trans. Michael Bullock (Routledge & Kegal Paul, London, 1953), p. 256.

25

tion need not be recounted here. What is certain is that we find ourselves at a point in human development where an historical reflux has already set in, and a return to barbarism can only be avoided by a return to the conditions which favour the development of lucid consciousness in the individual—not only in the exceptional individual, for he is merely a voice in the wilderness unless there is the same consciousness, in some degree, in every artisan. In this sense many an Athenian slave was as 'lucidly conscious' as Plato.

The only way to maintain the flux of history is to recover a vision of the future and a spirit of revolt against the present. The trouble about the piecemeal methods of science is that they are myopic: they are not inspired by a sense of direction, by a view of horizons. Such horizons are discovered by the inspiration of genius, by the divine madness of the poet, by the holy enthusiasm of the hero. Such horizons reveal the sun in its revolutionary splendour. Revolt, it will be said, implies violence; but this is an outmoded, an incompetent conception of revolt. The most effective form of revolt in this violent world we live in is non-violence. Gandhi temporarily inspired his followers to practise such a form of revolt, but we are still far from a full awareness of its potentialities.

Revolt is most effective when it is unpremeditated and spontaneous—an act of rebellion against the injustice of power. Revolt of that kind can only be advocated when the occasion for it arises. A general spirit of revolt, such as I advocate here, is directed against the totality of an absurd civilization—against its ethos, its morality, its economy, and its political structure. It does not necessarily find expression in isolated acts of rebellion, and such acts, by provoking reactionary forces, may actually retard the general revolution. The need is to effect a revolution in habits of thought and in moral habits. 'Changez d'abord vos mœurs; vous changerez ensuite vos lois', says Balzac. This is a little more precise than the usual exhortation to change our hearts. Habits are concrete; and they are often defiant. The growth of the habit of 'living in sin' brought about a change in the marriage and divorce laws—perhaps not an edifying example in some people's view, but nevertheless an effective demonstration of Balzac's law. Dr. Popper would no doubt point out that the process was nevertheless piecemeal, but it was inspired by motives which he would regard as irrational. One might give hundreds of examples of how habits have *haphazardly* transformed laws. If new habits were to be inspired by ideals, the consequent change in the laws would be historically coherent. A revolt would have taken place.

Our idealism must always centre imaginatively in the concept of freedom. 'Where leave is granted by fate,' wrote Santayana in his last major work, 'the love of life and of freedom is normal and noble. The psyche can then run its vital cycle with a happy zeal; and the spirit, from each moral hilltop, can select and fashion an inspired vision of the world.' But Santayana goes on to warn us that in the economy of nature there is no such thing as a *right*. 'Existence itself is an unearned gift and an imposed predicament. The privilege of more or less freedom is meted out to individuals and to nations temporally and unequally, not by an ideal justice or laws, but by the generative stress of a universal automatism. Primal Will pervades this movement; it is original and central at every point, in every atom or cell; and the confluence of all these impulses, in their physical medium, determines spontaneously the measure in which each may deploy its vital liberty.'[1]

Freedom, therefore, is an ideal that can never be surrendered, so long as our impulses remain vital. But it is not a vague energy animating society: liberty, Santayana also says, 'is not a source, but a confluence or harmony'.[2] It is a reconciliation or integration of impulses; a harmonization of haphazard and even conflicting forces. The authoritarian acts as though such order could only be effected by force: imposed on recalcitrant material. The libertarian believes that it can be effected by reason, by enlightenment, by the cultivation of right habits. The authoritarian believes in discipline as a means: the libertarian in discipline as an end, as a state of mind. The authoritarian issues instructions; the libertarian encourages self-education. The one tolerates a subjective anarchy below the smooth surface of his rule: the other has no need of rule because he has achieved a subjective harmony reflected in personal integrity and social unity.

[1] *Dominations and Powers* (Scribners, New York, 1951), pp. 63–4.
[2] Ibid., p. 237.

To the Western mind such a subjective harmony has never seemed possible, and for that reason we have to go to the East for a traditional doctrine, and for practical illustrations of its effectiveness. It will be said that the history of China is not particularly harmonious: wars and invasions, marches and countermarches, usurpations and revolutions are as frequent as in the history of any other part of the world. And yet the Chinese civilization has been and still is the most stable civilization in world history: and China has no epics to celebrate violence. If we seek for an explanation of this stability, we find that it is as Lin Yutang has said, 'partly constitutional and partly cultural'.

'Among the cultural forces making for racial stability must be counted first of all the Chinese family system, which was so well-defined and organized to make it impossible for a man to forget where his lineage belonged. . . . Another cultural force making for social stability was the complete absence of established classes in China, and the opportunity open for all to rise in the social scale through the imperial examination system. While the family system accounted for their survival through fecundity, the imperial examination system effected a qualitative selection, and enabled talent to reproduce and propogate itself. . . . What seems still more important is the fact that the ruling class not only came from the country but also returned to the country. This rural ideal in art, philosophy, and life, so deeply embedded in the Chinese general consciousness, must account in a large measure for the racial health today . . . the rural ideal of life is part of the social system which makes the family the unit and part of the politico-cultural system which makes the village the unit . . . this family ideal of industry and frugality and living the simple life persisted and was recognized as the soundest moral heritage of the nation. The family system somehow wove itself into the rural pattern of life and could not be separated from it. Simplicity was a great word among the Greeks, and simplicity, *shunp'o*, was a great word among the Chinese. It was as if man knew the benefits of civilization and knew also the dangers of it. Man knew the happiness of the joys of life, but also was aware of its ephemeral nature, fearful of the jealousy of the gods, and was willing to take the joys that were simpler but would last longer.'[1]

[1] *My Country and My People* (Heinemann, London, 1936), pp. 32–7.

The Western world has not shown itself very willing to learn from the East—the spiritual traffic, it is assumed, should be in the other direction. But that traffic is now disorganized, and if we consider our own great teachers, the Greeks, the early Christians, modern sages like Ruskin, Tolstoy, Giono, Simone Weil, we shall find that the wisdom of the West does not conflict in any essentials with the wisdom of the East. The only problem is the eternal problem of communication, of education. This problem has been treated most profoundly by Simone Weil, in *The Need for Roots*. The whole of the last section of that book (part three) is devoted to 'The Growing of Roots', and is far too long to summarize here. But Simone Weil's definition of education may perhaps be given as an indication of the extent of the problem. After first remarking that education, whether its object be children or adults, individuals or an entire people, or even oneself 'consists in creating motives . . . for no action is ever carried out in the absence of motives capable of supplying the indispensable amount of energy for its execution', she proceeds to classify the means of education as follows:

(1) Fear and hope, brought about by threats and promises.

(2) Suggestion.

(3) Expression, either officially or under official sanction, of some of the thoughts which, before being publicly expressed, were already in the hearts of the people, or in the hearts of certain active elements in the nation.

(4) Example.

(5) The modalities themselves of action, and those of organizations created for purposes of action.

She dismisses the first two methods as gross and unworthy. Her exposition of the other three methods is largely governed by the specific nature of her task in the book in question, which was to prepare the French people for the day of liberation from the tyranny of Hitler. Her book is a memorandum addressed to the French authorities in London—hence her use of such phrases as 'under official sanction'. In effect, the three modes of education which she recommends are very personal. She says of the third means, for example, that 'its foundations are laid in the hidden structure of human nature'. She recognizes that in normal circumstances 'all collective action . . . in the nature of things . . . stifles the resources concealed in the depths of each mind. . . .

The hatred of the State, which has existed in a latent, secret, but very powerful form in France since the days of Charles VI, makes it impossible for words emanating directly from a government to be welcomed by every individual Frenchman like the voice of a friend'. In normal circumstances:

'A truth can only present itself to the mind of a particular human being. How is he going to communicate it? If he tries to expound it, he won't be listened to; for other people have never heard of that particular truth, won't recognize it as such; they won't realize that what he is saying is true; they won't pay enough attention to enable them to see that it is so; for they won't have received any inducement to make the necessary effort of concentration.

'But friendship, admiration, sympathy or any other sort of benevolent feeling would naturally predispose them to give a certain amount of their attention. A man who has something new to say—for as far as platitudes are concerned no effort of attention is necessary—can only be listened to, to begin with, by those that love him.

'So it is that the transmission of truths among men depends entirely on the state of their feelings; and the same applies to no matter what kind of truth.'[1]

Simone Weil does not become much more precise than this in her description of the effective methods of education. What she is really saying—and it is a truth that has been more effectively stated by Martin Buber—is that the communication of any truth, of any 'lesson', depends on the existence of a condition of mutuality between the teacher and the pupil—all effective communication is a dialogue, and is based on mutual respect and love. This condition is created, in any particular relationship, by example and by trust. It is not sufficient 'to be an example'. A detached and would-be superior existence, remote from the common habits and social customs of people, is not a favourable relationship for the transmission of truth. I doubt if Simon Stylites converted many people by isolating himself on a pillar; and to live like an anchorite, except for purposes of self-purification, is a stultifying example. One should try, as Eric

---

[1] *The Need for Roots*. Trans. by Arthur Wills (Routledge & Kegan Paul, London, 1952), p. 198.

Gill did, to create a 'cell of good living'—the Chinese conception of the family is of such a 'cell'. But one can be too self-conscious even in that modest form of setting an example. To wear 'rational' clothes, to eat 'rational' foods, to establish 'rational' schools—these well-meaning exemplary methods too often tend to create a barrier between the exemplar and other people, a barrier of suspicion and reserve which makes the communication of any truth impossible. There are, of course, degrees of compromise which are also impossible because they demand participation in evil actions—participation in war, in my opinion, is one of these. But perfect love demands, not only that we should sup with publicans and sinners, but also that we should not offend them on such occasions by our ineffable superiority.

There remain what Simone Weil rather obscurely called 'the modalities of action'. In my lifetime I believe we have suffered a decisive disillusion in this respect: we have once more experienced the truth that revolution carried out by force leaves force in command of the ensuing situation. We should abandon the rhetoric of revolt, not changing anything in our hearts or our understanding. Our ideals must be as bold as ever, and our strategy must be realistic. But revolutionary realism, for an anarchist in an age of atom bombs, is pacific: the bomb is now the symbol, not of anarchy, but of totalitarian power. It is only to be released from the hands that hold it with the kiss that, in Dostoevsky's parable, the Prisoner gave the Grand Inquisitor.

THE PHILOSOPHY OF ANARCHISM

Ts'ui Chü said to Lao Tzu, 'You say there must be no government. But if there is no government, how are men's hearts to be improved?' 'The last thing you should do,' said Lao Tzu, 'is to tamper with men's hearts. The heart of man is like a spring; if you press it down, it only springs up the higher. . . . It can be hot as the fiercest fire; cold as the hardest ice. So swift is it that in the space of a nod it can go twice to the end of the world and back again. In repose, it is quiet as the bed of a pool; in action, mysterious as Heaven. A wild steed that cannot be tethered—such is the heart of man.'

CHUANG TZU (Trans. Waley).

Liberty, morality, and the human dignity of man consist precisely in this, that he does good, not because it is commanded, but because he conceives it, wills it, and loves it.

BAKUNIN.

A perfect society is that which excludes all private property. Such was the primitive well-being which was overturned by the sin of our first fathers.

SAINT BASIL.

If beans and millet were as plentiful as fire and water, such a thing as a bad man would not exist among the people.

MENCIUS.

THE PHILOSOPHY OF ANARCHISM

The characteristic political attitude of today is not one of positive belief, but of despair.

Nobody seriously believes in the social philosophies of the immediate past. There are a few people, but a diminishing number, who still believe that Marxism, as an economic system, offers a coherent alternative to capitalism, and socialism has, indeed, triumphed in one country. But it has not changed the servile nature of human bondage. Man is everywhere still in chains. The motive of his activity remains economic, and this economic motive inevitably leads to the social inequalities from which he had hoped to escape. In face of this double failure, of capitalism and of socialism, the desperation of the masses has taken shape as fascism—a revolutionary movement which aims at establishing a pragmatic organization of power within the general chaos. In this political wilderness most people are lost, and if they do not give way to despair, they resort to a private world of prayer. But others persist in believing that a new world could be built if only we would abandon the economic concepts upon which both socialism and capitalism are based. To realize that new world we must prefer the values of freedom and equality above all other values—above personal wealth, technical power, and nationalism. In the past this view has been held by the world's greatest seers, but their followers have been a numerically insignificant minority, especially in the political sphere, where their doctrine has been called *anarchism*. It may be a tactical mistake to try and restate the eternal truth under a name which is ambiguous—for what is 'without ruler', the literal meaning of the root of the word, is not necessarily 'without order', the meaning often loosely ascribed to it. The sense of historical continuity, and a feeling for philosophical rectitude cannot, however, be compromised. Any vague or romantic associations which the word has acquired are incidental. The doctrine itself remains absolute, and pure. There are thousands if not millions, of people who instinctively hold these ideas, and who would accept the doctrine if it were made clear to them. A doctrine must be recognized by a common name. I know of no better name than Anarchism. In this essay I shall attempt to restate the fundamental principles of the political philosophy denoted by this name.

I

Let us begin by asking a very simple question: What is the measure of human progress? There is no need to discuss whether such progress exists or not, for even to come to a negative conclusion we must have a measure.

In the evolution of mankind there has always been a certain degree of social coherence. The earliest records of our species point to group organizations—the primitive horde, nomadic tribes, settlements, communities, cities, nations. As these groups progressed in numbers, wealth and intelligence, they subdivided into specialized groups—social classes, religious sects, learned societies, and professional or craft unions. Is this complication or articulation of society in itself a symptom of progress? I do not think it can be described as such in so far as it is merely a quantitative change. But if it implies a division of men according to their innate abilities, so that the strong man does work requiring great strength and the subtle man does work requiring skill or sensibility, then obviously the community as a whole is in a better position to carry on the struggle for a qualitatively better life.

These groups within a society can be distinguished according to whether, like an army or an orchestra, they function as a single body; or whether they are united merely to defend their common interests and otherwise function as separate individuals. In one case an aggregation of impersonal units to form a body with a single purpose; in the other case a suspension of individual activities for the purpose of rendering mutual aid.

The former type of group—the army, for example—is historically the most primitive. It is true that secret societies of medicine-men appear quite early on the scene, but such groups are really of the first type—they act as a group rather than as separate individuals. The second type of group—the organization of individuals for the active promotion of their common interests—comes relatively late in social development. The point I am making is that in the more primitive forms of society the individual is merely a unit; in more developed forms of society he is an independent personality.

This brings me to my measure of progress. Progress is measured by the degree of differentiation within a society. If the individual is a unit in a corporate mass, his life will be limited, dull, and mechanical. If the individual is a unit on his own, with space and potentiality for separate action, then he may be more subject to accident or chance, but at least he can expand and express himself. He can develop—develop in the only real meaning of the word—develop in consciousness of strength, vitality, and joy.

All this may seem very elementary, but it is a fundamental distinction which still divides people into two camps. You might think that it would be the natural desire of every man to develop as an independent personality, but this does not seem to be true. Because they are either economically or psychologically predisposed, there are many people who find safety in numbers, happiness in anonymity, and dignity in routine. They ask for nothing better than to be sheep under a shepherd, soldiers under a captain, slaves under an overseer. The few that must expand become the shepherds, the captains, and leaders of these willing followers.

Such servile people exist by the million, but again I ask: What is our measure of progress? And again I answer that it is only in the degree that the slave is emancipated and the personality differentiated that we can speak of progress. The slave may be happy, but happiness is not enough. A dog or a cat can be happy, but we do not therefore conclude that such animals are superior to human beings—though Walt Whitman, in a well-known poem, holds them up for our emulation. Progress is measured by richness and intensity of experience—by a wider and deeper apprehension of the significance and scope of human existence.

Such is, indeed, the conscious or unconscious criterion of all historians and philosophers. The worth of a civilization or a culture is not valued in the terms of its material wealth or military power, but by the quality and achievements of its representative individuals—its philosophers, its poets, and its artists.

We might therefore express our definition of progress in a slightly more precise form. Progress, we might say, is the gradual establishment of a qualitative differentiation of the individuals within a society.[1] In the long history of mankind, the group is to be regarded as an expedient—an evolutionary aid. It is a means to security and economic well-being: it is essential to the establishment of a civilization. But the further step, by means of which a civilization is given its quality or culture, is only attained by a process of cellular division, in the course of which the individual is differentiated, made distinct from and independent of the parent group. The farther a society progresses, the more clearly the individual becomes the antithesis of the group.

At certain periods in the history of the world a society has become conscious of its personalities: it would perhaps be truer to say that it has established social and economic conditions which permit the free development of the personality. The great age of Greek civilization is the age of the great personalities of Greek poetry, Greek art, and Greek oratory: and in spite of the institution of slavery, it can be described, relatively to the ages which preceded it, as an age of political liberation. But nearer our time we have the so-called Renaissance, inspired by this earlier Hellenic civilization, and even more conscious of the value of free individual development. The European Renaissance is an age of political confusion; but in spite of tyrannies and oppression, there is no doubt that compared with the previous period,[2] it

[1] It is worth observing that this is Plato's measure of progress in the *Republic*, II, 369 ff.

[2] Stylistically it is no longer possible to regard the Renaissance as an epoch which begins arbitrarily about 1400. Giotto and Masaccio can fairly be regarded as the culmination of Gothic art no less than as the forerunners of Renaissance art. There was actually a continuous process of growth, which began imperceptibly as the new force of Christianity penetrated the dead forms of late Roman art, which reached maturity in the Gothic style of the twelfth and thirteenth centuries, and which then grew in richness and complexity as it became more personal and individual during the fourteenth and succeeding two centuries. From an aesthetic point of view the earlier

also was an age of liberation. The individual once more comes into his own, and the arts are cultivated and appreciated as never before. But still more significantly, there arises a consciousness of the very fact that the value of a civilization is dependent on the freedom and variety of the individuals composing it. For the first time the personality is deliberately cultivated as such; and from that time until today it has not been possible to separate the achievements of a civilization from the achievements of the individuals composing it. Even in the sciences we now tend to think of the growth of knowledge in particular and personal terms—of physics, for example, as a line of individuals stretching between Galileo and Einstein.

2

I have not the slightest doubt that this form of individuation represents a higher stage in the evolution of mankind. It may be that we are only at the beginning of such a phase—a few centuries are a short time in the history of a biological process. Creeds and castes, and all forms of intellectual and emotional grouping, belong to the past. The future unit is the individual, a world in himself, self-contained and self-creative, freely giving and freely receiving, but essentially a free spirit.

It was Nietzsche who first made us conscious of the significance of the individual as a term in the evolutionary process— in that part of the evolutionary process which has still to take place. Nevertheless, there exists in Nietzsche's writings a confusion which must be avoided. That it can be avoided is due mainly to scientific discoveries made since Nietzsche's day, so Nietzsche must to some extent be excused. I refer to the discoveries of psycho-analysis. Freud has shown one thing very clearly: that we only forget our infancy by burying it in the unconscious; and that the problems of this difficult period find their solution under a disguised form in adult life. I do not wish to import the technical language of psycho-analysis into this

---

and later phases of this process (Gothic and Renaissance) cannot be judged absolutely: what the one gains from co-operative unity it loses in variety, and vice versa.

discussion, but it has been shown that the irrational devotion which a group will show to its leader is simply a transference of an emotional relationship which has been dissolved or repressed within the family circle. When we describe a king as 'the Father of his People', the metaphor is an exact description of an unconscious symbolism. Moreover, we transfer to this figure-head all sorts of imaginary virtues which we ourselves would like to possess—it is the reverse process of the scapegoat, who is the recipient of our secret guilt.

Nietzsche, like the admirers of our contemporary dictators, did not sufficiently realize this distinction, and he is apt to praise as a superman a figure who is merely inflated with the unconscious desires of the group. The true superman is the man who holds himself aloof from the group—a fact which Nietzsche acknowledged on other occasions. When an individual has become conscious, not merely of his 'Eigentum', of his own closed circuit of desires and potentialities (at which stage he is an egoist) but also of the laws which govern his reactions to the group of which he is a member, then he is on the way to become that new type of human being which Nietzsche called the Superman.

The individual and the group—this is the relationship out of which spring all the complexities of our existence and the need for unravelling and simplifying them. Conscience itself is born of this relationship, and all those instincts of mutuality and sympathy which become codified in morals. Morality, as has often been pointed out, is antecedent to religion—it even exists in a rudimentary form among animals. Religion and politics follow, as attempts to define the instinctive conduct natural to the group, and finally you get the historical process only too well known to us, in which the institutions of religion and politics are captured by an individual or a class and turned against the group which they were designed to benefit. Man finds his instincts, already deformed by being defined, now altogether inhibited. The organic life of the group, a self-regulative life like the life of all organic entities, is stretched on the rigid frame of a code. It ceases to be life in any real sense, and only functions as convention, conformity, and discipline.

There is a distinction to be made here between a discipline imposed on life, and the law which is inherent in life. My own early experiences in war led me to suspect the value of discipline, even in that sphere where it is so often regarded as the first essential for success. It was not discipline, but two qualities which I would call initiative and free association, that proved essential in the stress of action. These qualities are developed individually, and tend to be destroyed by the mechanical routine of the barrack square. As for the unconscious obedience which discipline and drill are supposed to inculcate, it breaks as easily as eggshell in the face of machine-guns and high explosives.

The law which is inherent in life is of an altogether different kind. We must admit 'the singular fact', as Nietzsche called it, 'that everything of the nature of freedom, elegance, boldness, dance, and masterly certainty, which exists or has existed, whether it be in thought itself, or in administration, or in speaking and persuading, in art just as in conduct, has only developed by the means of the tyranny of such arbitrary law; and in all seriousness, it is not at all improbable that precisely this is "nature" and "natural".' (*Beyond Good and Evil*, §188.) That 'nature' is penetrated throughout by 'law' is a fact which becomes clearer with every advance of science; and we need only criticize Nietzsche for calling such law 'arbitrary'. What is arbitrary is not the law of nature, in whatever sphere it exists, but man's interpretation of it. The only necessity is to discover the true laws of nature and conduct our lives in accordance with them.

The most general law in nature is *equity*—the principle of balance and symmetry which guides the growth of forms along the lines of the greatest structural efficiency. It is the law which gives the leaf as well as the tree, the human body and the universe itself, an harmonious and functional shape, which is at the same time objective beauty. But when we use the expression: *the law of equity*, a curious paradox results. If we look up the dictionary definition of equity we find: 'recourse to principles of justice to correct or supplement law'. As so often, the words we use betray us: we have to confess, by using the word equity, that common and statute law which is the law imposed by the State is not necessarily the natural or just law; that there exist principles of justice which are superior to these man-made laws

—principles of equality and fairness inherent in the natural order of the universe.

The principle of equity first came into evidence in Roman jurisprudence and was derived by analogy from the physical meaning of the word. In a classical discussion of the subject in his book on *Ancient Law*, Sir Henry Maine points out that the Aequitas of the Romans does in fact imply the principle of equal or proportionate distribution. 'The equal division of numbers or physical magnitudes is doubtless closely entwined with our perceptions of justice; there are few associations which keep their ground in the mind so stubbornly or are dismissed from it with such difficulty by the deepest thinkers.' 'The feature of the Jus Gentium which was presented to the apprehension of a Roman by the word Equity, was exactly the first and most vividly realized characteristic of the hypothetical state of nature. Nature implied symmetrical order, first in the physical world, and next in the moral, and the earliest notion of order doubtless involved straight lines, even surfaces, and measured distances.' I emphasize this origin of the word because it is very necessary to distinguish between the laws of nature (which, to avoid confusion, we ought rather to call the laws of the physical universe) and that theory of a pristine state of nature which was made the basis of Rousseau's sentimental egalitarianism. It was this latter concept which, as Maine dryly remarked, 'helped most powerfully to bring about the grosser disappointments of which the first French Revolution was fertile'. The theory is still that of the Roman lawyers, but the theory is, as it were, turned upside down. 'The Roman had conceived that by careful observation of existing institutions parts of them could be singled out which either exhibited already, or could by judicious purification be made to exhibit, the vestiges of that reign of nature whose reality he faintly affirmed. Rousseau's belief was that a perfect social order could be evolved from the unassisted consideration of the natural state, a social order wholly irrespective of the actual condition of the world and wholly unlike it. The great difference between the views is that one bitterly and broadly condemns the present for its unlikeness to the ideal past; while the other, assuming the present to be as necessary as the past, does not affect to disregard or censure it.'

THE PHILOSOPHY OF ANARCHISM

I am not going to claim that modern anarchism has any direct relation to Roman jurisprudence; but I do claim that it has its basis in the *law* of nature rather than in the *state* of nature. It is based on analogies derived from the simplicity and harmony of universal physical laws, rather than on any assumptions of the natural goodness of human nature—and this is precisely where it begins to diverge fundamentally from democratic socialism, which goes back to Rousseau, the true founder of state socialism.[1] Though state socialism may aim at giving to each according to his needs, or, as nowadays in Russia, according to his deserts, the abstract notion of equity is really quite foreign to its thought. *The tendency of modern socialism is to establish a vast system of statutory law against which there no longer exists a plea in equity. The object of anarchism, on the other hand, is to extend the principle of equity until it altogether supersedes statutory law.*

This distinction was already clear to Bakunin, as the following quotation will show:

'When we speak of justice, we do not mean what is laid down in codes and in the edicts of Roman jurisprudence, founded for the most part on acts of violence, consecrated by time and the benediction of some church, whether pagan or christian, and as such accepted as absolute principles from which the rest can be deduced logically enough; we mean rather that justice which is based solely on the conscience of mankind, which is present in the conscience of each of us, even in the minds of children, and which is simply translated as *equalness* (équation).

'This justice which is universal but which, thanks to the abuse of force and to religious influences, has never yet prevailed, neither in the political nor in the juridical, nor in the economic world—this universal sense of justice must be made the basis of the new world. Without it no liberty, no republic, no prosperity, no peace!' (*Œuvres*, I (1912), pp. 54–5.)

[1] This is clearly demonstrated by Rudolf Rocker in *Nationalism and Culture* (New York, 1937).

3

Admittedly a system of equity, no less than a system of law, implies a machinery for determining and administering its principles. I can imagine no society which does not embody some method of arbitration. But just as the judge in equity is supposed to appeal to universal principles of reason, and to ignore statutory law when it comes into conflict with these principles, so the arbiter in an anarchist community will appeal to these same principles, as determined by philosophy or common sense; and will do so unimpeded by all those legal and economic prejudices which the present organization of society entails.

It will be said that I am appealing to mystical entities, to idealistic notions which all good materialists reject. I do not deny it. What I do deny is that you can build any enduring society without some such mystical ethos. Such a statement will shock the Marxian socialist, who, in spite of Marx's warnings, is usually a naïve materialist. Marx's theory—as I think he himself would have been the first to admit—was not a universal theory. It did not deal with all the facts of life—or dealt with some of them only in a very superficial way. Marx rightly rejected the unhistorical methods of the German metaphysicians, who tried to make the facts fit a pre-conceived theory. He also, just as firmly, rejected the mechanical materialism of the eighteenth century—rejected it on the grounds that though it could explain the existing nature of things, it ignored the whole process of historical development—the universe as organic growth. Most Marxians forget the first thesis on Feuerbach, which reads: 'The chief defect of all hitherto existing materialism—that of Feuerbach included—is that the object, reality, sensuousness, is conceived only in the form of the *object* but not as *human sensuous activity, practice*, not subjectively.' Naturally, when it came to interpreting the history of religion, Marx would have treated it as a social product; but that is far from treating it as an illusion. Indeed, the historical evidence must tend altogether in the opposite direction, and compel us to recognize in religion a social necessity. There has never been a civilization without its corresponding religion, and the appearance of rationalism and scepticism is always a symptom of decadence.

Admittedly there is a general fund of reason to which all civilizations contribute their share and which includes an attitude of comparative detachment from the particular religion of one's epoch. But to recognize the historical evolution of a phenomenon like religion does not explain it away. It is far more likely to give it a scientific justification, to reveal it as a necessary 'human sensuous activity', and therefore to throw suspicion on any social philosophy which arbitrarily excludes religion from the organization it proposes for society.

It is already clear, after twenty years of socialism in Russia, that if you do not provide your society with a new religion, it will gradually revert to the old one. Communism has, of course, its religious aspects, and apart from the gradual readmission of the Orthodox Church,[1] the deification of Lenin (sacred tomb, effigies, creation of a legend—all the elements are there) is a deliberate attempt to create an outlet for religious emotions. Still more deliberate attempts to create the paraphernalia of a new creed were made by the Nazis in Germany, where the necessity for a religion of some kind has never been officially denied. In Italy Mussolini was far too wily to do anything but come to terms with the Catholic Church, and a deep and frustrating ambiguity exists in the minds of many Italian communists. Far from scoffing at these irrational aspects of communism and fascism, we should rather criticize these political creeds for the lack of any real sensuous and aesthetic content, for the poverty of their ritual, and above all for a misunderstanding of the function of poetry and imagination in the life of the community.

It is possible that out of the ruins of our capitalist civilization a new religion will emerge, just as Christianity emerged from the ruins of the Roman civilization. Civilizations monotonously repeat certain patterns of belief in the course of their history, elaborate parallel myths. Socialism, as conceived by its pseudo-historical materialists, is not such a religion, and never will be.

[1] For an account of the relations between the Soviet Government and the Church, see A. Ciliga, *The Russian Enigma* (Routledge, London, 1940), pp. 160–5.

And though, from this point of view, it must be conceded that fascism has shown more imagination, it is in itself such a phenomenon of decadence—the first defensive awareness of the fate awaiting the existing social order—that its ideological superstructure is not of much permanent interest. For a religion is never a synthetic creation—you cannot select your legends and saints from the mythical past and combine them with some kind of political or racial policy to make a nice convenient creed. A prophet, like a poet, is born. But even granted a prophet, we are still far from the establishment of a religion. It needed five centuries to build the religion of Christianity on the message of Christ. That message had to be moulded, enlarged, and to a considerable extent distorted until it conformed with what Jung has called the archetypes of the collective unconscious—those complex psychological factors which give cohesion to a society. Religion, in its later stages, may well become the opium of the people; but whilst it is vital it is the only force which can hold a people together—which can supply them with a natural authority to appeal to when their personal interests clash.

I call religion a natural authority, but it has usually been conceived as a supernatural authority. It is natural in relation to the morphology of society; supernatural in relation to the morphology of the physical universe. But in either aspect it is in opposition to the artificial authority of the State. The State only acquires its supreme authority when religion begins to decline, and the great struggle between Church and State, when, as in modern Europe, it ends so decisively in favour of the State, is from the point of view of the organic life of a society, eventually fatal. It is because modern socialism has been unable to perceive this truth and has instead linked itself to the dead hand of the State, that everywhere socialism is meeting its defeat. The natural ally of socialism was the Church, though admittedly in the actual historical circumstances of the nineteenth century it was difficult to see this. The Church was so corrupted, so much a dependency of the ruling classes, that only a few rare spirits could see through appearances to the realities, and conceive socialism in the terms of a new religion, or more simply as a new reformation of Christianity.

Whether, in the actual circumstances of today, it is still possible to find a path from the old religion to a new religion is doubtful. A new religion can arise only on the basis of a new society, and step by step with such a society—perhaps in Russia, perhaps in Spain, perhaps in the United States: it is impossible to say where, because even the germ of such a new society is nowhere evident and its full formation lies deeply buried in the future.

I am not a revivalist—I have no religion to recommend and none to believe in. I merely affirm, on the evidence of the history of civilizations, that a religion is a necessary element in any organic society.[1] And I am so conscious of the slow process of spiritual development that I am in no mood to look for a new religion, and have no hope of finding one. I would only venture one observation. Both in its origins and development, up to its zenith, religion is closely associated with art. Religion and art are, indeed, if not alternative modes of expression, modes intimately associated. Apart from the essentially aesthetic nature of religious ritual; apart, too, from the dependence of religion on art for the visualization of its subjective concepts; there is, besides, an identity of the highest forms of poetic and mystic expression. Poetry, in its intensest and most creative moments, penetrates to the same level of the unconscious as mysticism. Certain writers—and they are among the greatest—Saint Francis, Dante, Saint Teresa, Saint John of the Cross, Blake— rank equally as poets and as mystics. For this reason it may well happen that the origins of a new religion will be found if not in mysticism, then in art rather than in any form of moralistic revivalism.[2]

What has all this to do with anarchism? Merely this: socialism of the Marxist tradition, that is to say, state socialism, has so completely cut itself off from religious sanctions and has been driven to such pitiful subterfuges in its search for substitutes for religion, that by contrast anarchism, which is not without its

[1] For a sociological explanation of this fact see *Egrégores*, by Pierre Mabile (Jean Flory, Paris, 1938).

[2] It may not be without significance that the most authentic types of modern art—the paintings of Picasso or the sculpture of Henry Moore— succeed in creating symbols whose nearest parallels are to be found in the magical accessories of primitive religions. Cf. my essay, 'The Dynamics of Art', in the *Eranos Jahrbuch*, xxi (Rhein Verlag, Zurich, 1953); and *Le Mythe de l'éternel retour*, by Mircea Eliade (Gallimard, Paris, 1949).

mystic strain, is a religion itself. It is possible, that is to say, to conceive a new religion developing out of anarchism. During the Spanish Civil War many observers were struck by the religious intensity of the anarchists. In that country of potential renaissance anarchism has inspired, not only heroes but even saints— a new race of men whose lives are devoted, in sensuous imagination *and in practice*, to the creation of a new type of human society.

4

These are the resounding phrases of a visionary, it will be said, and not the practical accents of 'constructive' socialism. But the scepticism of the so-called practical man is destructive of the only force that can bring a socialist community into existence. It was always prophesied, in the pre-war years, that State socialism was a visionary ideal, impossible of realization. Apart from the fact that every industrial country in the world has been moving rapidly towards State socialism during the last quarter of a century, there is the example of Russia to prove how very possible a central organization of production and distribution is, provided you have visionaries ruthless enough, and in this case inhuman enough, to carry an ideal into practice. I do not believe that this particular kind of social organization can endure for long, simply because, as I have already suggested, it is not organic. But if such an arbitrary (or, if you prefer the word, logical) form of society can be established even for a few years, how much more likely it is that a society which does not contradict the laws of organic growth can be established and will endure. A beginning was being made in Spain, in spite of the Civil War and all the restrictions that a condition of emergency implied. The textile industry of Alcoy, the wood industry in Cuenca, the transport system in Barcelona—these are a few examples of the many anarchist collectives which were functioning efficiently for more than two years.[1] It has been demonstrated beyond any possibility of denial that whatever may be the merits or demerits of the anarcho-syndicalist system, it can and does work. Once it

[1] See *Social Reconstruction in Spain*, by Gaston Leval. Also *After the Revolution*, by D. A. de Santillan.

prevails over the whole economic life of the country, it should function better still and provide a standard of living far higher than that realized under any previous form of social organization.

I do not intend to repeat in any detail the syndicalist proposals for the organization of production and distribution. The general principle is clear: each industry forms itself into a federation of self-governing collectives; the control of each industry is wholly in the hands of the workers in that industry, and these collectives administer the whole economic life of the country. That there will be something in the nature of a parliament of industry to adjust mutual relations between the various collectives and to decide on general questions of policy goes without saying, but this parliament will be in no sense an administrative or executive body. It will form a kind of industrial diplomatic service, adjusting relations and preserving peace, but possessing no legislative powers and no privileged status. By such means the antagonism of producer and consumer, so characteristic of capitalistic economy, will disappear, and the cadres of a competitive economy will be rendered obsolete by an interflow of mutual aid.

Admittedly there will be all sorts of practical difficulties to overcome, but the system is simplicity itself compared with the monster of centralized State control, which sets such an inhuman distance between the worker and the administrator that there is room for a thousand difficulties to intervene. On the other hand, if the motive for association and mutual aid is the wellbeing of the community, then that end is most effectively assured by an economy decentralized on a regional or local basis. There will be complexities (such as those involved in the exchange of surpluses) but they will be resolved by methods which secure the maximum benefit for the community as a whole. No other method will exist, but this motive will create the necessary enterprise.

The only other practical problem to consider at this stage is what I will call the interpretation of equity rather than the administration of justice. Obviously the great mass of civil and criminal proceedings will simply disappear with the disappearance of the profit motive; such as remain—unnatural acts of acquisitiveness, of anger, and self-indulgence—will to a great extent be dealt with by the collectives, just as the old manor courts dealt with all offences against the peace of the parish. If it is true that certain dangerous tendencies will persist, these must be kept in check. 'Kept in check' is the cliché that first springs to the mind, but it indicates the repressive methods of the old morality. The more fashionable word would be 'sublimated', and by this we mean the devising of harmless outlets for emotional energies which, when repressed, become evil and anti-social. The aggressive instincts, for example, are expended in competitive games of various kinds—the most playful nation is even now the least aggressive.

The whole case for anarchism rests on a general assumption which makes detailed speculations of this kind quite unnecessary. The assumption is that the right kind of society is an organic being—not merely analogous to an organic being, but actually a living structure with appetites and digestions, instincts and passions, intelligence and reason. Just as an individual by a proper balance of these faculties can maintain himself in health, so a community can live naturally and freely, without the disease of crime. Crime is a symptom of social illness—of poverty, inequality, and restriction.[1] Rid the social body of these illnesses and you rid society of crime. Unless you can believe this, not as an ideal or fancy, but as a biological truth, you cannot be an anarchist. But if you do believe it, you must logically come to anarchism. Your only alternative is to be a nihilist and authoritarian—a person who has so little faith in the natural order that he will attempt to make the world conform to some artificial system of his own devising.

[1] By this last word I mean the general restriction of emotional maturity due to social conventions and the petty tyrannies of the family. For a scientific demonstration of the social origins of crime, see *What We Put in Prison*, by G. W. Pailthorpe, M.D. (London, 1932) and the same author's official report on *The Psychology of Delinquency* (H.M. Stationery Office). An earlier treatment of the subject from the anarchist point of view is Edward Carpenter's *Prisons, Police and Punishment.* Cf. also Alex Comfort *Authority and Delinquency in the Modern State* (Routledge & Kegan Paul, London, 1950).

5

I have said little about the actual organization of an anarchist community, partly because I have nothing to add to what has been said by Kropotkin and by contemporary syndicalists like Dubreuil;[1] partly because it is always a mistake to build *a priori* constitutions. The main thing is to establish your principles— the principles of equity, of individual freedom, of workers' control. The community then aims at the establishment of these principles from the starting-point of local needs and local conditions. That they must be established by revolutionary methods is perhaps inevitable. But in this connection I would like to revive the distinction made by Max Stirner between *revolution* and *insurrection*. Revolution 'consists in an overturning of conditions, of the established condition or *status*, the State or society, and is accordingly a *political* or *social* act'. Insurrection 'has for its unavoidable consequence a transformation of circumstances, yet does not start from it but from men's discontent with themselves, is not an armed rising, but a rising of individuals, a getting up, without regard to the arrangements that spring from it'.[2] Stirner carried the distinction farther, but the point I wish to make is that there is all the difference in the world between a movement that aims at an exchange of political institutions, which is the bourgeois socialist (Fabian) notion of a revolution; and a movement that aims at getting rid of these political institutions altogether. An insurrection, therefore, is directed against the State as such, and this aim will determine our tactics. It would obviously be a mistake to create the kind of machinery which, at the successful end of a revolution, would merely be taken over by the leaders of the revolution, who then assume the functions of a government. That is out of the frying-pan into the fire. It is for this reason that the defeat of the Spanish Government, regrettable in that it leaves the power of the State in still more ruthless hands, is to be looked upon with a certain indifference; for in the process of defending its existence the

---

[1] See *A chacun sa chance*, by Hyacinthe Dubreuil (Grassel, Paris, 1935).
[2] Cf. p. 17 above, and Albert Camus, *L'homme révolté* (Paris, 1952); English trans. *The Rebel* (Hamish Hamilton, London, 1953).

Spanish Government had created, in the form of a standing army and a secret police, all the instruments of oppression, and there was little prospect that these instruments would have been discarded by the particular group of men who would have been in control if the war had ended in a Government victory.

The natural weapon of the working classes is the strike, and if I am told that the strike has been tried and has failed, I must reply that the strike as a strategic force is in its infancy. This supreme power which is in the hands of the working classes has never yet been used with intelligence and with courage. It has been conceived in the narrow terms of class warfare, a war of trade unions against bosses. As the General Strike of 1926 showed with a logic that the strikers themselves had to accept, a third party is involved—the community. It is merely stupid for a group of workers—even for the workers organized as a national group— to invite the making of a distinction between themselves and the community. The real protagonists in this struggle are the community and the State—the community as an organic and inclusive body and the State as the representative of a tyrannical minority. The strike, as a weapon, should always be directed against the State—a strategy that has been made easier by the State taking over, in several industries, the functions and practices of the capitalist. The General Strike of the future must be organized as a strike of the community against the State. The result of that strike will not be in doubt. The State is just as vulnerable as a human being, and can be killed by the cutting of a single artery. But the event must be catastrophic. Tyranny, whether of a person or a class, can never be destroyed in any other way. It was the Great Insurgent himself who said: 'Be ye wise as serpents.'

An insurrection is necessary for the simple reason that when it comes to the point, even your man of good will, if he exercises power, will not sacrifice his personal advantages to the general good. In the rapacious type of capitalism existing in Europe and America, such personal advantages are the result of an exercise of low cunning hardly compatible with a sense of justice; or they are based on a callous speculation in finance which neither knows nor cares what human elements are involved in the abstract movement of market prices. For the last fifty years it has been obvious to anyone with an inquiring mind that the capitalist system has reached a stage in its development at which it can only continue under cover of imperial aggression—at which it can only extend its markets behind a barrage of high explosives. But even that realization—the realization that capitalism involves a human sacrifice beyond the lusts of Moloch—even that realization has not persuaded our rulers to humanize the social economy of nations. Nowhere—not even in Russia—have they abandoned the economic values upon which every society since the Middle Ages has vainly tried to base itself. It has only been proved, again and again, that on the question of spiritual values there can be no compromise. Half-measures have failed and now the inevitable catastrophe has overwhelmed us. Whether that catastrophe is the final paroxysm of a doomed system, leaving the world darker and more despairing than ever; or whether it is the prelude to a spontaneous and universal insurrection, will depend on a swift apprehension of the destiny that is upon us. Faith in the fundamental goodness of man; humility in the presence of natural law; reason and mutual aid —these are the qualities that can save us. But they must be unified and vitalized by an insurrectionary passion, a flame in which all virtues are tempered and clarified, and brought to their most effective strength.

POETRY AND ANARCHISM

The first philosophers, the original observers of life and nature, were the best; and I think only the Indians and the Greek naturalists, together with Spinoza, have been right on the chief issue, the relation of man and his spirit to the universe.

SANTAYANA

By governing the people with love it is possible to remain unknown.

LAO-TZE

I tell you I had rather be a swineherd upon the flats of Amager and be understood of the swine, than be a poet and be misunderstood of men.

KIERKEGAARD

I

NO PROGRAMME

To declare for a doctrine so remote as anarchism at this stage of history will be regarded by some critics as a sign of intellectual bankruptcy; by others as a sort of treason, a desertion of the democratic front at the most acute moment of its crisis; by still others as merely poetic nonsense. For myself it is not only a return to Proudhon, Tolstoy, and Kropotkin, who were the predilections of my youth, but a mature realization of their essential rightness, and a realization, moreover, of the necessity, or the probity, of an intellectual confining himself to essentials.

I am thus open to a charge of having wavered in my allegiance to the truth. In extenuation I can only plead that if from time to time I have temporized with other measures of political action —and I have never been an active politician, merely a sympathizing intellectual—it is because I have believed that such measures were part way to the final goal, and the only immediately practical measures. From 1917 onwards and for as long as I could preserve the illusion, communism as established in Russia seemed to promise the social liberty of my ideals. So long as Lenin and Stalin promised a definitive 'withering away of the State' I was prepared to stifle my doubts and prolong my faith. But when, five, ten, fifteen, and then twenty years passed, with the liberty of the individual receding at every stage, a break became inevitable. It was only delayed so long because no other country in the world offered a fairer prospect of social justice. Then for a few breathless months it became possible to transfer our hopes to Spain, where anarchism, so long oppressed and obscured, emerged as a predominant force in constructive socialism. For the time being the forces of reaction have established an uneasy dictatorship, but it is impossible to believe that the conscience of a modern people, once roused to a sense of its human rights, will always endure this tyranny. The struggle in Spain was the first phase of the world struggle against fascism, and the defeat of Hitler and Mussolini should involve the eventual overthrow of their ally Franco. Anarchism will then re-manifest its possibilities in Spain, and justify a renewal of our faith in human humility and individual grace. The will to power, which has for so long warped the social structure of Europe, and which has even possessed the minds of socialists, has been renounced by people who can claim to represent the vital forces of a nation. For that reason I do not see why intellectuals like myself, who are not politicians pledged to an immediate policy, should not openly declare ourselves for the only political doctrine which is consistent with our love of justice and our need for freedom.

I speak of doctrine, but there is nothing I so instinctively avoid as a static system of ideas. I realize that form, pattern, and order are essential aspects of existence; but in themselves they are the attributes of death. To make life, to insure progress, to create interest and vividness, it is necessary to break form, to distort pattern, to change the nature of our civilization. In order to create it is necessary to destroy; and the agent of destruction in society is the poet. I believe that the poet is necessarily an anarchist, and that he must oppose all organized conceptions of the State, not only those which we inherit from the past, but equally those which are imposed on people in the name of the future. In this sense I make no distinction between fascism and marxism.

This tract is a personal confession of faith. It is not a programme, nor a party pronunciamento. I have no deliberate design on mankind. I have arrived at a personal equation: *Yo sé quién soy*—my ideas relate to myself. They are conditioned by my origin, my environment, and my economic condition. My happiness consists in the fact that I have found the equation between the reality of my being and the direction of my thoughts.

In spite of my intellectual pretensions, I am by birth and tradition a peasant. I remain essentially a peasant. I despise this foul industrial epoch—not only the plutocracy which it has raised to power, but also the industrial proletariat which it has drained from the land and proliferated in hovels of indifferent brick. The class in the community for which I feel a natural sympathy is the agricultural class, including the genuine remnants of a landed aristocracy. This perhaps explains my early attraction to Bakunin, Kropotkin, and Tolstoy, who were also of the land, aristocrats and peasants. A man cultivating the earth—that is the elementary economic fact; and as a poet I am only concerned with elementary facts.

Deep down, my attitude is a protest against the fate which has made me a poet in an industrial age. For it is almost impossible to be a poet in an industrial age. In our own language, there have only been two genuine major poets since the industrial age established itself—Whitman and Lawrence. And they are great in their protestations—rarely in their positive expressions of joy. Whitman, it is true, was only half caught in the trap; he was born in a raw undeveloped country, which explains why he was so much more positive than Lawrence.

Nevertheless I realize that industrialism must be endured; the poet must have bowels to digest its iron aliment. I am no yearning medievalist, and have always denounced the sentimental reaction of Morris and his disciples. I have embraced industrialism, tried to give it its true aesthetic principles, all because I want to be through with it, want to get to the other side of it, into a world of electric power and mechanical plenty when man can once more return to the land, not as a peasant but as a lord. The ether will deliver us the power which the old landlords extracted from serfs: there will be no need to enslave a single human soul. But we shall be in contact with the land; we shall have soil and not cement under our feet; we shall live from the produce of our fields and not from the canned pulp of factories.

I am not concerned with the practicability of a programme. I am only concerned to establish truth, and to resist all forms of dictation and coercion. I shall endeavour to live as an individual, to develop my individuality; and if necessary I shall be isolated in a prison rather than submit to the indignities of war and collectivism. It is the only protest an individual can make against the mass stupidity of the modern world. He can do it—if he can afford it—from the safe distance of a New Mexican Thebaid; but if he is poor he must cut a wry romantic figure on the ash-heaps of his own outraged country.

In the parochial atmosphere of England, to profess a belief in anarchism is to commit political suicide. But there are more ways than one of committing suicide, of escaping from the unendurable injustice of life. One way is the mortal and effective way of a poet like Mayakovsky. I shall consider it in the next chapter. Another way is the way of the Thebaid—the way taken by the Christian intellectuals at a similar crisis in the world's history and the way taken in our own age by an artist like Gauguin. Gauguin is perhaps not a very important painter, but he is a pioneer in this particular mode of escape. He was the type of artist who, realizing the necessity of imagination and appreciating as keenly as anyone its qualities, set out consciously to seek it. He sought above all to create the material conditions in which it would function. He gave up his bourgeois occupation and his bourgeois marriage; he tried to avoid the most elementary economic and practical activities. 'My mind is made up: I want soon to go to Tahiti, a little island in Oceania, where material life has no need of money. A terrible epoch is being prepared in Europe for the coming generation: the reign of Gold. Everything is rotten, both men and the arts. Here one is incessantly distracted. There, at least, the Tahitian, under a summer sky and living on a wonderfully fertile soil, needs only to put out his hand to find food. Consequently he never works. Life, to the Tahitian, consists of singing and making love, so that once my material life is well organized, I shall be able to give myself up entirely to painting, free from artistic jealousy, and without any necessity for shady dealing.' Gauguin went to Tahiti, but he was bitterly disappointed. He found that even in the South Seas you cannot escape 'the reign of Gold'. You merely find yourself at its outposts, and have to fight its most degraded exponents single-handed. You can, in short, only escape from civilization by entirely renouncing civilization—by giving up the struggle for beauty and fame and wealth—all bourgeois values to which Gauguin still pathetically clung. It was his friend, the poet Arthur Rimbaud, who accepted the only immediate alternative: complete renunciation, not merely of civilization, but of all attempts to create a world of the imagination.

Civilization has gone from bad to worse since Gauguin's time, and there are many young artists today whose only desire is to escape to some fertile soil under a summer sky, where they may devote themselves entirely to their art free from the distractions of an insane world. But there is no escape. Apart from the practical difficulty of finding a secure refuge in this world, the truth is that modern man can never escape from himself. He carries his warped psychology about with him no less inevitably than his bodily diseases. But the worst disease is the one he creates out of his own isolation: uncriticized phantasies, personal symbols, private fetishes. For whilst it is true that the source of all art is irrational and automatic—that you cannot create a work of art by taking thought—it is equally true that the artist only acquires his significance by being a member of a society. The work of art, by processes which we have so far failed to understand, is a product of the relationship which exists between an individual and a society, and no great art is possible unless you have as corresponding and contemporary activities the spontaneous freedom of the individual and the passive coherence of a society. To escape from society (if that were possible) is to escape from the only soil fertile enough to nourish art.

The escape of Gauguin and the escape of Mayakovsky are thus the only alternative methods of committing suicide. There only remains the path I have chosen: to reduce beliefs to fundamentals, to shed everything temporal and opportunist, and then to stay where you are and suffer if you must.

2

POETS AND POLITICIANS

On the 14th of April 1930, Vladimir Mayakovsky, then acknowledged as the greatest poet of modern Russia, committed suicide. He is not the only modern Russian poet who has taken his own life: Yessenin and Bagritsky did the same, and they were not inconsiderable poets. But Mayakovsky, by all accounts, was exceptional—the inspiration of the revolutionary movement in Russian literature, a man of great intelligence, and of inspired utterance. The circumstances leading to his death are obscure, but he left behind him a piece of paper on which he had written this poem:

> *As they say*
> *'the incident is closed'.*
> *Love boat*
> *smashed against mores.*
> *I'm quits with life.*
> *No need itemizing*
> *mutual griefs*
> *woes*
> *offences.*
> *Good luck and good-bye.*[1]

There is no need to itemize. There is no need to detail the circumstances leading to this poet's death. Obviously there was a love affair, but to our surprise there were also the *mores*—the social conventions against which this love-boat smashed. Mayakovsky was in a very special sense the poet of the Revolution: he celebrated its triumph and its progressive achievements in verse which had all the urgency and vitality of the event. But he was to perish by his own hand like any miserable in-grown subjectivisit of bourgeois capitalism. The Revolution had evidenlty not created an atmosphere of intellectual confidence and moral freedom.

We can understand and draw courage and resolution from the death of Garcia Lorca, who was shot by fascists at Granada in 1936. On the whole, an undisguised hatred of poets is preferable to the callous indifference of our own rulers. In England poets are not regarded as *dangerous* individuals—merely as a type that can be ignored. Give them a job in an office, and if they won't work let them starve. . . .

In England or in Russia, in America or in Germany, it is the same: in one way or another poetry is stifled. That is the world-wide fate of poetry. It is the fate of poetry in our civilization,

[1] Trans. by Max Eastman, *Artists in Uniform* (Allen & Unwin, 1934).

and Mayakovsky's death merely proves that in this respect the new civilization of Russia is only the same civilization in disguise. Nor are poets the only artists to suffer—composers, painters, and sculptors, are in the same love-boat, smashed against the *mores* of the totalitarian State. War and revolution have achieved nothing for culture because they have achieved nothing for freedom. But that is too vague and grandiloquent a way of expressing the simple truth: what I really mean is that the doctrinaire civilizations which are forced on the world—capitalist, fascist, and marxist—by their very structure and principles exclude the values in which and for which the poet lives.

Capitalism does not challenge poetry in principle—it merely treats it with ignorance, indifference, and unconscious cruelty. But in Russia, Italy, Germany, as still in fascist Spain, there was neither ignorance nor indifference, and cruelty was a deliberate persecution leading to execution or suicide. Both fascism and marxism[1] are fully aware of the power of the poet, and because the poet is powerful, they wish to use him for their own political purposes. The conception of the totalitarian State involves the subordination of all its elements to a central control, and not least among such elements are the aesthetic values of poetry and of the arts in general.

This attitude towards art goes back to Hegel, in whom both marxism and fascism have their source. In his anxiety to establish the hegemony of the spirit or the Idea, Hegel found it necessary to relegate art, as a product of sensation, to a past historical stage in human development. Art he regarded as a primitive mode of thought or representation which had been gradually superseded by the intellect or reason; and consequently, in our present stage of development, we ought to put art away like a discarded toy.

Hegel was fairly just in his estimate of art; where he went wrong was in thinking that it could be dispensed with. He was a victim of the evolutionary concepts of his time, and applied these concepts to the human mind, where they do not work. The

---

[1] I always use 'marxism' to designate the centralized totalitarian conception of communism as distinct from the devolutionary types which I call 'anarchism'.

intellect does not develop by improving or eliminating the primary sensations or instincts, but by suppressing them. They remain submerged but clamant, and art is if anything more necessary today than in the Stone Age. In the Stone Age it was a spontaneous exercise of innate faculties, as art still is with young children and savages. But for civilized man art has become something much more serious: the release (generally vicarious) of repressions, a compensation for the abstraction of the intellect. I am not implying that this is the only function of art—it is also a necessary mode of acquiring a knowledge of certain aspects of reality.

When Marx turned Hegel upside down, or inside out, he accepted this evolutionary scheme—accepted, that is to say, Hegel's dismissal of art to the childhood of mankind. His dialectic of materialism is a reversal of Hegel's dialectic of the spirit, but since art had already been eliminated from the domain of the spirit, it was left out of the negation of that domain. It is true that you will find in the works of Marx and Engels a few vague (and even uneasy) references to art; it is one of the ideological superstructures to be accounted for by the economic analysis of society. But there is no recognition of art as a primary factor in human experience, of art as a mode of knowledge or as a means of apprehending the meaning or quality of life.

In a similar way, that development of Hegel's thought which has accepted and affirmed his hierarchy of the spirit and has put into practice his notion of a supreme authoritarian State, this development has necessarily reduced art to a subordinate and slavish role. Fascism has perhaps done more and worse than that: it has insisted on a purely rational and functional interpretation of art. Art becomes, not a mode of expressing the life of the imagination, but a means of illustrating the concepts of the intelligence.

At this point, marxism and fascism, the prodigal and the dutiful sons of Hegel, meet again; and will inevitably become reconciled. There is not the slightest difference, in intention, in control and in final product, between the art of marxist Russia and the art of fascist Germany. It is true that the one is urged to celebrate the achievements of socialism, and the other to celebrate the ideals of nationalism; but the necessary method is the same—a rhetorical realism, devoid of invention, deficient in imagination, renouncing subtlety and emphasizing the obvious.

I am not going to repeat here the familiar arguments against socialist realism as such. Its products are so poor by every standard known to the history of art that such arguments are not really necessary. It is more important to show the positive connection between art and individual freedom.

If we consider the world's great artists and poets—and the question of their relative greatness does not matter: what I am going to say is true of any poet or painter who has survived the test of time—we may observe in them a certain development. Indeed, to trace this development in a poet like Shakespeare or a painter like Titian or a composer like Beethoven is partly an explanation of the enduring fascination of their work. We may correlate such development with incidents in their lives and with circumstances of their time; these are not without their effects. But the essential process is that of a seed falling on fertile ground, germinating and growing and in due course reaching maturity. Now just as certainly as the flower and the fruit are implicit in the single seed, so the genius of a poet or painter is contained within the individual. The soil must be favourable, the plant must be nourished; it will be distorted by winds and by accidental injuries. But the growth is unique, the configuration unique, the fruit unique. All apples are very much alike, but no two are exactly the same. But that is not the point: a genius is the tree which has produced the unknown fruit, the golden apples of Hesperides. But Mayakovsky was a tree which one year was expected to produce plums of a uniform size and appearance; a few years later apples; and finally cucumbers. No wonder that he broke down under such an unnatural strain!

In Soviet Russia any work of art that is not simple, conventional, and conformist is denounced as 'leftist distortion'. Any originality is described as 'petty bourgeois individualism'. The artist must have one aim and only one aim—to supply the public with what it wants. The phrases varied in Germany and Italy, but they were to the same effect. The public is the undifferentiated mass of the collectivist State, and what this public wants is what it has wanted throughout history—sentimental tunes, doggerel verse, pretty ladies on chocolate-box lids: all that which the Germans call by the forceful word *Kitsch*.

The marxist may protest that we are prejudging the result of an experiment. The arts must return to a popular basis and from that basis, by a process of education, be raised to a new universal level such as the world has never known. It is just conceivable—an art as realistic and as lyrical as, say, that of Shakespeare, but freed from all those personal idiosyncrasies and obscurities which mar the classical perfection of his drama; or an art as classically perfect as Racine's, but more human and more intimate; the scope of Balzac allied to the technique of Flaubert. We cannot assume that the individualistic tradition which has produced these great artists has attained the highest possible peak of human genius. But is there in the history of any of the arts any evidence that such superlative works will be produced to a programme? Is there any evidence to show that the form and scope of a work of art can be predetermined? Is there any evidence that art in its highest manifestations can appeal to more than a relatively restricted minority? Even if we admit that the general level of education can be raised until there is no excuse for ignorance, will not the genius of the artist by this very fact be compelled to seek still higher levels of expression?

The artist in the U.S.S.R. is classed as a worker. That is all to the good, for the social exclusiveness of the artist has nothing to do with the quality of his work, and may be decidedly harmful. But it shows a fundamental misunderstanding of the faculty of artistic creation if the artist is treated like any other kind of producer, and compelled to deliver a specified output in a specified time. The vein of creation or inspiration is soon exhausted under such duress. That should be obvious. What is not so obvious is that the laws of supply and demand in art are very different from those in economics. Admittedly at a certain level art becomes entertainment, and admittedly at that level it is a matter of supplying a popular article of a specified kind. But whereas we go to an entertainment to be taken out of ourselves, to forget for an hour or two our daily routine, to escape from life, we turn to a work of art in a very different mood. To express it crudely, but forcibly, we expect to be uplifted. The poet or the painter or the composer, if he is more than an entertainer, is a man who moves us with some joyful or tragic interpretation of the meaning of life; who foretells our human destiny or who celebrates the beauty and significance of our natural environment; who creates in us the wonder and the terror of the unknown. Such things can only be done by a man who possesses a superior sensibility and insight; and who by virtue of his special gifts stands apart from the mass—not disdainfully, but simply because he can only exercise his faculties from a distance and in a solitude. The moments of creation are still and magical, a trance or reverie in which the artist holds communion with forces which lie below the habitual level of thought and emotion. That is what the man of action, the politician and fanatic, cannot appreciate. They bully and shout at the artist and force him into the hubbub of practical activities, where he can only produce mechanically to an intellectually predetermined pattern. Art cannot be produced under such conditions, but only a dry and ineffectual semblance of it. Compelled to produce under such conditions, the more sensitive artist will despair. *In extremis*, like Mayakovsky he will commit suicide.

3
WHY WE ENGLISH HAVE NO TASTE

The title of this chapter is deliberate, and exact. I do not say that the English have bad taste—that, perhaps, might be said of other nations—but simply that they do not exercise those faculties of sensibility and selection which make for good taste. Our condition is neutral—an immense indifference to questions of art. It is true that we have magnificent museums, unrivalled in the whole world: but if we inquire into their origin, we find that they were founded ' to encourage manufactures'. It is true that we have produced great artists like Gainsborough, Constable, and Turner; but we find, when we look into their lives, that they were regarded as socially inferior beings, and were always treated with neglect. Occasionally an artist is honoured, but it is always an official artist—the President of the Royal Academy, the painter of the King's official portraits, the designer of our telephone boxes. From its very inception, our Academy has opposed original talent, and never more obstinately than today, when we can say without fear of contradiction that not a single artist of international reputation is included among its members. When there is no question of an art being used 'to encourage manufacture', as in the case of music, then it is completely unrecognized by the State.[1]

A superficial observer jumps to the conclusion that our lack of taste is a racial defect. We are ready ourselves to confess that we are not an artistic nation (thank God!). But this, the readiest explanation, is the least true. There is the obvious contradiction of our past—our Gothic cathedrals, and all our minor arts in the Middle Ages. It can be claimed with good reason that in the twelfth century England was the most artistic country in the whole of Europe. Even in the art of music, in which we have for so long been completely impotent, we were once supreme (from the time of John Dunstable in the fifteenth century to that of Purcell in the seventeenth century). And though the gulf between the plastic arts (in which, for the purposes of this argument, we may include music) and the art of poetry is so great that it cannot be bridged by any logic, yet our poetry is sufficient evidence of an organic sensibility, of an inherent artistic nature. We must, therefore, dismiss the racial factor as largely irrelevant, and look first into the historical factor.

But before we leave the racial question, it is worth observing that the English race is not a simple unity; apart from various subdivisions, there is the broad distinction between the Celtic and Germanic elements. About these two races we can make certain generalizations based on our knowledge of their history.

[1] Since this chapter was first written, the Arts Council of Great Britain has come into existence, and has as its function the direct encouragement of the arts. With the limited funds at its disposal it can do little more than keep alive institutions (such as the Covent Garden Opera House) which would otherwise have disappeared in the economic stress of the post-war period.

We know, for example, that Celtic art through all the centuries of its separate existence was an abstract art, very vital and rhythmical, but shunning the representation of natural forms. In the modern sense, it was non-figurative. We also know that the Germanic peoples were not given to plastic expression; their modes of thought were conceptual, and their typical art is therefore verbal. If, in the subsequent history of a country which combines two such divergent races, we find an alternation of plastic and verbal arts, it may well be due to the supremacy of one or other of these constituent racial elements.

Actually, of course, these racial elements got obscured by other factors, chiefly economic. The movement which in England brought an end to our plastic modes of expression was partly economic and partly religious; the religious aspect is known as Puritanism, the economic aspect as Capitalism, and there is now a general agreement that these two aspects were inter-active. Puritanism provided Capitalism with a moral atmosphere within which it could develop unchecked by conscience and the rule of the Church. Whether the economic motive called the moral values into being, or the moral values encouraged latent impulses for the acquisition of individual power, is a problem in the dialectic of history into which we need not inquire now.

To say that England, during the last four hundred years, has shown the least evidence of artistic taste is therefore but another way of saying that during the same period England has been the most highly developed capitalist state. But such a simple materialistic explanation will not altogether suffice to explain the facts. For at other times, and in other countries, the fine arts have been used to express material wealth and power. But not in England. At the most, the successful industrialist would commission an artist to paint his portrait, and the portraits of members of his family; sometimes the patronage would be extended to include his favourite racehorse, or even a prize bull. But the notion of buying works of art for their own sake, and for the sake of the owner's aesthetic enjoyment, was confined to a few members of the aristocracy.

For an explanation of this difference between England and other capitalist countries, we must turn from social economics to social psychology. During this same period the Englishman has developed, and has shown himself consciously proud of, certain characteristics which are summed up in the terms *common sense*, and *sense of humour*. The terms are closely related, and denote a certain ideal of normality to which every Englishman aspires, and to which the whole of his upbringing and education is directed. His sense of humour is his perception of any deviation from the normal. The 'gentleman' is the apotheosis of the normal. Common sense is normal sense—accepted opinion, agreed conventions, perfected habits. In his house and his clothes, in his food and his women, the Englishman of the capitalist-puritan era endeavoured to attain the normal. The definition of a well-dressed gentleman is 'one whose clothes you do not remember'; a man who in every detail, from the colour of the cloth to the number of buttons on his sleeve, is so normal that he is unnoticeable, unseen. Just as a gentleman's clothes must be distinguished by their lack of distinction, so with all his possessions. To possess works of art would be odd; to frequent artists would be odd, for to the Englishman the artist is essentially odd, abnormal.

But the matter is deeper than this. Psychologists are beginning to suspect that this normality we value so much is no more than the most common neurosis; that normality is itself a neurosis, a retreat from the reality of life, a nervous mask. Everything in English life supports this view; the normal man *is* nervous—his laughter is an expression of nervousness. For English laughter (or, as I should more accurately call it, capitalist laughter) is not bodily laughter—not *belly laughter*, like the laughter of Chaucer and Rabelais; it is mental laughter, caused by an unconscious disturbance of suppressed instincts. From the same social suppression of instinct (and it is, of course, the sexual instinct that is most in question) come our other characteristics —our so-called hypocrisy, which is not pure hypocrisy, just because it is unconscious; our prudishness; our coldness in love; our lack of wit (it is significant that our wittiest writers come from Ireland, the least Protestant and the least capitalist part of the kingdom).

From the same source comes the prevalent indifference to the plastic arts. For the ideal of normality alone will not explain

70

this fact; it would be equally normal if everyone were interested in the plastic arts. But there was never any chance of that, for the same forces of repression which determine the neurosis of normality, are at the root of a plastic anesthesia in the individuals suffering from such a neurosis.

The complete demonstration of this correspondence must be left to the psycho-analysts. Empirically we can see that the least suppressed societies—those least addicted to normality in conduct—are also the most plastically conscious people; the Greeks, for example. But the most convincing demonstration would be in the sphere of individual psychology; for though the neurosis is determined by societal pressure, the effects reach beyond social activities and rule the individual in his purely personal modes of expression. Plastic expression is the most objective mode of expression; it involves giving fixed material expression to a personal impulse. Fear of infringing the limits of normality will tend to inhibit such a mode of expression. It will be far safer to express the individual impulse in the comparatively transitory and fluid material of music and poetry. For some obscure reason the other great Puritan section of Europe expressed its individual longings mainly in music; the English mainly in words, in poetry. But the great distinction of this poetry, compared with the poetry of other modern nations, is that it is a pure poetry. Its greatest beauty is inherent in its sound; it too is a kind of music, as far removed as possible from the visual and the plastic.

Some foreign observers, puzzled by this complete lack of the plastic sense in the English, have attempted to find it in unexpected places. A few years ago a Danish architect made an exhibition of the real, the unrecognized, English arts. The *chef d'œuvre* was the English football; there were English boots and English tennis-rackets; suitcases and saddles, and probably a water-closet. In such articles, it was maintained, we showed a supreme sense of form, of abstract *form*. It was a charming idea, but the Englishman was not flattered; he laughed in his nervous manner. To him, it was a *stunt*, a good joke. 'You never know', they said to one another, 'what these foreigners will be up to next!'

So the neurosis of normality is preserved; it is impregnable. Its latest manifestation is illustrated in the term *highbrow*, which in recent years has become a supreme term of abuse. For the normal man recognizes in his midst, not merely odd fellows who can be dismissed as artists, but also odder fellows who use a non-plastic medium, words, and who in poems, articles, books, and speeches, revolt against the ideal of normality; fellows who defend the artist and all his works; fellows who refuse to accept his economic system, his ideal of gentleman, his public-school education, his whole outfit of normality. Such dangerous eccentrics must be stigmatized, ridiculed, made into figures of fun— something to laugh at, something to sneer at, something to snigger at. And so the word highbrow is invented, and becomes an efficient label. You have only to call a man a highbrow to damn him in the eyes of the public, to make his books unsaleable, and his life impossible. For in his clumsy bovine way the normal man, the poor dupe of capitalism, recognizes in the highbrow a disturber of the peace; if not of the peace of society, then of the peace of his mind. 'Peace of mind' is another revealing phrase; it is the proud possession of every normal Englishman.

Those who wish to study our national neurosis must do so on the spot, but it is very doubtful if a foreigner could ever appreciate its ramifications in our society. A useful guide to its obvious aspects is that famous journal of national humour, *Punch*. There every week the highbrow is guyed, the normal is exalted, and the existence of sex is suppressed. Even the poor are resented, and their illiteracy exposed to the mirth of the public-school mind. Any daily paper will reveal the more aggressive aspects of our normality; an absolute poverty of ideas, a complete absence of any intellectual interests. But it is only in the English *home*, the Englishman's castle, as he proudly calls it, that the full horror of the neurosis will be revealed. All over the world capitalism has spread its net of mental debauchery; its standardization of taste, its imposition of material values. But in England the natural instincts have been so long deformed, that they no longer function. Sensibility is dead, and the only criterion of judgement is convention: the acceptance of a standard imposed by manufacturers, whose only criterion is profit.

The conclusion is inevitable: the conclusion we come to whichever way we turn. We are the victims of an historical process, and our lack of taste is merely our lack of social freedom. With the growth of individualism began the growth of capitalism; the public good, the common-wealth, was subordinated to private good, private wealth. Religion and morality were adapted to the new economic order; which is to say that spiritual values were divorced from worldly values. Such is the general aspect of the change. But the individual suffers; no longer a cell within the spiritual and economic womb of the community, he develops a new kind of consciousness—the protective mechanism of a mind exposed to criticism. He grows this shell of normality, a hard opaque exterior which admits no light; beneath which the senses stir like blind maggots.

Therefore the cause of the arts is the cause of revolution. Every reason—historical, economic, and psychological—points to the fact that art is only healthy in a communal type of society, where within one organic consciousness all modes of life, all senses and all faculties, function freely and harmoniously. We in England have suffered the severest form of capitalist exploitation; we have paid for it, not only in physical horror and destitution, in appalling deserts of cinders and smoke, in whole cities of slums and rivers of filth—we have paid for it also in a death of the spirit. We have no taste because we have no freedom; we have no freedom because we have no faith in our common humanity.[1]

4

ESSENTIAL COMMUNISM

When an artist, a poet, or a philosopher—the kind of person we often describe as an intellectual—ventures to take part in the political controversies of his own time, he always does so at a certain risk. It is not that such ques-

---

[1] I have dealt more positively with the subject of this chapter in a later pamphlet: *To Hell with Culture* (Kegan Paul, 1941). Reprinted in *The Politics of the Unpolitical* (Routledge, 1945).

tions are beneath his notice; for they involve, in the end, the very problems of art and ethics which are his particular concern. But the immediate application of general principles is rarely possible in politics, which are ruled by expediency and opportunism—modes of conduct which the intellectual cannot decently adopt. Nevertheless, in so far as his intellectual detachment, which is quite simply the scientific method, does lead to definite conclusions, to that extent the intellectual should declare his political position.

The poet, however, is in a more embarrassing situation than most of his kind. He is a creature of intuitions and sympathies, and by his very nature shrinks from definiteness and doctrinaire attitudes. Pledged to the shifting process of reality, he cannot subscribe to the static provisions of a policy. He has two principal duties: to mirror the world as it is, and to imagine the world as it might be. In Shelley's sense he is a legislator, but the House of Poets is even more incapacitated than the House of Lords. Disfranchized by his lack of residence in any fixed constituency, wandering faithlessly in the no-man's-land of his imagination, the poet cannot, without renouncing his essential function, come to rest in the bleak conventicles of a political party. It is not his pride that keeps him outside; it is really his humility, his devotion to the complex wholeness of humanity—in the precise sense of the word, his magnanimity.

Special causes have intensified the indecision of my own generation. I do not wish to exaggerate the effects of war; in my case I can see quite clearly that experience of war was not the immediate cause of political disillusion and inactivity. But it would be absurd entirely to discount the psychological effects of that experience, in so far as it was the direct experience of death and destruction. It will be recalled how Dostoevsky keyed himself up to face death one cold morning in 1849; and how he was at the last moment reprieved. It was an experience which his critics have found highly significant for his subsequent development. But that was an experience endured tens or hundreds of times by intellectuals in the war—not by intellectuals only, of course, but by intellectuals in common with others less liable to register their psychological reactions. But in spite of such experiences, I remember that when peace came in 1918, I personally still retained the youthful idealism which had been mine in 1914. The disillusion came with the peace—with the slow-motion farce of the Treaty negotiations, with the indifference which people in power felt for the opinion of the men who had fought, with the general spread of false sentiment and hypocrisy. We had fought for Peace, for a decent world; we found we had won trophies of hatred and greed, of national passion and commercial profiteering, of political reaction and social retrenchment—not one voice, not one party, not even a Christian Church, openly declaring itself for a world of economic justice, a world free from the faults that had led us into the horrors of a world war.

Only in Russia there was a difference—a withdrawal from the scramble, a struggle for a new order of some sort. But from the depths of imposed ignorance and hopelessness, it seemed impossible to believe in the reality and the permanence of that revolution; impossible to estimate its significance.

My difficulty then was to find an immediate active role for the intellectual in politics. The only guide I found in this personal dilemma was the French philosopher and critic, Julien Benda. This very sharp and subtle mind had first attracted me by an attack on Bergson, at a time when Bergson was very much my enthusiasm. He was not just to Bergson, but he weaned me from my allegiance, and my mind was fully prepared for the sterile intellectualism of Benda's subsequent works. That expression is perhaps too strong, for Benda's main contention, in such a book as *La Trahison des Clercs*, is unassailable. I shared his desire to occupy a detached position; quite simply, to be left alone to get on with my job as a poet, an intellectual, a 'clerk'. Unfortunately, as Benda admitted in his book, modern economic conditions scarcely permit the clerk to fulfil his function; and so 'the true evil to deplore in our time is perhaps not the treason of the clerks, but the disappearance of the clerks—the impossibility of leading the life of a clerk under present conditions'.

Trotsky has said that all through history the mind limps after reality. It is another way of saying that the intellectual cannot avoid the economic conditions of his time; he cannot ignore them —for they will not ignore him. In one way or another he must compound with circumstances. But to describe the exact nature of the dilemma, a metaphor more elaborate than Trotsky's is necessary. Reality is manifold: a magnetic field with lines of force passing through all points in the compass of human sensibility.

The material organization of life is the basic fact: to that extent an intellectual can accept the marxian dialectic. But though I admit the virtues of this method of reasoning, it would be better for me to drop all pretensions of generality and approach the matter as an intellectual, as one who has definite preferences in art and therefore in life. The marxian would call such preferences bourgeois prejudices, but that is precisely where we differ. Art is a discipline—'a symbolic discipline', as Wyndham Lewis has so well described it. Now a discipline is always practised for the purpose of directing a force into some definite channel. The discipline of art directs our sensibility, our creative energy, our intuitions, into formal patterns, symbolic shapes, allegorical fables, dramatic myths—into *works* (literally constructions) of art. But discipline, and the order it gives, does not exist for itself: it is not an end, but a means. It is not even a general or universal form which can be imposed on a multitude of phenomena. It is, rather, an individual sense of rhythm or harmony. There are metres but not metre; forms, but not form. It is only by *variation* that the artist achieves beauty. The discipline of art, therefore, is not static; it is continually changing, essentially revolutionary.

What in the attitude of our between-war socialists probably repelled me most directly was their incapacity to appreciate the significance of the artist's approach. To me it seemed elementary that a belief in Marx should be accompanied by a belief in, say, Cézanne; and that the development of art since Cézanne should interest the completely revolutionary mind as much as the development of socialist theory since Proudhon. I wanted to discuss, not only Sorel and Lenin, but also Picasso and Joyce. But no one saw the connection. Each isolated on his separate line denied the relevance of the force animating the other lines. No one could see that it was the same force that was transforming the whole of reality—making it possible to give different interpretation of reality. To me it seemed just as important to destroy the established bourgeois ideals in literature, painting, and

76

architecture as it was to destroy the established bourgeois ideals in economics.

In a preface to a book on the principles of modern art,[1] under the shadow, then oppressive, of the German counter-revolution, I made an attempt to dissociate revolutionary art and revolutionary politics. It is quite true, as I stated, that the majority of modern artists are 'neither Jews nor Communists, not racialists or politicians of any kind. They are just artists, and, if anything, the more *modern* they are in spirit as artists, the more disinterested and detached they become'. That cannot be denied; and my further statement is equally true—that the modernity of modern art is the result of developments within the technique and science of art. 'The great artists who have determined the course of modern art,' I wrote, 'Constable, Turner, Cézanne, Matisse, Picasso—have been, and are, singularly devoid of ideologies of any kind. They live in their vision and their paint, and follow the inevitable course dictated by their sensibility.' These statements, I repeat, are true enough, and in their context at least rhetorically justified. But in another context—the narrow context of the conditions deplored by Benda, the wider contexts of the general conditions of historical necessity—my statements ignore the fundamental (and fundamentally true) thesis of the marxian dialectic—the thesis expressed by my image of the four-pronged magnet.

That the marxian dialectic, as applied to art, is by no means clear in its workings is shown by the marxian critics themselves. On the other hand, we have, for example, Carl Einstein interpreting the Cubist movement in general, and Braque in particular, as an inevitable outcome of the transition from individual to collective values in society.[2] The images of reality characteristic of capitalist society must be discarded and in their place the modern artist must create the images of a new conception of reality. Cubism in its first phase is the first step in the process of destruction, but its tectonic element—what it retains of formal structure and geometric measure—is a residue of old prejudices, a last safeguard against the unknown; it still shows a trace of the classical fear of ecstasy. But in his later work an artist like

[1] *Art Now* (Faber & Faber, 1933).
[2] *Georges Braque* (Zwemmer, London, 1934).

Braque passes beyond such limitations, into a world of hallucination. The conscious or reasoning self is entirely destroyed, or superseded, and the painter expresses a visionary reality, devoid of any mundane (bourgeois) associations. The aesthetic criterion is overcome by the force of the creative invention; the picture becomes a 'psychogram'. And by the force of the same argument it ceases, presumably, to be a work of art! Thus the dialectical method in art criticism leaves us with an art which is not so much art as an instrument of derationalization, and we are bound to ask how such an art can ever become the synthetic expression of a proletarian culture. Mr. Einstein would argue that a proletarian art is for the moment impossible, and therefore the question does not arise. The importance of contemporary art is purely negative: it aims at a dissolution of conventional notions of reality. It clears the deck for the collective art of the future.

The examination which another marxian critic, Max Raphael, makes of another modern painter, Picasso, leads to a different conclusion.[1] Picasso is a more complicated case than Braque, but so far as his descriptive analysis of this most typical of modern artists goes, Raphael's Picasso does not differ greatly from Einstein's Braque. The difference lies in the interpretation of the facts. For whereas Einstein sees in Braque a forerunner of the future proletarian art, Raphael finds in Picasso merely the last phase of a decadent bourgeois art—at best, a substitution of metaphysical intuition for impressionistic sensualism; but definitely within the European tradition, and definitely reactionary. His recourse to negro art, to classical art, to 'super-reality', are so many flights from reason—from the implications of a rational view of life. His art is not a simple eclecticism, but a new form of reactionary bourgeois art. The series: negroid, antique, medieval—all phases of Picasso's development—expresses first his fear of tradition, then his precipitate flights back into its bosom. According to this view, Picasso's many-sided development only displays so many futile efforts to solve the problem left unsolved by the nineteenth century—the creation of an art based on economic reality, on the emergent social

[1] *Proudhon, Marx, Picasso: trois études sur la sociologie de l'art* (Editions Excelsior, Paris, 1933).

forces of the modern period. Which is to say no more than that Picasso has remained completely unconscious of the class struggle —a supposition which was not confirmed by his attitude towards the struggle in Spain.

Trotsky somewhere warns us of the necessity, the difficult necessity, of distinguishing between the true and the false revolutionary. That discrimination is just as necessary in modern art as in modern politics. In the modern tradition of painting— ever since painting revolted, like poetry, against the artificiality and irrelevance of the academic tradition of the eighteenth century—there are a number of individual artists whose aims and whose achievements have step by step built up a new conception of reality—a conception of reality totally opposed to the bourgeois standards of the period. Constable began a movement which includes Courbet, Daumier, Van Gogh, Cézanne, and Seurat. The perspective this side of Cézanne is more difficult to see, but in that tradition I would place an artist so coherent and so consistent as Juan Gris, and for the present the tradition is in the miraculous hands of Picasso. Against that tradition, catering for quite a different public (for a *bourgeois* public, in short) you have not only the commonplace art of the academies, but various aspects of dilettantism (neo-classicism, pseudo-romanticism, impressionism) all of which have little to do with the art of the future. The main tradition, the only tradition which is revolutionary in essence, in its fundamental vision of life, that is the tradition which must be integrated with the social revolution.

The issue, as presented by a consideration of these facts, has clearly to do with the relation of the individual to society. The artist is always an individualist, in some sense. But the sense is very different at different times. It is not the same sense in the twelfth century and in the nineteenth century. There is, in fact, an important distinction to be made between individuality and individualism—between the unique capacity of the individual as artist and what Gorky calls 'the instinctive anarchy of the individual', which latter meaning is the basis of Plato's objection to the poet. I am not sure that this distinction will not resolve, in the end, into the general contrast between classicism and romanticism, but I do not, on this occasion, wish to be tempted by such a dangerous analogy. My immediate object is to suggest that the main tradition of modern art is a coherent attitude towards reality—that reality which, to quote Gorky once more, 'is created by the inexhaustible and intelligent will of man'.

Trotsky, who has dealt with these questions more intelligently than most modern critics, has a clear definition of the artist's individuality. 'The truth is,' he writes in *Literature and Revolution*,[1] 'that even if individuality is unique, it does not mean that it cannot be analysed. Individuality is a welding together of tribal, national, class, temporary, and institutional elements, and, in fact, it is the uniqueness of this welding together, in the proportions of this psycho-chemical mixture, that individuality is expressed. One of the most important tasks of criticism is to analyse the individuality of the artist (that is, his art) into its component elements, and to show their correlations. In this way, criticism brings the artist closer to the reader, who also has more or less of a "unique soul", "artistically" unexpressed, "unchosen", but none the less representing a union of the same elements as does the soul of the poet. So it can be seen that what serves as a bridge from soul to soul is not the unique, but the common. Only through the common is the unique known; the common is determined in man by the deepest and most persistent conditions which make up his "soul", by the social conditions of education, of existence, of work, and of associations.'

With this passage I should like the reader to compare Gorky's statement on the same subject, in a letter from which I have already quoted:[2]

'Individualism sprang from the soil of "private ownership". Generations upon generations of men have created collectives, and always the individual, for one reason or another, has stood apart, breaking away from the collective and at the same time from reality where the new is ever in the making. He has been creating his own unique, mystical, and incomprehensible god, set up for the sole purpose of justifying the right of the individual to independence and power. Here mysticism becomes indispensable, because the right of the individual to absolute rule, to

---

[1] Trans. Rose Strunsky (Allen & Unwin, London, 1925), pp. 59–60.
[2] 'Reply to an Intellectual', in *On Guard for the Soviet Union*. English trans. (Martin Lawrence, London, 1933), p. 90.

"autocracy", cannot be explained by reason. Individualism endowed its god with the qualities of omnipotence, infinite wisdom and absolute intelligence—with qualities which man would like to possess, but which develop only through the reality created by collective labour. *This reality always lags behind the human mind,* for the mind which creates it is slowly but constantly perfecting itself. If this were not so, reality would, of course make people contented, and the state of contentment is a passive one. Reality is created by the inexhaustible and intelligent will of man, and its development will never be arrested.'

I must apologize for these long quotations, but this question of the relation of the individual to the collective society of which he is a member is the fundamental issue, in art as well as in politics. It is the fundamental question *within* religion too, for what is the Reformation but the affirmation of the autocratic will of the individual against the collective rule of the Church? Philosophically it is the issue between Scholasticism and Cartesianism, between materialism and idealism. But before passing on to the general issue, I should like to point out a curious contradiction between the statements quoted from Trotsky and Gorky—something more serious than their (or their translators') inconsistent use of the words 'individuality' and 'individualism'. I have previously quoted Trotsky's blunt summary of his general point of view: 'all through history, mind limps after reality.' 'Reality', says Gorky in the sentence I have italicized, 'always lags behind the human mind.' Presumably these two statements could be reconciled by the dialectical method, for dialectics, in the words of Lenin,[1] is 'the study of how there can be and are . . . identical opposites'.

Dialectics apart, there is a sense in which both Gorky and Trotsky may be right. The relation between mind and reality, between the individual and the community, is not one of precedence; it is more one of action and reaction, a process of tacking against the wind. The current of reality is strong, and troubles the mind; but the mind embraces this contrary force, and is lifted higher, and carried farther, by the very opposition. And so with the individual and the community. Complete freedom means inevitable decadence. The mind must feel an opposition,

[1] Quoted by Max Eastman, *Artists in Uniform,* p. 189.

must be tamped with hard realities if it is to have any blasting power.

For this reason I think we must look askance at the word 'liberal', preferring perhaps the title 'realist'. A realist I would define as a man who has learnt to distrust any term to which he cannot attach a perfectly definite meaning. He particularly distrusts those ideological phrases, catch-words, slogans, and symbols under cover of which most of the political activities of today take place. He has a very bitter memory of phrases like 'a war to end war', and 'making the world safe for democracy'. As a realist I look with intense suspicion on words like 'democracy', 'race', 'nation', 'empire', 'proletariat', 'party', 'unity', 'decency', 'morality', 'tradition', 'duty', etc. I prefer words like 'reason', 'intelligence', 'order', 'justice', 'action', and 'objective'; words equally abstract, but representing tidier habits of mind. The word 'liberalism' would naturally be suspect; but it has associations with the word 'liberty', and in the name of liberty most of what I value in life and literature has been achieved. What, then, of this word 'liberty'?

I admit that it represents an idea to which I am passionately attached; at the same time it is a word which I have looked at with a disenchanted eye. I know that it denotes different things to different people, and that many interpretations of it are worthless. In short, I know that the idealistic implications of the word are quite devoid of reality. Liberty is always relative to man's control over natural forces, and to the degree of mutual aid which he finds necessary to exert this control. That is why, in face of the material problems of existence, the ideal of anarchy becomes the practical organization of society known as anarcho-syndicalism. Government—that is to say, control of the individual in the interest of the community—is inevitable if two or more men combine for a common purpose; government is the embodiment of that purpose. But government in this sense is far removed from the conception of an autonomous State. When the State is divorced from its immediate functions and becomes an entity claiming to control the lives and destinies of its subjects—then liberty ceases to exist.

What might be called the tyranny of facts—the present necessity which most of us are under to struggle for our very existence, our food, our shelter, and other no less essential amenities of life—this tyranny is so severe that we ought to be prepared to consider a restriction of liberty in other directions if in this respect some release is promised. But it is no less essential to realize that this tyranny is to a large extent due to the inefficiency of our present economic system, and that liberty now and always depends on a rational organization of production and distribution.

In all that concerns the planning of economic life, the building up of a rational mode of living in a social community, there can be no question of absolute liberty. For, so long as we live in a community, in all practical affairs the greatest good of the greatest number is also the greatest good of the individual. As individuals we must be willing to surrender all material rights—to put all our property into the common fund. Even if we have wealth, we can do this with a happy conscience, for material possessions were always a menace to spiritual liberty. To a certain degree, therefore, we must admit that the social contract implies an economic structure, possessing legitimacy—as an efficient machine designed to facilitate the complex business of living together in a community. But actually the scope of this rational and practical concept—a concept that need be nothing but rational and practical and strictly functional—is extended and combined with various distinct ideologies: in Russia with the marxian ideology of dialectical materialism, in Italy with the ideology of nationalism, in Germany with the even more dangerous ideology of race. In the name of these ideologies, the intellectual liberty of the individual is sacrificed. And that is too much. Whether we accept Trotsky's or Gorky's 'identical opposite', whether we regard the individual as determined by the community, or the community as determined by the individual, the sacrifice is in either case intolerable.

Intellectual liberty—the liberty to pursue individual trends of thought and to publish these for the interest or amusement of our fellow-men—is not defended by me in a spirit of vague idealism. The political ideology of liberty is liberalism, or *laissez-faire*, which is the doctrine most suited to a predatory capitalism. But the pure doctrine of liberty, or libertarianism, will be a living doctrine as long as our civilization survives; for on our liberty depends the life of our civilization. And depends in the most practical and demonstrable way. The proof must naturally be historical; and from history, in all its aspects, emerges the incontrovertible law which Mill expressed in these words: 'The initiation of all wise or noble things comes and must come from individuals; generally at first from some one individual.' Or, negatively: 'The despotism of custom is everywhere the standing hindrance to human advancement, being in unceasing antagonism to that disposition to aim at something better than customary, which is called, according to circumstances, the spirit of liberty, or that of progress or improvement.' I am not as fond as Mill of the word 'progress'; it is not very real as a concept applied to the last five thousand years of history, and it is foolish to indulge in anything but relatively short-term policies for the human race. But I do cling to the fact of vitality; for on the vitality of a civilization depends just simply the will to live—at least, for an intellectual. I know that some of my contemporaries can complacently sacrifice this will; but that is a form of spiritual treachery in which I have no desire to participate. In history, the stagnant waters, whether of custom or of despotism, support no life; life depends on the agitation set up by a few eccentric individuals. For the sake of that life, that vitality, a community must take certain risks, must admit a modicum of heresy. It must live dangerously if it would live at all.

At first sight it would seem that countries like Germany, Italy, and Russia satisfy this condition. One could hardly complain of social stagnation in any of them; and the effects of intellectual stagnation require a few years to show themselves. The economic issues in such countries have been confused by political opportunism. But one issue, and one only, emerges when all temporary and tactical considerations have been dismissed: the issue between capitalism and communism. Even fascism, if we are to believe its theoretical exponents, is socialistic, the aim being to control the means of production and distribution for the general benefit of the community, and therefore to restrict all forms of monopoly and individual power. The essential doctrine of all reforming parties is communism; they only differ in the sincerity with which they profess the ideal, and in the means they adopt

84

to realize it. Some find the means more attractive than the end.

But I must explain what is meant by this essential communism, for it has little to do with the existing communist parties. In the famous Manifesto of the Communist Party, published by Marx and Engels in 1848, the theory of communism was summed up in a single sentence: *Abolition of private property*. There is, it will at once be seen, nothing ideological, nothing in any way mystical, about such a doctrine. But one might criticize it for being merely negative in expression. *The provision of equal and sufficient property for all*, or simply *The abolition of poverty*, gives a more positive expression to the same aim. The doctrine is fundamentally single and practical and can be given an economic sanction if an ethical one is regarded as too idealistic.

The difficulty is to agree on a definition of terms, and on the practical application of theory. There, I think, the politicians fail us. All alike refuse to make a realistic analysis of the factors involved. They talk of capitalism, but make no distinction between financial capital and industrial capital, between liquid and fixed assets, between the bank and the factory. They talk of the proletariat or the working class, without realizing that these are only empty ideological phrases. There is a proletariat in Russia (or was), but if we have any imagination at all, or any knowledge of the difference between the two countries, we must recognize that the word 'proletariat' has no realistic application for us; for us the term is mythical. In Russia the proletariat was a social reality; it is possibly a reality in Japan and China, and in those countries we may perhaps legitimately expect a communist revolution on the Russian plan. But in this country, and in advanced industrial countries all over the world, the proletariat is becoming more and more insignificant. It is the Ten Little Nigger Boys of our economic system: unit by unit rejected by the dehumanizing machine. Some of it goes into the skilled technical classes, some into the petty bourgeois class, some into that growing class, the permanently unemployed. Immense developments of energy and invention since Marx's days have completely transformed the economic situation; so transformed it that, frankly, a revolution of the kind which that prophet envisaged is no longer necessary, and will never be desired by a coherent proletariat in this country. Naturally the abolition of poverty and the consequent establishment of a classless society is not going to be accomplished without a struggle. Certain people have to be dispossessed of their autocratic power, and of their illegitimate profits. But now that the true drift of capitalism has become so evident in the world-wide paradox of 'poverty in the midst of plenty', the real evil stands revealed; and against that evil, the money monopoly, not one class but the whole of the rest of the community will be united.

No man in his senses can contemplate the existing contrasts with complacency. No one can measure the disparity between poverty and riches, between purchasing power and productive capacity, between plan and performance, between chaos and order, between ugliness and beauty, between all the sin and savagery of the existing system and any decent code of social existence (Christian or moral or scientific)—no man can measure these disparities and remain indifferent. Our civilization is a scandal and until it is remade all our intellectual activities are vain. As poets and painters we are futile until we can build on the basis of a unified commonality. Again I do not imply any mystical factor; I merely want to point to the obvious truth that you cannot play to an audience in an uproar—however attentive the people in the stalls.

The problem, in its broad outlines, is simple enough. On the one side we have mankind, needing for its sustenance and enjoyment a certain quantity of goods; on the other side we have the same mankind, equipped with certain tools, machines, and factories, exploiting the natural resources of the earth. There is every reason to believe that with modern mechanical power and modern methods of production, there is or could be a sufficiency of goods to satisfy all reasonable demands. It is only necessary to organize an efficient system of distribution and exchange. Why is it not done?

The only answer is that the existing inefficient system benefits a small minority of people who have accumulated sufficient power to maintain it against any opposition. That power takes various forms—the power of gold, the power of tradition, the power of inertia, the control of information—but essentially it is the power to keep other people in a state of ignorance. If the superstitious credulity of the masses could be shaken; if the fantastic dogmas of the economists could be exposed; if the problem could be seen in all its simplicity and realism by the simplest worker and peasant, the existing economic system would not last a day longer. The creation of a new economic system would take more than the following day; but it would be better to begin with a revolution, as in Spain, than to go through the slow-motion agony of a so-called 'transitional period'. A transitional period is merely a bureaucratic device for postponing the inevitable.

The inevitable is the classless society—the society without a bureaucracy, without an army, without any closed grade or profession, without any functionless components. A hierarchy of talent, a division of labour, there must be; but only within the functional group, the collective organization. Whether responsibility and efficiency should be rewarded is a nice problem for the future; what is certain is that it should not be rewarded by any kind of money or tokens of exchange which could give one man power to command the services of another outside the collective organizations. The tokens of exchange should only be redeemable in goods, and should have a limited period of validity. The hoarding of money and all forms of usury should be regarded as unnatural vices, tendencies to be prevented by the psychologist in infancy. The only object of work should be immediate enjoyment; and there should be no work done in excess of immediate needs, except such as may be required to insure against the risks of natural calamities. Work in general should be subordinated to the enjoyment of life—it should be regarded as a necessary interval in the day's leisure. But this very distinction between work and leisure is born of our slave-ridden mentality; the enjoyment of life is the activity of life, an undifferentiated performance of mental and manual functions: things done and things made in response to a natural impulse or desire.

The phrase, 'a classless society', no doubt has terrors for any thoughtful person. It calls up immediately the image of a dull level of mediocrity: no masters and no servants, no palaces and no cottages, no Rolls-Royces and no donkey-carts—all one uniform scale of self-sufficient individuals, living in model-houses, travelling in uniform Fords along endless uniform roads. I admit that a society in which every individual has an inalienable right to a living dividend will, by the abolition of poverty, create some pretty problems for the snobs of Mayfair and Kensington, even for the snobs of every suburban villa. But even if, eventually, the products of the labour of the community were more or less equally divided, the sharing of this wealth would not produce a uniformity of life, simply because there is no uniformity of desire. Uniformity is an unintelligent nightmare; there can be no uniformity in a free human society. Uniformity can only be created by the tyranny of a totalitarian regime.

The only kind of levelling we need really fear is an intellectual levelling. But again we must take into consideration the facts—that is to say, human nature. The society I desire and will and plan is a leisure society—a society giving full opportunity for the education and development of the mind. Mind only requires time and space—to differentiate itself. The worst conditions of intellectual uniformity and stupidity are created by conditions of poverty and lack of leisure. The ordinary man under our present unjust system has to have his education stopped before his mind is fully opened. From the age of fourteen he is caught up in an endless treadmill; he has neither time nor opportunity to feed his undeveloped senses—he must snatch at the diuretic pabulum of the newspapers and the radio, and as a consequence, tread the mill with more urgency.

In the classless society, the mind of every individual will have at least the opportunity to expand in breadth and depth, and culture will once more be the natural product of economic circumstances, as it was in Ancient Greece, in China, in Medieval Europe, and indeed in all the great epochs of civilization. Whether the same circumstances will lead to an intensified religious life is a speculation I must leave to others; but I will present those who are interested in this aspect of the question with the following dilemma: if religion is a consolation or compensation for the insufficiencies of this vale of tears (the 'romanticism of pessimism', as Benda calls it), then no doubt it will suffer by the abolition of poverty; if, on the other hand, religion is the life of contemplation, the fruit of pure meditation, spiritual joy, then it cannot help but prosper in a society free from poverty, pride, and envy.

5

THE NECESSITY OF ANARCHISM

There is nothing to be gained by disguising the fact that the post-revolutionary history of Russia has created among socialists, if not a state of open disillusionment, at any rate some degree of secret embarrassment. It began with the first of the great trials for treason in Moscow; for whatever the rights and wrongs of the parties in question, we were left with this inescapable dilemma: either the accused were guilty, in which case their treason was evidence of a lack of unity within the Soviet Union—even of a widespread revolt against the policy of Stalin; or they were innocent, in which case Stalin becomes a sinister dictator in no way distinguishable from Hitler or Mussolini. Meanwhile various other tendencies in Russia, which we had condoned so long as they could be ascribed to the stress of intensive economic production, became stabilized and to some extent codified in the new constitution. These tendencies I shall presently refer to in more detail. But it is not in Russia alone that disturbing events have taken place. We have witnessed very significant developments in Spain. There we saw the outbreak of a fascist revolt against a democratic socialist government, and the emergence, in defence of that government, not of any clearly defined marxist party on the Russian model, but of a heterogeneous group of parties of the left who were barely kept from flying at each others' throats by the danger which threatened them all alike. Including federalists and anarchists, these parties of the left in Spain were overwhelmingly opposed to a totalitarian state on the Russian model. Even if, in the course of the undying struggle against fascism, owing to their command of Russian or so-called democratic aid, the communists had gained temporary control of the machine of government, we may be sure that the end of civil war would have been the end of that advantage. The demand for provincial autonomy, for syndicalist autonomy, for the abolition of the bureaucracy and the standing army, springs from the deepest instincts of the Spanish people.

The journals of this country, and the leading political publicists who serve them, showed at the time little comprehension of this situation in Spain. At the mention of anarchism the bourgeois press conjures up a bearded figure wearing a wide-brimmed hat and carrying a home-made bomb in his pocket, and is quite capable, it seems, of crediting Spain with two million such melodramatic characters. As for our socialistic pressmen, either they have assumed that anarchism was buried when Marx defeated Bakunin at the Hague Congress of 1872, and they will not write or act on any other assumption; or, knowing that in Italy and Spain anarchism has never died, they have deliberately obscured the issue, pretending that anarchism was merely an infantile disorder of the Latin temperament, and not to be taken seriously. They will watch the final outcome of the Spanish struggle with some anxiety, for what if, after all, anarchism becomes a power in one European country? What if, in the west of Europe, there came into existence a form of socialism which presented an alternative to the form of socialism already established in the east? At present many accept Stalin's regime and the Third International because, whatever its faults and shortcomings, it is the only established system of communism in the world. What if, in Spain, another system were established which claimed to be a more essential kind of communism?

We cannot anticipate the events, but we can at least prepare our minds for an unprejudiced reception of them. My only object at present is to contrast some of the transitional aspects of communism in Russia with some of the aspirations of anarchism in Spain.

I began by speaking of a general state of disillusionment or doubt among socialists, but I have already confessed that my own misgivings were first aroused by the suicide of Mayakovsky, which took place in 1930. I know that most communists, even those among them who might claim to be fellow-poets, have been able to explain away this suicide to their own satisfaction; in view of the magnitude of the Russian experiment a certain amount of rough-shod trampling over the tender shoots of poetry was perhaps to be expected. But if it had been merely a case of clumsiness, it might have been met with forgiveness. It soon appeared, however, that the 'liquidation' of such poets as Mayakovsky was to be justified on aesthetic grounds. They were accused of formalism, individualism, and subjectivism, and all true communist poets were required to subscribe to a doctrine of realism, naturalism, and objectivity. Political power was invoked to enforce an aesthetic programme; time-serving journalists like Radek and Bukharin were called upon to relate this aesthetic programme to the true gospel of dialectical materialism—an exercise in scholasticism which they carried out with medieval thoroughness.

The fall of Radek and Bukharin did not bring to an end the persecution of poets and artists. Pasternak, since Mayakovsky's death the most important poet in Russia, has been imprisoned, and his present fate is uncertain; and Shostakovich, one of the few modern composers with a European reputation, is continually in disgrace. There is no question of their complicity in any political manœuvres; their only sin is 'formalism', by which is meant their inability to degrade their art to the level of the sensibility of the masses.

It will be objected that these are relatively small incidents to pit against the achievements—military, industrial, and educational—of the Soviet Union. But that is to adopt a short-sighted view of what it takes to make a civilization and a culture. When Stalin and his works are trampled into the dust by new generations of men, the poetry of Pasternak and the music of Shostakovich will still be as real as on the day they emerged from the minds of their creators.

This should make my own fundamental attitude clear enough. I do not want to pose as a politician. I am not ignorant of political economy nor of political philosophy, but I am not advancing a political doctrine. To accuse me of Trotskyism, for example, is quite meaningless. For Trotsky as a writer and a dialectician I had a considerable admiration. In his political aspirations and intrigues I did not take the slightest interest; for I had no guarantee that a doctrinaire like Trotsky would be any improvement on a doctrinaire like Stalin. Fundamentally I renounce the whole principle of leadership and dictatorship to which Stalin is and Trotsky was personally committed.

The essential principle of anarchism is that mankind has reached a stage of development at which it is possible to abolish the old relationship of master-man (capitalist-proletarian) and substitute a relationship of egalitarian co-operation. This principle is based, not only on ethical grounds, but also on economic grounds. It is not merely a sentiment of justice, but also a system of economic production. The ethical anarchism of Bakunin has been completed by the economic anarchism of the French syndicalists. There may still be ethical anarchists of the Tolstoyan type who are convinced that we must reverse the whole tendency of our technical development and return to handcraft and individual workmanship. But the more realistic anarchist of to-day has no desire to sacrifice the increased power over nature which modern methods of production have developed. And actually he has now realized that the fullest possible development of these methods of production promises a greater degree of individual freedom than has ever hitherto been secured by mankind.

Marx and Engels always represented communism, in its final stage, as a free association of co-operators, exempt from the control of any central government or bureaucracy. Engels describes the State as 'withering away'—it is one of the key passages in the formulation of marxism:

'The proletariat seizes State power, and then transforms the means of production into State property. But in doing this, it puts an end to itself as the proletariat, it puts an end to all class differences and class antagonisms, it puts an end also to the State as a State. . . . As soon as there is no longer any class of society to be held in subjection; as soon as, along with class domination and the struggle for individual existence based on the former anarchy of production, the collisions and excesses arising from these have also been abolished, there is nothing more to be repressed, and a special repressive force, a State, is no longer necessary. The first act in which the State really comes forward as the representative of society as a whole—the seizure of the means of production in the name of society—is at the same time its last independent act as a State. The interference of a State power in social relations becomes superfluous in one sphere after another, and then becomes dormant of itself. Government over persons is replaced by the administration of things and the direction of the processes of production. The State is not "abolished", *it withers away*.'

As if conscious that this theory of Engels might be treated as a brilliant paradox and no more, Lenin himself wrote a special treatise, *The State and Revolution*, which he finished between the March and October revolutions, 1917, with the express purpose of substantiating Engels. It is true that he is also concerned to make clear that a revolution is a precedent and necessary condition for this withering away of the State; the proletariat must seize State power before it can establish the conditions for its gradual dissolution. But that is not in question. What we are to note is Lenin's most explicit affirmation of the non-governmental nature of the final phase of communism. In his own words:

'From the moment when all members of society, or even only the overwhelming majority, have learned how to govern the State *themselves*, have taken this business into their own hands, have "established" control over the insignificant minority of capitalists, over the gentry with capitalist leanings, and the workers thoroughly demoralized by capitalism—from this moment the need for any government begins to disappear. The more complete the democracy, the nearer the moment when it begins to be unnecessary. The more democratic the "State" consisting of armed workers, which is "no longer a State in the proper sense of the word", the more rapidly does *every* State begin to wither away.

'While the State exists there is no freedom. When there is freedom, there will be no State.'

In view of such explicit statements, it is not possible for the present rulers in Russia to do other than announce their own approaching dissolution. Stalin himself, in his speech to the Sixteenth Congress of the U.S.S.R., said:

'We are for the withering away of the State. . . . To keep on developing State power in order to prepare the conditions for the withering away of State power—that is the marxist formula.'

Or is there an equivocation in this utterance? We are for the withering away of the State—yes, but first we must develop the State to unheard-of dimensions in order to prepare the conditions for this withering away. Like the frog in the fable, the State must inflate itself till it bursts. Certainly since the revolution of 1917 the State machine has year by year grown in size and importance, and the hope that it will eventually wither away, which must have replaced the hope of Paradise in the hearts of all true Russians, becomes every day more remote. For in the very process of developing the power of the State new classes are born which usurp this power and use it to oppress the people at large.

In Russia this decisive turn was taken—not with any appeal to first principles, not with any overt consciousness of the significance of the event—when payment by piecework was re-established in the Soviets. This step was justified, as all departures from the true doctrine of communism have been justified, on the grounds of economic necessity. It became apparent that the socialist system could only be established in Russia by increasing the rate of industrial production. In a socialist state it is not possible to increase the level of individual well-being, however equally you divide the common goods, unless you increase the total amount of production.[1] Now whether because the actual machinery of production in Russia is inadequate, or because the natural aptitude of the Russian for production is below the general standard, the fact is that the productivity of labour in Russia has been, and still is, lower than the productivity of labour in capitalist countries like Great Britain, Germany, and the United States. There are many explanations, but the one which has most significance is the one which Stalin has not failed to use—the fact that man will not produce to the full extent of his abilities unless he can thereby gain some advantage over his fellow-men. This allegation—I am going to submit that it is no more than an allegation—if it is accepted, undermines the

[1] Theoretically there is the alternative of maintaining the amount of production and decreasing the population, but that too involves an increased *rate* of production.

whole doctrine of communism. For what, if it is true, becomes of the most sacred of all marxian formulas: *From each according to his abilities, to each according to his needs*? That phrase means, if it means anything at all, that each member of the community will work in accordance with his individual will and inclination —his physical and psychological capacity—and that no compulsion will be used to make him work beyond his abilities. The *necessity*, as Lenin put it, of observing the simple, fundamental rules of everyday social life in common will have become a *habit*.

Have we, then, to admit that in Russia in particular or in the world in general this sacred formula has to be abandoned? Have we to come to the humiliating conclusion that without compulsion men will not work sufficiently to satisfy the total requirements of the community? Have we to assume that with all the vast increase of means and methods of production—collective farms, tractors, standardization, rationalization, electric power —that with all these gifts civilized man is no better off than the savage, who even in the arctic wastes will work according to his abilities and receive according to his needs?

Such a conclusion is impossible. We must rather conclude that there is something very wrong with the state of Russia. The most charitable assumption is that the country is still in such a backward condition of economic development that it must resort to methods of labour exploitation which even in capitalist countries are rapidly disappearing. The uncharitable assumption is that such a method of exploitation has been introduced to subsidize a scarcely disguised system of state capitalism, with the bureaucracy as a privileged controlling class. Trotsky and other critics of the Stalinist régime already make that charge, and point to many subsidiary proofs. It is certainly difficult, on any other assumption, to justify such measures as the rehabilitation of the rouble, the new laws protecting private property, the revival of military titles and decorations, the establishment of separate military colleges and special schools for the children of the privileged classes.

But it is not my intention to detail all the shortcomings of the present régime in Russia; some of its failings are admittedly of a transitional nature, and others can be set off against the manifold benefits which communism has brought to the Russian people. But even if the system were perfect in its functioning, it would still be in complete contradiction with the principles of anarchism. For essential to the communist policy as it has developed in Russia is the concept of leadership—a concept which it shares with fascism, let it be noted. It may be, of course, that men of destiny like Lenin and Stalin, Hitler and Mussolini, are created by historical events—that their stature is, as it were, inflated by special economic conditions. But however produced, communists as well as fascists never doubt the necessity, nor even the desirability, of such leaders. They are extolled as the creators and the controlling minds of the political movements of which they are the figureheads.

Freud has shown what an important part is played by the leader in the psychology of the group. 'The uncanny and coercive characteristics of group formations, which are shown in their suggestive phenomena, may . . . be traced back to the fact of their origin from the primal horde. The leader of the group is still the dreaded primal father; the group still wishes to be governed by unrestricted force; it has an extreme passion for authority; in Le Bon's phrase, it has a thirst for obedience.' As for the leader himself, 'he, at the very beginning of the history of mankind, was the Superman whom Nietzsche only expected from the future. Even today the members of a group stand in need of the illusion that they are equally and justly loved by their leader; but the leader himself need love no one else, he may be of a masterly nature, absolutely narcissistic, but self-confident and independent.'[1]

I would define the anarchist as the man who, in his manhood, dares to resist the authority of the father; who is no longer content to be governed by a blind unconscious identification of the leader and the father and by the inhibited instincts which alone make such an identification possible. Freud, who at this point is merely adopting the ideas of Otto Rank, sees the origin of the heroic myth in such a longing for independence. 'It was then, perhaps, that some individual, in the exigency of his longing, may have been moved to free himself from the group and take

[1] Sigm. Freud, *Group Psychology and the Analysis of the Ego.* English trans. (1922), pp. 99–100, 93 and passim.

over the father's part. He who did this was the first epic poet; and the advance was achieved in his imagination. This poet disguised the truth with lies in accordance with his longing. He invented the heroic myth. The hero was a man who by himself had slain the father—the father who still appeared in the myth as a totemistic monster. Just as the father had been the boy's first ideal, so in the hero who aspires to the father's place the poet now created the first ego ideal.' But the further step which the anarchist now takes is to pass from myth and imagination to reality and action. He comes of age; he disowns the father; he lives in accordance with his own ego-ideal. He becomes conscious of his individuality.

How far the communists are from taking that further step in human development is shown, not merely by historical events in Russia, but also by their theories and pronouncements. There is no need to repeat the numerous exaltations of leadership which appear with monotonous regularity in the communist press; but it is interesting to note the deliberate adoption of the leadership principle by a communist who happens at the same time to be a psycho-analyst—I refer to Mr. R. Osborn's book on *Marx and Freud*. Mr. Osborn gives an account of Freud's theory of leadership and then, without once questioning the necessity for the particular type of group organization which demands a leader, assumes that the need for leadership is universal, and that the Communist Party would be well advised to adopt a strategy based on a realization of this fact. 'The first necessity', he says, 'would seem to be to crystallize the leadership in the shape of a leader—someone who may be referred to in such term as will awaken the required emotional attitudes. In other words, we must idealize for the masses some one individual to whom they will turn for support, whom they will love and obey.' He gives Lenin and Stalin as admirable examples of such individuals and concludes that 'it is a psychologically sound measure to keep such people before the masses as an incentive and guide to the overcoming of difficulties on the road of social progress'. He declares that the problem must be tackled 'in a consciously-thought-out manner which utilizes all that modern psychology has to offer on the subjective characteristics involved. . . . If Hitler and Mussolini, by deliberate publicity and propaganda methods, can be presented as saviours of the people, so too can Communist leaders.'

I will not comment on the somewhat scornful attitude towards the 'masses' which such tactics imply. The dictatorship of the proletariat is one thing—it is a fine-sounding phrase which conjures up a picture of politically conscious individuals acting rationally and objectively; but what has it in common with this other picture of a dumb horde which blindly worships and obeys a modern and scientifically concocted equivalent of the primitive tyrant? Surely it is the depth of political despair to conclude that there is no possible escape from this particular psychological pattern. We know that the mass of people is psychologically disposed to accept a leader or dictator. We are all children who are willing to leave our destinies in the hands of a father, and discover too late that this father is tyrannical. If we revolt, must it be merely for the purpose of placing another father in the place of the one deposed? Is it not rather time that we grew up, became individually conscious of our manhood, asserted our mutual independence?

If we now pass from the people to the leader, we are forced to recognize the complementary fact that *power corrupts*. It does not matter whether the chosen leader was originally a man of good intentions, like Stalin or Mussolini; or whether he was a vulgar and pretentious demagogue like Hitler: it is only a rare superman, such as Lenin may have been, who is by nature so essentially humble that he is incorruptible. It is not necessary to enlarge on this truth; it is a commonplace of history, and has been embodied in the ethical teachings of all the great religions. In Greek mythology this corruption in tyrants was recognized as a particular kind of sin (*hybris*) and visited by inevitable retribution.

The obsessive fear of the father which is the psychological basis of tyranny is at the same time the weakness of which the tyrant takes advantage. We all know the spectacle of the bully goaded into sadistic excesses by the very docility of his victim. The tyrant or dictator acts in exactly the same way. It is not psychologically credible that he should act in any other way. The only alternative to the principle of leadership is the

98

principle of co-operation or mutual aid; not the father-son relationship which has persisted from primitive times, but the relationship of brotherhood; in political terms, the free association of producers working for the common good. This is the essential doctrine of anarchism, and far from having been discredited by marxian economics or the achievements of the Soviet Union, it has everywhere received overwhelming confirmation in the events of the last twenty years, until we may now claim that the realization of this principle of brotherhood is the only hope of civilization.

I do not say that we must go back to Bakunin—you find many noble sentiments in his writings, and his life was immensely heroic, but he has no practical message for the present age. Kropotkin, who was also a noble and heroic figure, is more practical, but his plans too have been overtaken by the intensive development of modern methods of production. Since Kropotkin's time anarchism has evolved to meet modern conditions, and as a practical policy is known as syndicalism; wherever anarchism is a considerable political force, as in Spain, it is combined with syndicalism. Anarcho-syndicalism is a clumsy mouthful, but it describes the present-day type of anarchist doctrine.

Outbreaks of 'unofficial' strikes, strikes against the authority of the Trade Unions and against the State as employer, are now a characteristic of our time. These developments are devolutionary—revolts against centralization and bureaucratic control —and as such essentially anarchist. For the anarchist objects, not merely to the personal tyranny of a leader like Stalin, but still more to the impersonal tyranny of a bureaucratic machine.

What is wrong with bureaucracy? In the vast and extremely complicated conditions of modern civilization, is not a bureaucracy necessary merely to hold that civilization together, to adjust relationships, to administer justice and so on?

Actually, of course, in a society of rich and poor nothing is more necessary. If it is necessary to protect an unfair distribution of property, a system of taxation and speculation, a monopolist money system; if you have to prevent other nations from claiming your ill-gotten territorial gains, your closed markets, your trade routes; if as a consequence of these economic inequalities you are going to maintain pomp and ceremony, ranks and orders; if you are going to do any or all these things you will need a bureaucracy.

Such a bureaucracy consists of armed forces, police forces, and a civil service. These are largely autonomous bodies. Theoretically they are subordinate to a democratically elected Parliament, but the Army, Navy, and Air Forces are controlled by specially trained officers who from their schooldays onwards are brought up in a narrow caste tradition, and who always, in dealing with Parliament, can dominate that body by their superior technical knowledge, professional secrecy, and strategic bluff. As for the bureaucracy proper, the Civil Service, anyone who has had any experience of its inner workings knows the extent to which it controls the Cabinet, and through the Cabinet, Parliament itself. We are really ruled by a secret shadow cabinet, the heads of the Treasury, the Foreign Office, the Home Office, the Service Departments, and the Permanent Secretary to the Cabinet. Below this select club of Old Wykehamists we have a corps of willing and efficient slaves—beetle-like figures in striped trousers, black coats, winged collars, and bow ties. All these worthy servants of the State are completely out of touch with the normal life of the nation: they are ignorant of the methods and conditions of industrial production, unaware of the routine and atmosphere of proletarian life—or life of any real kind.

Every country has the bureaucracy it deserves. Ours, trained in public school and university, is efficient, unimaginative, unfeeling, dull, and honest. In other countries the bureaucracy has no such gentlemanly traditions; it is lazy, lousy, and corrupt. In any case, lazy or efficient, honest or corrupt, a bureaucracy has nothing in common with the people; it is a parasitic body, and has to be maintained by taxation and extortion. Once established (as it has been established for half a century in England and as it is newly established in Russia) it will do everything possible to consolidate its position and maintain its power. Even if you abolish all other classes and distinctions and retain a bureaucracy you are still far from the classless society, for the bureaucracy is itself the nucleus of a class whose interests are totally opposed to the people it supposedly serves.

As an example of the power and selfish interest of the bureaucracy, consider the fate of the League of Nations. It is commonly assumed that the League was frustrated first by Japan and then by Italy, and that France and England refused to enforce its authority on these test occasions because they were not sufficiently armed to fight. Such may have been the actual catastrophe, but the ground had been slowly and deliberately undermined. The League of Nations was destroyed by a rival League —the League of Diplomats. Ambassadors and secretaries the world over saw in the League of Nations a rival organization, which when perfected would reduce their embassies to post offices and replace their several provinces by a single central authority. So on every possible occasion the permanent officials of every Foreign Office in Europe did all in their power to frustrate the activities of the League. They have been only too successful!

What we have to ask, then, is how can the bureaucracy be abolished in a communist society? If we cannot answer that question, we have to admit that our ideal of a classless society can never be realized.

The syndicalist—the anarchist in his practical rather than his theoretical activity—proposes to liquidate the bureaucracy first by federal devolution. Thereby he destroys the idealistic concept of the State—that nationalistic and aggressive entity which has nearly ruined Western civilization. He next destroys the money monopoly and the superstitious structure of the gold standard, and substitutes a medium of exchange based on the productive capacity of the country—so many units of exchange for so many units of production. He then hands over to the syndicates all other administrative functions—fixing of prices, transport, and distribution, health, and education. In this manner the State begins to wither away! It is true that there will remain local questions affecting the immediate interests of individuals—questions of sanitation, for example; and the syndicates will elect a local council to deal with such questions—a council of workers. And on a higher plane there will be questions of co-operation and exchange between the various productive and distributive syndicates, which will have to be dealt with by a central council of delegates—but again the delegates will be workers. Until anarchism is complete there will be questions of foreign policy and defence, which again will be dealt with by delegated workers.

But no whole-time officials, no bureaucrats, no politicians, no dictators. Everywhere there will be cells of workers, working according to their abilities and receiving according to their needs.

I realize that there is nothing original in this outline of an anarchist community: it has all the elements of essential communism as imagined by Marx and Engels; it has much in common with Guild Socialism and Christian Socialism. It does not matter very much what we call our ultimate ideal. I call it anarchism because that word emphasizes, as no other, the central doctrine—the abolition of the State and the creation of a co-operative commonwealth. But against all these forms of socialism, challenging the possibility of this ultimate ideal, is the cry that it can never be established because of the natural depravity of mankind. Even if one non-governmental community could be established, it is said, some predatory tribe or nation would descend on it and annexe it.

To that objection we must reply that anarchism naturally implies pacifism. I would therefore propose to avoid that issue for the moment. I do not shirk the question: I shall discuss it more fully in the next chapter.

The objections raised by the state socialist (he now usually calls himself a communist) are based on grounds of practicability. Modern existence, he says, has become so immensely complicated that it cannot be simplified now without causing great suffering and chaotic disorganization. Apart from retorting that no disorganization or suffering could conceivably be greater than that caused by the collectivization of agriculture in Russia, the answer to this charge must be that it is precisely the charge which has been brought against every attempt to reform the social system. When the communists object to the anarchists on grounds of impracticability, unreality, idealism, and so on, they are merely repeating, at an interval of thirty or forty years, the arguments used against themselves by the reactionaries of the past.

What matters in politics—what matters in history—is clarity of vision, force of reason. Nothing, in the slow course of civilization, has ever been won by any other means. A man has contemplated existence; has seen its elements clearly and discretely; has seen how these elements could be rearranged to better effect, to greater well-being. In that way—entirely realistically—a vision is born, and a man who has seen this vision has shown it to his friends and neighbours, who have then become inspired with the same vision. And so a group, a sect, a party has been formed, the necessary enthusiasm has been aroused, and the vision has in due time been realized. That is the only way in which progress takes place—the only way in which a civilization is built up. When there are no longer men who have such visions, then progress ceases and a civilization decays. Such is the essential law of history—a law to which the theory of dialectical materialism is but a corollary.

It will be seen that there is nothing in this conception of anarchism to prevent the emergence of an aristocracy of the intellect. Anarchism is not in this respect an egalitarian doctrine, any more than communism is. The distinction is that anarchism would not confer any special powers upon such an élite. Power corrupts even the intellect, and an aristocracy plus power is no longer an aristocracy, but an oligarchy. The seer, the visionary, the poet will be respected and honoured as never before in the history of mankind; but that dreadful confusion between the man of imagination and the man of action will be avoided. Imagination renders a man incapable of determinate action; determinate action inhibits imagination—such is the dialectic of the human personality.

Anarchism is a rational ideal—an ideal common to Marx, Bakunin, and Lenin. It is only because that ideal has been lost sight of in the collective socialism of contemporary Russia that it becomes necessary to reaffirm it under its most uncompromising name. Socialism is dynamic: it is a movement of society in a definite direction and it is the direction that matters most. In our conception of socialism, are we moving towards centralization, concentration, depersonalization; or are we moving towards individualization, independence, and freedom? It seems to me that there can be no possible doubt as to which direction is the more desirable; and I am afraid that, at the moment, everywhere in the world we are moving in the wrong direction.

It is often said, by advocates of fascism and the totalitarian state, that democracy has failed because the electorate has proved unworthy of the responsibility which that system of government places upon it. At election times it acts either capriciously or ignorantly, or even refuses to act at all. This observation is based on certain true facts: it is the deduction only which is wrong. Even in my own lifetime, I am conscious of a great slackening of political consciousness. Politics do not occupy the space they used to in the Press, and parliamentary proceedings are no longer followed with any great interest. For the most part, though their fate may depend on the result of their voting, the electors are bored and apathetic. Even with all the machinery of party organizations, publicity campaigns, door-to-door canvassing, open-air meetings, broadcasting, etc., it is difficult to get more than 50 per cent of the electorate into the polling booths. Without these artificial stimulants, it is doubtful if as much as 30 per cent of the electorate would exercise the right to vote.

But the reason for this apathy is not strictly political. It may be a case of democracy not functioning, but you cannot blame a vehicle for not moving if you overload it. The degeneration of political consciousness in modern democratic states is not a moral degeneration. It is due to this very process of centralization and collectivization which is taking place independently, and in spite of the particular political system we supposedly enjoy. There was a time when the relationship between the citizen and his representative in Parliament was direct and human; there was a time when the relationship between a member of Parliament and the government was direct and human; but all that has passed. We have been the victims of a process of dehumanization in our political life. Parties have become obedient regiments of mercenaries; delegates have been replaced by committees; the paid official, the omnipresent bureaucrat, stands between the citizen and his Parliament. Most departments of national life are controlled by vast and efficient bureaucratic machines which would continue to function to a large extent independently—that is to say, irrespective of political control.

Universal political franchise has been a failure—that we have to confess. Only a minority of the people is politically conscious, and the remainder only exist to have their ignorance and apathy exploited by an unscrupulous Press. But do not let us confuse universal franchise, which is a system of election, with democracy, which is a principle of social organization. Universal franchise is no more essential to democracy than divine right is to monarchy. It is a myth: a quite illusory delegation of power. Justice, equality, and freedom—these are the true principles of democracy, and it is possible—it has been amply proved by events in Italy and Germany—that the universal franchise can in no sense guarantee these principles, and may, indeed, impose a fiction of consent where in effect no liberty of choice exists.

If you go into a village and propose to introduce electric power; if you go into a city street and propose to widen it; if you raise the price of bread or curtail the hours of drinking licences—then you touch the immediate interests of the citizen. Put these questions to the voter and without any coaxing or canvassing he will run to the poll.

In short, real politics are local politics. If we can make politics local, we can make them real. For this reason the universal vote should be restricted to the local unit of government, and this local government should control all the immediate interests of the citizen. Such interests as are not controlled by the local council should be controlled by his local branch of the syndicate or soviet to which he belongs. His remoter interests—questions of co-operation, intercommunication, and foreign affairs—should be settled by councils of delegates elected by the local councils and the syndicates. Only in that way shall we ever get a democracy of vital articulation and efficient force.

It is important, however, to make one qualification without which any democratic system will fail. A delegate should always be an *ad hoc* delegate. Once a delegate separates himself from his natural productive function, once he becomes a *professional* delegate, then all the old trouble sets in again. The bureaucratic parasite is born; the evil principle of leadership intervenes; the lust for power begins to corrode these chosen people. They are consumed by pride.

The professional politician is an anomalous figure, and should some day be subjected to a thorough critical analysis. The professional economist is one thing—he is an expert in one department of knowledge and should be capable of supplying a specific need in the community. The local man of standing—a landowner or active industrialist who allows himself to be elected to Parliament from a sense of responsibility and duty—he too is a justifiable type. But there exists this other type of politician who has no such functional status. He is the man who deliberately adopts politics as a career. He may incidentally be a lawyer or a trade-union secretary or a journalist; but he is in politics for what he can get out of it. He means to climb to office and to power, and his motive throughout is personal ambition and megalomania. Owing to the preoccupations of the other types of parliamentary representatives, this professional politician is only too likely to succeed. It is he in particular who is a danger in a socialist society, for with the disappearance of the disinterested man of leisure, he becomes the predominant type of politician. Unchecked by rival types, he monopolizes all offices of power, and then, intoxicated with the exercise of this power, turns against his rivals within his own category, ruthlessly exterminates those who threaten to supplant him, and enforces the strict obedience of all who promise to serve him. Such is the process by which dictators rise and establish themselves; such is the process by which Mussolini, Stalin, and Hitler established themselves. It is a process which the social democratic state unconsciously but inevitably encourages. The only safeguard against such a process is the abolition of the professional politician as such and the return to a functional basis of representation. It ought to be axiomatic in a communist society that power is never delegated to an individual as such, to be exercised arbitrarily. Power should be an abstraction, a grace invested in an office, exercised impersonally. An elected delegate or representative should never confuse his authority with his individuality—it is the old distinction which the Church made between the divine grace and the human vessel.

Generally I would suggest that in many respects parliamentary socialism, which is the final expression of a subjective and individualistic doctrine of power which began its fatal course at the Renaissance, has to return to concepts of grace, freedom, and function which are more in line with scholastic Christian philosophy than with modern philosophy. I have always tended to see in communism a reaffirmation of certain metaphysical doctrines which Europe possessed in the Middle Ages, and then lost in the rising tide of humanism, liberalism, and idealism. I do not believe that we can go back to the religious formulas of the Middle Ages, and for that reason I do not believe that we can be saved by a revival of Catholicism; in the theory of anarchism the organized Church is as much an anathema as the State. But it is very necessary that we should once again admit the universalism of truth and submit our lives to the rule of reason. This universalism and this reason, as Catholic philosophers insist, are aspects of realism.[1] There can only be one kind of truth because there is only the single reality of our experience, and we arrive at the true nature of that experience by the process of reasoning. Communists speak of dialectical materialism, but dialectical realism would be a better phrase. The negation of the idealism of Hegel is realism; the realism of Aristotle, of Albertus and Aquinas; the realism of modern science with its insistence on the universality of law and design.

When we follow reason, then, in the medieval sense, we listen to the voice of God: we discover God's order, which is the Kingdom of Heaven. Otherwise there are only the subjective prejudices of individuals, and these prejudices inflated to the dimensions of nationalism, mysticism, megalomania, and fascism. A realistic rationalism rises above all these diseases of the spirit and establishes a universal order of thought, which is a necessary order of thought because it is the order of the real world;

---

[1] For a brilliant restatement of the Catholic doctrine, see Professor Etienne Gilson's essay on 'Medieval Universalism and its Present Value' in *Independence, Convergence and Borrowing in Institutions, Thought and Art* (Harvard University Press, 1937). Here are a few sentences which give the gist of his conclusions: '. . . mental liberty consists in a complete liberation from our personal prejudices and in our complete submission to reality . . . Either we shall be free from things, and slaves to our minds, or free from our minds because submitted to things. Realism always was and still remains the source of our personal liberty. Let us add that, for the same reason, it remains the only guarantee of our social liberty. . . . Our only hope is therefore in a widely spread revival of the Greek and medieval principle, that truth, morality, social justice, and beauty are necessary and universal in their own right. Should philosophers, scientists, artists, make up their minds to teach that principle and if necessary to preach it in time and out of time, it would become known again that there is a spiritual order of realities whose absolute right it is to judge even the State, *and eventually to free us from its oppression.* . . . In the conviction that there is nothing in the world above universal truth lies the very root of intellectual and social liberty.'

and because it is necessary and real, it is not man-imposed, but natural; and each man finding this order finds his freedom.

Modern anarchism is a reaffirmation of this natural freedom, of this direct communion with universal truth. Anarchism rejects the man-made system of government, which are instruments of individual and class tyranny; it seeks to recover the system of nature, of man living in accordance with the universal truth of reality. It denies the rule of kings and castes, of churches and parliaments, to affirm the rule of reason, which is the rule of God.

The rule of reason—to live according to natural laws—this is also the release of the imagination. We have two possibilities: to discover truth, and to create beauty. We make a profound mistake if we confuse these two activities, attempting to discover beauty and to create truth. If we attempt to create truth, we can only do so by imposing on our fellow-men an arbitrary and idealistic system which has no relation to reality; and if we attempt to discover beauty we look for it where it cannot be found—in reason, in logic, in experience. Truth is in reality, in the visible and tangible world of sensation; but beauty is in unreality, in the subtle and unconscious world of the imagination. If we confuse these two worlds of reality and imagination, then we breed not only national pride and religious fanaticism, but equally false philosophies and the dead art of the academies. We must surrender our minds to universal truth, but our imagination is free to dream; is as free as the dream; is the dream.

I balance anarchism with surrealism, reason with romanticism, the understanding with the imagination, function with freedom. Happiness, peace, contentment—these are all one and are due to the perfection of this balance. We may speak of these things in dialectical terms—terms of contradiction, negation, and synthesis—the meaning is the same. The world's unhappiness is caused by men who incline so much in one direction that they upset this balance, destroy this synthesis. The very delicacy and subtlety of the equilibrium is of its essence; for joy is only promised to those who strive to achieve it, and who, having achieved it, hold it lightly poised.

6

THE PREREQUISITE OF PEACE

My approach to this problem must again be personal. It may be that there is an abstract ethical question, and that the answer is unequivocally in favour of universal peace. It may be that there is a concrete biological question, and that the answer is unequivocally in favour of periodic wars. I doubt very much whether all the answers to all the questions that can be raised on this issue can be unanimous. There is not only a conflict of values involved, but also a hopeless confusion of motives. Some of the most aggressive and egotistical people I know are active pacifists; some of the gentlest and most sensitive men I have ever met were professional soldiers. They, too, hated war; but they accepted it.

I do not accept war. I consider that it is an insult to the life of reason, and that it is cruel and senseless and wholly evil in its effects. Of its economic and social consequences I do not propose to speak—it is surely obvious enough to all who have lived in the post-war epoch that these have been disastrous. I seem to remember that Mr. Douglas Jerrold, one of our ablest apologists for war, once maintained that the First World War had been worth while because it had achieved the westernization of Turkey; but most of us find it hard to believe that the abolition of the harem and the fez was worth the sacrifice of twelve million lives.

In my opinion the most convincing arguments for war are not logical at all, but based on certain obscure psychological motives. I do not mean that the arguments are convincing because they are obscure (not an unknown state of affairs): I mean that certain rationalizations of war persist because they are the expression of an emotional energy which would otherwise be repressed. When these rationalizations take a definite and elaborate form, the process of sublimation is obvious enough to anyone with a psychological training. But it is more difficult to explain a far

109

more general attitude towards war and peace, which is not active opposition or defence, but uncertainty or apathy. There may be two hundred thousand pacifists; there are a few hundred active militarists; but the mass of people are morbidly indifferent to the fate that threatens them, and remain so in the midst of war itself.

My own case, which is one of doubt rather than apathy, is perhaps typical enough. I belong to the generation which did the fighting in the 1914–18 war and I hated it from the minute it began until the end. When the war broke out, I was completely unmoved by the general enthusiasm for the Allied cause, and could have had no enthusiasm for war in any cause. The war seemed to me to be just a meaningless interruption in the great struggle for social justice. I was annoyed that my thoughts should be diverted from what I considered the real problems of life, and was full of impotent rage when I found that all my time and bodily activities were involved in that madness. But like most people in 1914 (for I had read *The Great Illusion*) I did not believe that the war could last for many weeks and after an interlude of training and camping, I expected that I should be able to return to my books.

But the war did not end so soon. It drifted on, and I with it. I was given a commission and drafted to a battalion of infantry, and in due course went to France and had the normal experience of a front-line infantry officer. I do not wish to disguise the fact that in some ways I gained from that experience. I found that I had as much courage and endurance as most men, and that was a valuable discovery. But otherwise the experience was for me one of overwhelming horror, and in 1919 I left the Army a more convinced pacifist than ever—a pacifist who could speak of the horrors of war with the authority of experience.

What was to be done about it? As writing was to be my business in life, I felt I must first write about this experience of war—tell the truth about it with calmness and detachment. But I found, much to my surprise, that no one wanted to know the truth about war. People were either sick to death of the subject and wanted to find a mental refuge in peace-time activities, or they wanted to boost our so-called victory. I published, at my own expense, some realistic poems under the title *Naked War-*

riors, but although they were well reviewed, not more than 300 or 400 copies were sold. I wrote an account of the Retreat of March 1918, and though (or because!) I made it as objective as possible, and kept it quite free from propaganda of any kind, I could not find a publisher for it—it was not published until five years later. This was all very discouraging, and though I have since written one or two other descriptions of war incidents, I feel that this method is not effective, and that, in short, the more effectively war is represented *as literature,* the more attractive war itself becomes. It is obvious that its horrors fascinate people (even women), and it sometimes seems that if one wants to prevent war, it is better to act as if it had never existed.

The self-confidence which is one of the positive values gained by the personality in war may possibly come in the course of an active life in peace-time, though not, I think, so quickly. I do not for a moment entertain the idea that it is worth the sacrifice of life exacted by modern warfare. But the effects of war on the individual go deeper. I can only hint at some of the obscurer manifestations of its influence. For example, it developed my sensibility in such a way that I know instinctively which among the people I meet are cowards. Not merely which *were* cowards in the war, but which would be cowards in any position of danger. It is not a very comforting knowledge to have of one's fellow-men; and certainly it does not add to one's social complacency, for under the present economic dispensation it is certain that the coward often rises to a place of authority and power. But it is reasonable to believe that in the long run courage adds to the sum total of human happiness, and if war sharpens our sensibility to this element in life, it awakens in us the desire to cultivate it.

Such a peculiar sensibility could not be developed in any conditions but those of prolonged common danger. It may be that there are certain peace-time callings, such as coal-mining, which develop the same qualities, but these only affect a small minority of the population. I am not sure that the same is not true of that other quality which war develops so conspicuously—comradeship. The pacifists themselves are so conscious of this virtue in war, that they propose to establish all kinds of group activities to inculcate it under peaceful conditions. They even, to a large extent, set out to imitate the organization and training of the military machine.[1]

Comradeship is a group feeling, and apart from its sentimental associations, we may assume that its value, like courage, is of a biological nature. It is the little man's defensive gesture in the face of the cold comfort of the material world. But however many of these biological virtues we may find in war, their value is obviously relative to the evil which is called into existence by the same circumstances. No amount of courage and comradeship will avail us if in the end all our brave men are exterminated and our civilization is destroyed. We must ask ourselves whether the virtues which arise from modern warfare are biologically of more value than the corresponding vices. ' 'Tis strange to imagine that *War*,' wrote Shaftesbury in his *Characteristics*, 'which of all things appears the most savage, shou'd be the Passion of the most heroick Spirits. But 'tis in War that the Knot of Fellowship is closest drawn. 'Tis in War that mutual Succour is most given, mutual Danger run, and *common Affection* most exerted and employ'd. For *Heroism* and *Philanthropy* are almost one and the same. Yet by a small misguidance of the Affection, a Lover of Mankind becomes a Ravager: A Hero and Deliverer becomes an Oppressor and Destroyer.'

On examination, it will be found that the biological case for war rests on a certain apotheosis of 'Life' or 'Nature' which has no reasonable sanction. It is a great error in philosophy (to my way of thinking) to ascribe independent existence and overriding authority to creations of the mind or imagination. The process of evolution, so far as the scientists have been able to reconstruct it, seems to have been anything but certain and determinate in its course; and though by acquiring consciousness the human race has been able to nurse an illusion of controlling its own destiny, the very question we are discussing shows how ineffective that control has been. The only certain purpose of life is the process of living; the only awareness of this process is in individual sensibility; and since war destroys the individual life, it would seem to be biologically indefensible save when the only means of securing a living is to take another's life.

[1] See *Training for Peace: a Programme for Peaceworkers*, by Richard B. Gregg.

But though the economic causes of war are evident enough, few apologists for war resort to this argument. It is too obvious that with modern methods of production there is potentially enough for everybody's need. What then remains of the biological argument?

It is worth recalling the work of a French writer whose influence, though not often acknowledged, is still active among the few who openly defend war. René Quinton, who died in 1925, was a French biologist who took a distinguished part in the First World War. When war broke out he was already in his forty-eighth year, and though an officer of the reserve, no longer liable for active service, he volunteered and served continuously with the artillery. He was wounded eight times, received high Belgian, British, and American decorations as well as the French Croix de Guerre, and was appointed successively Officer and Commander of the French Legion of Honour. After the war Quinton returned to his scientific work, and only in 1924 began to put together the maxims which were subsequently published in book form. He did not live to see the publication of this book.

Mr. Douglas Jerrold wrote a long introduction to the English translation of Quinton's book,[1] presenting his maxims as a coherent philosophy of war, a philosophy which he has since developed in his own writings. Maxims are a very elusive type of literature, and the maxim-writer is always more concerned for the truth of his particular observations than for their consistency one with another. Many of these maxims are direct observations from experience, and strike us immediately as acute. This distinction between brave men and heroes, for example: 'The brave man gives his life when it is asked of him; the hero offers it.' 'The hero is a mystic and perhaps it takes a hero to understand him.' 'Courage comes from the exact computation of probabilities.' 'Bravery is an intellectual rather than a moral quality.' 'There is no discipline in the firing-line; there is mutual consent. Discipline begins behind the line.' In such maxims the soldier is speaking, but in the majority of them it is an elderly biologist. Mr. Jerrold says: 'The keystone of Quinton's thesis is the doctrine that the end of life, for the male, is something beyond life, and that until this instinct to serve the race, or more widely, the

[1] *Soldier's Testament* (Eyre & Spottiswoode, 1930).

universal purpose behind life, is dominant, man is not truly masculine, not truly mature. Pacifism and malthusianism alike are regarded as definitely unnatural, an attempt to defy, with results ultimately disastrous, the fundamental biological instincts of the female and the male.' And again: 'An idea for which a man is not prepared to die is not an idea sufficient dynamic to stimulate the instinct to serve, and it is on the stimulation of this instinct, on its predominance over all else that, as a matter of mere biological necessity, the health of the race depends. For it is only in serving that the male can attain moral dignity, without which the race must deteriorate and ultimately decay.'

The fallacy on which this doctrine is based is derived from the romantic biologists of the last century; it is a version of the pathetic fallacy which takes the form of a personification of an imaginary force called Nature. 'It is the intention of *Nature*', reads Quinton's first maxim, 'that man should die in his prime.' '*Nature* creates species, she does not create individuals', runs the second. And so on, throughout the whole book, we have this unconscious assumption, and if the reader does not care to accept it, the philosophy of war based on it falls to the ground.

Hitherto I have referred to pacifists generally, but actually there are two schools of thought among the opponents of war. One is humanitarian, maintaining the dignity and sanctity of life, regarding war as a barbaric survival; the object of life, one must suppose, is more life, and a better life. These are the pacifists proper, and their doctrine rests on practically the same assumption as René Quinton's—a conception of Man as part of a purposive life-force. Another doctrine, which Mr. Jerrold confuses with this, has no such sentimental bias. 'Life' may be purposive or not; it is beside the point. But 'life' cannot be reduced to a single concept. There are different kinds of life— mineral, vegetable, animal, and human. Human life is distinguished by the possession of unique faculties which we commonly call reason. In the hierarchy of life, reason involves a difference, not of degree only, but of kind; so that no proposition that is true for the life of instinct is necessarily true for the life of reason. But reason, not being prejudiced, can admit the insecurity of its tenure; it is for ever challenged by the ineradicable passions which we inherit with our animal frame. It must therefore defend itself, and in that defence it must be willing to sacrifice life. Only those who unconsciously prefer death (and call their preference 'non-attachment') are unwilling to sacrifice life. The rational opponent of war, it follows, is not a pacifist, for he believes that there are ideals for which in the last resort he must wage war. But as part of his fight against his own instincts, he will fight against the instinct to fight. He knows that that instinct is a mark of decadence, for wars mean economic waste, racial debility, and intellectual poverty. Mr. Jerrold seems to accept Spengler's theory of history, and no doubt some such fatalism is necessary if you are to justify war. But it is far more reasonable to suppose that civilizations have perished from too much war rather than from too little of it. This is the view expressed by George Santayana in his book *Reason in Society*:

'Internecine war, foreign and civil, brought about the greatest set-back which the life of reason has ever suffered: it exterminated the Greek and Italian aristocracies. Instead of being descended from heroes, modern nations are descended from slaves; and it is not their bodies only that show it. After a long peace, if the conditions of life are propitious, we observe a people's energies bursting their barriers; they become aggressive on the strength they have stored up in their remote and unchecked development. It is the unmutilated race, fresh from the struggle with nature (in which the best survive, while in war it is often the best that perish), that descends victoriously into the arena of nations and conquers disciplined armies at the first blow, becomes the military aristocracy of the next epoch and is itself ultimately sapped and decimated by luxury and battle, and merged at last into the ignoble conglomerate beneath. Then, perhaps, in some other virgin country a genuine humanity is again found, capable of victory because unbled by war. To call war the soil of courage and virtue is like calling debauchery the soil of love.'

This conception of war agrees with the record of history and is not dependent on any fanciful apotheosis of the life-force. It also emphasizes the fact that it is not necessary to be military to be masculine. All the virtues that are necessary for the preservation of a civilization are naturally evolved in the process of building up that civilization. It requires far more courage to preserve a civilization than to destroy it. The life of reason is itself a sufficient safeguard against decadence.

Another curious confusion arises out of Mr. Jerrold's misunderstanding of the rational pacifist's position. He says, in effect, that the rationalist cannot believe in any absolute values because the only effective way of believing in such values is to establish them by force. But reason achieves its end by persuasion. Force is only necessary to establish irrational values. If the word 'absolute' has any meaning in this connection, it implies a quality that is universal. It is inconceivable, therefore, that nation should fight against nation for the establishment of universal values. If such values exist, they will be obvious to all men of reason; and if it is necessary to establish them by force, they will be supported by men of reason irrespective of race or country. A war in that sense is a crusade, and a crusade is the only kind of war which a reasonable man might countenance.

Both fascism and marxism claim to be crusades in this sense, but the very fact that these doctrines claim to be universal and yet oppose each other shows that they cannot both be based on reason. Either one or both must be invalid as a crusade. It is almost inconceivable that a truth should be so universally accepted by men of reason that it would justify a crusade to establish it. War in practice is always an attempt to circumvent the process of reasoning, which is slow and difficult. Fighting and reasoning are different means to the same end, and if we assume that the life of reason is an absolute value and war merely a means sanctioned by the values it aims to establish, and not in itself an absolute value, then we must agree with Santayana that the only rational war is a war to end war. The only valid crusade is a crusade to establish universal peace.

At first sight, this conclusion would seem to justify those who argue that if we would ensure peace we must prepare for war: that peace can only be guaranteed by force of arms. Such a position ignores, as pacifists have often pointed out, the positive evils of a state of war-mindedness. You cannot sit on a powder-magazine and smoke your pipe in peace. Sooner or later a spark sets fire to it. If peace can only be guaranteed by force then that force must be super-national. But by the time we have arrived at a political and economic organization of the world which will allow the creation of such a force, we shall have arrived at a state of civilization which will render such a force unnecessary.

I will leave these well-worn and irrefutable arguments on one side to consider a more difficult aspect of the problem. Some time ago the League of Nations sponsored the publication of a discussion on our subject by two of the greatest scientists of our time—Albert Einstein and Sigmund Freud.[1] Einstein put forward the point we have just been considering; he realizes that the practical solution of the problem of war is superficially simple. 'The quest of international security involves the unconditional surrender by every nation, in a certain measure, of its liberty of action, its sovereignty, that is to say, and it is clear beyond all doubt that no other road can lead to such security.' But 'the ill-success, despite their obvious sincerity, of all the efforts made during the last decade to reach this goal leaves us no room to doubt that strong psychological factors are at work, which paralyse these efforts'. Einstein therefore calls on Freud to bring the light of his 'far-reaching knowledge of man's instinctive life' to bear upon the problem.

Einstein asks his questions simply and modestly; Freud's answer is, it must be confessed, a little pretentious and evasive. He supposes the existence in man of two innate and opposite tendencies—the will to create and the will to destroy, Love and Hate, the polarities of attraction and repulsion which operate the whole of the vital, and perhaps of the physical universe. But he sees no simple or innocuous way of controlling the destructive instinct; he is led to the conclusion, rather, that this instinct is present in every living being, striving to work its ruin and reduce life to its primal state of inert matter. For that reason we might well call it the 'death instinct'. This death instinct becomes destructive when it directs its action outwards, against external objects. But sometimes it directs itself inwards, and Freud traces the origin of a number of normal and pathological phenomena to such an introversion of the destructive instinct. Obviously, he argues, when this internal tendency operates on too large a scale, a positively morbid condition arises;

[1] *War, Sadism and Pacifism* (Allen & Unwin, 1933). A new and enlarged edition was published in 1947.

whereas the diversion of the destructive impulse towards the external world must have beneficial effects on the individual. And such is the biological justification for the aggressive impulses in mankind. What is much more difficult to explain, says Freud, is why we should make a stand against these malicious but natural propensities.

There Freud, for the moment, leaves the question, and there Dr. Edward Glover, an English psycho-analyst, takes it up. He begins by quoting a passage from this letter of Freud's, and his short book,[1] which is of quite exceptional importance, is an attempt to trace the psychological complexities involved in the problem of war and peace. His thesis is, briefly, that there is a fundamental identity between some of the impulses promoting peace and the impulses giving rise to war, and that no effective peace propaganda will be possible until we realize this fact. When the destructive instinct is suppressed in man (it is usually frustrated in infancy), then we are liable to get psychological reactions of two kinds: sadistic when the destructive impulse is turned outwards and fused with the erotic impulse, masochistic when to some degree the destructive impulse is turned inward against the self. As applied to the problem of war and peace, Dr. Glover's thesis is briefly this: 'The psycho-analyst alleges that *concentration of peace propaganda on ethical or economic arguments*, on measures of inhibition, pacts, disarmament treaties or limitations, to the neglect of unconscious motivations, *is in a very real sense a reactionary policy.* He alleges that *peace and war manifestations are both essentially end products, the results obtained by passing the same psychic energies through different mental systems.* Or to put it another way, that peace and war activities are both solutions of mental tension, the apparent and actual difference being due to the different defensive mechanisms employed. He states that *the driving energy in both cases belongs to the destructive group of instincts,* in particular that variety which when fused with some love components is known as sadism. And in illustration of this he points out that the fanatical pacifist under certain circumstances may be a danger to peace. He also points out, however, that in addition to this active form of destructive impulse an element of confusion is introduced by a

[1] *War, Sadism and Pacifism* (Allen & Unwin, 1933).

passive form, namely masochism, in which destructive impulses are fused with passive love components. These *passive destructive impulses* are more silent in operation than the active sadistic components; nevertheless they *contribute considerably to an unconscious readiness to tolerate or even welcome situations of war.* And they do so not merely by paralysing the operation of self-preservative impulses, but because the acceptance of suffering, in addition to being a primary form of gratification, represents a primitive method of overcoming " unconscious guilt ".'

This thesis has done much to discredit the present methods of pacifist propaganda; moreover, it explains why some of us, who are pacifists in reason, have never been able to be pacifists in practice. We have been aware of the fact that most of our fellow-pacifists are actuated, not by rational motives, but by an obscure perversion of the very instinct that should be recognized and rationally controlled.

Dr. Glover has no ready alternative to propose, and admits that there is no agreement among psychologists—that there is, in fact, at present no scientific remedy for the evil of war. He confines himself to his diagnosis and calls for a more realistic inquiry. As a psycho-analyst he believes that the instincts giving rise to war are obscured in childhood; the foundations of peace reactions are laid in the same period. The remedy, presumably, is in the hands that rock the cradles all over the world. But how instil the right virtues into such hands? Dr. Glover does not know. Dr. Freud does not know. Nobody knows, and meanwhile war is threatening the very existence of our civilization.

Freud's theory of the destructive instinct is, of course, only an hypothesis; but to accept merely the general psychological notion of an instinct predisposing the mass of mankind to war-like activities is to admit the futility of all our present pacifist methods. To arm for peace, even internationally, is to ensure that plenty of weapons will be at the disposal of those instincts once they can no longer be restrained. To be content with a policy of non-resistance (Gregg, De Ligt, Aldous Huxley, and the Peace Pledge Union) is to assume that the obvious does not exist. It is particularly significant that Mr. Huxley, who is not innocent of psychology, should so completely ignore the psychological problem. He does, it is true, note Dr. J. D. Unwin's theory according to which the rise of war may be correlated with the increased sexual continence of an emergent ruling class; and freely admits what from my own point of view is an immediate symptom of war psychology—the rise of self-conscious leaders preoccupied with the ideas of personal domination and personal survival after death. But his general attitude is governed by his doctrine of non-attachment, which is in itself a typical product of the death instinct.

What then shall we do? We can undertake the research programme outlined by Dr. Glover, but its outcome is admittedly doubtful, and in any case it demands a period of experiment and educational training measured in centuries. Moreover, that programme can only be realized under conditions which are absolutely inconsistent with present systems of government and present economic structures. It involves, in fact, handing over the supreme power in each country to the modern equivalent of the philosopher-king—to the psychological expert. I think that most nations would rather perish than do that.

The only realistic approach, because the only approach which promises immediate and far-reaching changes in the structure of society, is the revolutionary approach. Economic imperialism is so demonstrably dependent on the support of armed force that only the most prejudiced capitalist can pretend to ignore its importance as a factor in the encouragement of latent warlike instincts. But the capitalist is quite logical (and for once he has the support of the psychologist) when he points out that warfare has a longer history than capitalism, and that the establishment of socialism in Russia, for example, has by no means been accompanied by a decline of the martial spirit. It may be argued that militarism in the U.S.S.R. is purely defensive; but it is militarism none the less, and there are few countries where the pacifist is less free to preach his doctrine of non-resistance. So long as nationalism persists as a sentiment, so long as collectivism masquerades as socialism, so long will socialist units be nothing more than militarist units magnified and intensified.

War increases in intensity and effect as society develops its central organization. The greatest intensification of the horrors of war is a direct result of the democratization of the State. So long as the army was a professional unit, the specialist function of a limited number of men, so long war remained a relatively harmless contest for power. But once it became every man's duty to defend his home (or his political 'rights') warfare was free to range wherever that home might be, and to attack every form of life and property associated with that home.

The economic foundations of peace will never be secure so long as collective units such as the nation exist. So long as it is possible to unite men in the name of an abstraction, war will exist; for the possibility of uniting the whole of mankind under the same abstraction is too remote to be worth considering, and as long as more than one abstraction exists with collective forces organized behind it, the possibility of war will exist.

The only pacifist peoples are certain so-called savage tribes living under a system of communal land tenure in a land of plenty: communities where the accumulation of capital and the power it gives has no purpose and therefore does not exist, and where there is no possibility of one man exploiting the labour of another. These conditions create, not only the social and economic possibilities of peace, but also the far more important psychological possibilities. Such communities are, in the precise meaning of the word, *anarchist* communities.

There is no problem to which, during the last thirty years, I have given more thought than this problem of war and peace; it has been an obsession with my generation. There is no problem which leads so inevitably to anarchism. Peace is anarchy. Government is force; force is repression, and repression leads to reaction, or to a psychosis of power which in its turn involves the individual in destruction and the nations in war. War will exist as long as the State exists. Only an anarchist society can offer these economic, ethical, and psychological conditions under which the emergence of a peaceful mentality is possible. We fight because we are too tightly swathed in bonds—because we live in a condition of economic slavery and of moral inhibition. Not until these bonds are loosed will the desire to create finally triumph over the desire to destroy. We must be at peace with ourselves before we can be at peace with one another.

7

THE IMPORTANCE OF LIVING

A modern Chinese philosopher, Lin Yutang, has written a valuable book under this title. It is a book that expresses, as well as any I know, the outlook on life with which I most sympathize. It is not entirely my philosophy, because it is Oriental, and has many small incidental peculiarities which I do not share. It is also a philosophy with a tradition of many centuries of meditation behind it, and it has therefore a ripeness or maturity to which I cannot pretend. The tradition of the Western world is quite different, and anyone who revolts against it, as I do, must necessarily stand in isolation.

I am so imbued with the spirit of toleration—and toleration is an essential aspect of anarchism as I conceive it—that religion as such does not seem to me to enter into the discussion of public affairs. It is only when religion is organized and assumes dictatorial powers over the lives and conduct of everyone that I resent it. I resent the government of the Church in the same way that I resent the government of the State. It is an intolerable interference with my liberty.

I cannot conceive religion as anything but the expression of individual emotions. I look around and see that some people 'profess' religion, others do not. I examine myself and find that I do not feel this religious need. I remember experiencing such a feeling in my youth, but it passed and left me serener and happier. I can only conclude that this feeling is the product of certain emotional stresses in the individual; and I am quite willing to admit that people who have the stresses are entitled to have the emotional or imaginative compensations which they need. But it is utterly fantastic to admit that they should have any right to impose their particular compensation on people who have no need of it.

But religion, it will be said, is far more than such a subjective

122

fantasy: it is, for example, a system of ethics or an explanation of the universe.

Ethics is the science of good conduct. As such it implies a theory, or at least a sense, of values. But I fail to see how this sense can be imposed from above or from outside. The sense of right and wrong is a subjective sense: if I do not *feel* what is right and what is wrong, I cannot act rightly or wrongly, except under compulsion. To *know* a code of right and wrong is to know someone else's conception of right and wrong. Truth, justice, goodness, beauty—these are the universals of the philosopher, and I have more than once assumed the reality of their existence. But when we try to define the *mode* of their existence, we are either reduced to dogmatic affirmations and the evidence of mystics, or are compelled to admit that there are only particular cases of truth, justice, goodness, and beauty. But to admit that truth, for example, is only the sum of particular truths at a particular time is to base all our speculations on a morass of relativism. That truth, single and invariable, does exist is the premiss of all science and philosophy. But is it not possible that the only truth is the law and structure of the universe, so far as we can observe it, and that all other truths are analogies derived from aspects of this physical order? Justice, for example, on this assumption, is an analogy of equal quantities; beauty is an analogy of symmetry and balance; goodness is perfect growth. With the Pythagoreans we can once more assert that the nature of all things is number. This would give the highest value to reason, which is the faculty by means of which we discover the laws of the universe and attempt to relate them to some general conception of its organization. Such a faculty, we may conclude, is well able to look after our morals.

The origin of conscience, and the knowledge of good and evil, can be explained within the terms of individual psychology. What is not within the scope of the subjective sense of good and evil—certain wider aspects of social justice, for example—is invariably a projection of this subjective sense into the analogous body of the community. I believe that we have acquired in the course of our human history feelings of sympathy and mutuality which compel us to subordinate our purely egoistic impulses to the general good. Such feelings are often most evident in simple uncivilized communities, and most distorted or repressed in highly complex civilizations.

As for our knowledge of the external world, in so far as we can be certain of the objectivity of such knowledge, I observe that it reveals a certain structural harmony in the universe which is of the greatest significance, and which we may, if we have use for the symbol, identify with God. We cannot yet and probably will never be able to grasp the system of the universe in its completeness and in its farthest ramifications. We have to confess our ignorance and the limitations of our human faculties. But the degree of our knowledge of the universe is the guarantee of our liberty of action. We can only act freely in a familiar environment.

It is tempting to identify our aesthetic emotions with our awareness of the structural harmony of the universe, but a closer examination of the aesthetic creations of mankind shows that their forms tend to depart in some degree from the structural patterns which result from physical processes. The emotion we experience when we perceive the form of a crystal or of the solar system is not the same as the emotion we experience when we read Shakespeare's poetry or listen to Beethoven's music. This latter emotion is rather the vertigo we experience in daring to depart from the patterns inherent in the universe. Art is thus an adventure into the unknown, and essentially subjective. This has not always been perceived, and a confusion has arisen between the imitation of the universal harmony (the 'beauty' of classical philosophy) and the creation of new patterns of reality (which is art properly so-called).

Kierkegaard observes that we tend to experience the universe either aesthetically or ethically; and he supposed that these mutually exclusive attitudes could only be reconciled in a synthesis which is religion. But that seems to me to impose a totally unnecessary strain on the individual mind. The ethical and the aesthetic are but two aspects of the one reality—two methods of establishing a relationship with reality. Kierkegaard's third way may exist, but it implies such an intense degree of subjectivity that it can only be cultivated by a minority of mystics.

From whatever angle we approach it life is thus an individual adventure. We enter the world as the world's most sensitive instrument. We are immediately subjected to thousands of sensations, some of them pleasant, some painful. By our nature we seek the pleasant, and though we soon discover that the path of least resistance is not necessarily or finally the path of most pleasure, we endeavour to order our life so that it may contain the maximum intensity of pleasure. We become connoisseurs of the varieties of pleasure, experts in the integration of sensations and gradually evolve a hierarchy of values which constitutes our culture. If that hierarchy is well built, our culture survives; if it is too selfish or too harmful to our health, our culture perishes.

Natural catastrophes—famine, disease, floods, storms, eclipses —these, before men could explain them rationally, inspired terror. The struggle for food inspired rivalry and hatred. The leader was the man who succeeded against all rivals, and he exploited not only his strength, but the terror which was latent in his fellow-men. Lust for power and the fear of death are the original sins. They alone are sufficient to explain the repression of natural instincts and the creation of gloomy fantasies from which all the melancholy of the world proceeds. When we can cast out the fear of death and renounce any desire to dominate the least of our fellow-men, then we can live in peace and happiness. And that is the final aim: neither to believe, nor suffer, nor renounce; but to accept, to enjoy, to realize the anarchy of life in the midst of the order of living.

THE PARADOX OF ANARCHISM

The highest perfection of society is found in the union of order and anarchy.

PROUDHON

THE PARADOX OF ANARCHISM

It has been the fashion, especially among orthodox marxists, to hold in contempt any theory of politics which did not justify itself in action, and this emphasis on action has often led to a confusion of means and ends—the means too often overshadowing the ends and becoming a substitute for them. The dictatorship of the proletariat, for example, at first put forward as a means towards the classless society, becomes stabilized in Russia as the sovereignty of a new class.

Anarchism does not confuse means and ends, theory and practice. As a theory it relies on reason alone, and if the conception of society which it thus arrives at seems utopian and even chimerical, it does not matter, for what is established by right reasoning cannot be surrendered to expediency. Our practical activity may be a gradual approximation towards the ideal, or it may be a sudden revolutionary realization of that ideal, but it must never be a compromise. Proudhon was often accused of being an anarchist in theory, but only a reformist in practice: he was, in fact, an anarchist all the time, who refused to commit himself to the hazards of dictatorship. He would not play the game of politics because he knew that economics were the fundamental reality. And so today it is conceivable that a change in the control of financial credit, or a new system of land tenure, might bring us nearer to anarchism than a political revolution which merely transferred the power of the State into the hands of a new set of ambitious gangsters.

Anarchism means literally a society without an *arkhos*, that is to say, without a ruler. It does not mean a society without law, and therefore it does not mean a society without order. The anarchist accepts the social contract, but he interprets that contract in a particular way, which he believes to be the way most justified by reason.

129

The social contract, as expounded by Rousseau, implies that each individual in society surrenders his independence for the common good, with the assumption that only in this way can the liberty of the individual be guaranteed. Liberty is guaranteed by law, and law, to use Rousseau's phrase, is the expression of the general will.

So far we are on common ground, not only with Rousseau, but with the whole democratic tradition which has been built up on the theoretical foundation laid by Rousseau. Where the anarchist diverges from Rousseau, and from that aspect of the democratic tradition which has found expression in parliamentary socialism, is in his interpretation of the manner in which the general will should be formulated and enforced.

Rousseau himself was not consistent on this question. He was quite convinced that some form of State must exist as an expression of the general will, and that the power invested in the State by general consent must be absolute. He was equally convinced that the individual must retain his liberty, and that upon the individual's enjoyment of liberty depended all progress and civilization. He realized that as an historical fact the State and the individual had always come into conflict, and for a solution of this dilemma he fell back upon his theory of education. If every citizen could be brought up to appreciate the beauty and harmony of the laws inherent in nature, he would be as incapable of establishing a tyranny as of enduring one. The society in which he lived would automatically be a natural society, a society of free consent in which law and liberty are but two aspects of the same reality. But such a system of education implies a pre-existing authority to establish it and that authority must be absolute.

The system of government recommended by Rousseau in *The Social Contract* is an elective aristocracy rather than a true democracy, and to control this aristocracy he imagines a State so small that every individual within it would be able to watch and criticize the government. He probably had something like the Greek city-state in mind as the ideal unit. He certainly had no prevision of the vast complexes of millions of individuals which constitute most modern States, and we can be quite sure that he would have been the first to admit that his system of checks on authority would not work under such conditions.

But his theory of the State, which has had such a profound influence on the development of modern socialism, has been taken over as applicable to these vast conglomerates, and it thus becomes a justification for the most absolute kind of authoritarianism. This danger was recognized as long ago as 1815 by Benjamin Constant, who described *The Social Contract* as 'le plus terrible auxiliaire de tous les genres de despotisme'.

If what Rousseau calls an aristocratic form of government is more or less identical with modern democracy, what he calls democracy is more or less identical with the modern theory of anarchism, and it is interesting to see why he rejects democracy. He does so for two reasons—first because he regards it as an executive impossibility. A people cannot be continuously assembled to govern itself; it must delegate authority as a mere matter of convenience, and once you have delegated authority, you no longer have a democracy.

His second reason is a typical example of his inconsistency. If there were a people of gods, he says, they could govern themselves democratically, but a government so perfect is unsuitable for men.

But if the reason establishes democracy as the perfect form of government, it is not for one who has proclaimed his faith in the perfectability of man to restrict it to the gods. What is good enough for the gods is all the better for man—as an ideal. If the ideal exists we must recognize it and strive however approximately to attain it.

But the fundamental question in all this sophistry is ignored by Rousseau. It is the unreality of the notion of the general will. There is probably only one issue on which a people ever expresses unanimous or general will: the defence of their physical liberty. Otherwise they divide according to their temperaments, and though these are limited in number, they are sufficiently diverse and so mutually opposed that in any given geographical area they will give rise to incompatible groups.

On that very account, say Rousseau and many other philosophers, a democracy is impossible.

But they are forced to this conclusion because they adhere

obstinately to the arbitrary boundaries of the modern State—boundaries established by rivers, seas, mountains, and military treaties, and not by reason.

Suppose we were to ignore these boundaries, or abolish them. The realities are, after all, human beings with certain desires: with certain primitive needs. These human beings, according to their needs and sympathies, will *spontaneously* associate themselves into groups for mutual aid, will *voluntarily* organize an economy which ensures the satisfaction of their needs. This is the principle of mutual aid, and it has been explained and justified with much historical and scientific evidence by Kropotkin. It is this principle which the anarchist makes the foundation of his social order, and upon which he believes he can build that democratic form of society which Rousseau felt was reserved for the gods.

It is not necessary here to repeat the empirical evidence for this belief: Kropotkin's great book is a work whose scholarship is acknowledged by sociologists of all schools. The difficulty is not to justify a principle which has sound psychological and empirical evidence to support it, but to apply this principle to the existing state of society.

This we do tentatively by taking the voluntary organizations that already exist and seeing to what extent they are capable of becoming the units in a democratic society. Such organizations are trade unions, syndicates, professional unions, academies, etc.—all those groups which crystallize around a human function. We then consider the functions which are now performed by the State, and which are necessary for our well-being, and we ask ourselves to what extent these functions could be entrusted to such voluntary organizations. We come to the conclusion that there are no *essential* functions which could not thus be transferred. It is true that there are functions like making war and charging rent which are not the expression of an impulse towards mutual aid, but it does not need much consideration of such functions to see that they would naturally disappear if the central authority of the State was abolished.

The mistakes of every political thinker from Aristotle to Rousseau have been due to their use of the abstract conception *man*. Their systems assume the substantial uniformity of this creature of their imaginations, and what they actually propose are various forms of authority to enforce uniformity on man.

But the anarchist recognizes the uniqueness of the person, and only allows for organization to the extent that the person seeks sympathy and mutual aid among his fellows. In reality, therefore, the anarchist replaces the *social* contract by the *functional* contract, and the authority of the contract only extends to the fulfilling of a specific function.

The political unitarian or authoritarian conceives society as one body compelled to uniformity. The anarchist conceives society as a balance or harmony of groups, and most of us belong to one or more such groups. The only difficulty is their harmonious interrelation.

But is it so difficult? It is true that trade unions sometimes quarrel with one another, but analyse these quarrels and you will find, either that they proceed from causes outside their function (such as their different conceptions of their place in a non-functional, i.e., capitalist society) or from personal rivalries, which are a reflection of the struggle for survival in a capitalist world. Such differences of aim bear no relation to the principle of voluntary organization and are indeed excluded by that very concept. In general, trade unions can agree with one another well enough even in a capitalist society, in spite of all its incitement to rivalry and aggressiveness.

If we go outside our own time to the Middle Ages, for example, we find that the functional organization of society, though imperfectly realized, was proved to be quite possible, and its gradual perfection was only thwarted by the rise of capitalism. Other periods and other forms of society, as Kropotkin has shown, fully confirm the possibility of the harmonious interrelationships of functional groups.

Admitted, it may be said, that we can transfer all the economic functions of the State in this way, what about other functions—the administration of criminal law, relationships with foreign countries not at the same stage of social development, education, etc.?

To this question the anarchist has two replies. In the first place he argues that most of these non-functional activities are incidental to a non-functional State—that crime, for example, is largely a reaction to the institution of private property, and that foreign affairs are largely economic in origin and motivation. But it is agreed that there are questions, such as certain aspects of common law, infant education, public morality, which are outside the province of the functional organizations. These, he argues, are matters of common sense, solved by reference to the innate good will of the community. But the community for this purpose need not necessarily be anything so impersonal and so grandiose as a State—in fact, it will be effective in inverse ratio to its size. The most effective community is the smallest—the family. Beyond the family is the parish, the local association of men in contiguous dwellings. Such local associations may form their courts and these courts are sufficient to administer a common law based on common sense. The manor courts in the Middle Ages, for example, dealt with all crimes and misdemeanours save those committed against the artificial entities of the State and the Church.

In this sense anarchism implies a universal decentralization of authority, and a universal simplification of life. Inhuman entities like the modern city will disappear. But anarchism does not necessarily imply a reversion to handicraft and outdoor sanitation. There is no contradiction between anarchism and electric power, anarchism and air transport, anarchism and the division of labour, anarchism and industrial efficiency. Since the functional groups will all be working for their mutual benefit, and not for other people's profit or for destructive armaments, the measure of efficiency will be the appetite for fullness of living. The anarchist collectives in Spain gave a convincing demonstration of this progressive tendency during their brief existence.

There is a further consideration of a more topical and more pressing nature. In a remarkable book, *The Crisis of Civilization*, Alfred Cobban has shown that the disasters which have fallen on the Western world are a direct consequence of the adoption by Germany of the theory of popular or national sovereignty, in place of the theory of natural law which had been evolved by the rational movement of thought in the eighteenth century known as the Enlightenment. German thought, writes Mr. Cobban, 'substituted historical rights for natural rights, and the will of the nation, or the *Volk*, for reason as the basis of law and government . . . The ultimate result of the theory of popular sovereingty was thus the substitution of history for ethics. This tendency was present in the contemporary thought of all countries. It has only achieved a complete triumph in Germany. The distinguishing mark of modern German thought is the dissolution of ethics in the *Volkgeist*; its practical conclusion is that the state is the source of all morality, and the individual must accept the laws and actions of his own state as having ultimate ethical validity.'

I will not repeat the detailed evidence which Mr. Cobban, who is a professional historian, offers in support of this statement, but its truth is obvious enough. 'Sovereignty, whether it adopts the democratic, nationalist, or socialist disguise, or some amalgam of all three, is the political religion of today.' It follows that if we are to rid Europe permanently of the menace to peace which Germany represents, we must first of all destroy the German conception of sovereignty. So long as this conception remains, as a national religion, there will be a continual resurgence of the instruments of such a policy—armed might and arbitrary aggression.

Germany can, of course, be disarmed, but we have tried that remedy once before, and it gave Europe only a short respite. Reparations also proved to be a capitalist illusion, and did no good, least of all to the recipients. A reconstituted democratic republic, once again a member of a reconstituted League of Nations, or European Federation? Nothing in the history of Germany can allow any realist to suppose that Germany would play such a nice political game. So long as her present social structure remains intact, Germany will seek the economic and political advantages which she believes to be her right and destiny.

There is only one way to prevent a third resurgence of German power, and that is the way of anarchism. It is necessary to destroy the German State as such. The German people are made up of as many diverse elements as any other people, but the great majority of them (workers included) are sustained in their fanatical beliefs by the most centralized State in Europe; and the most fanatical of all their beliefs is their belief in the sovereignty of this State. It is difficult for anyone unfamiliar with German thought, or with even the ordinary run of German people, to realize the force and philosophic strength of this belief—a belief common to all parties, from the militarists on the right to the communists on the left. Germany, in all her menace and neurotic frenzy, is obsessed by this uncritical worship of the State, and she can only be immunized and rendered harmless by the systematic destruction of that concept. This can be done in stages, first by the restoration of independence to the provinces whose union made the German State possible, and then by the devolution within these separate provinces of all economic power to trade unions and other voluntary organizations. Other measures, such as the abolition of national banks and national currency, would follow as a matter of course. The principles of anarchism would be introduced into one country in Europe and the demonstration of their pacific and civilizing influence would be so effective that other countries would quickly and voluntarily hasten to follow the same path. Force would have abolished force and individual life would once more expand in freedom and beauty.

It was a great German, already alarmed by the tendencies then taking shape, as an immediate reaction from the French Revolution, who warned his countrymen against the monster they were creating. 'It is thus', wrote Schiller, 'that concrete individual life is extinguished, in order that the abstract whole may continue its miserable life, and the State remains for ever a stranger to its citizens, because feeling does not discover it anywhere. The governing authorities find themselves compelled to classify, and thereby simplify, the multiplicity of citizens, and only to know humanity in a representative form and at second hand. Accordingly they end by entirely losing sight of humanity, and by confounding it with a simple artificial creation of the understanding, whilst on their part the subject classes cannot help receiving coldly laws that address themselves so little to their personality. At length society, weary of having a burden that the State takes so little trouble to lighten, falls to pieces and is broken up—a destiny that has long since attended most European States. They are dissolved in what may be called a state of moral nature, in which public authority is only one function more, hated and deceived by those who think it necessary, respected only by those who can do without it.'[1] In these pre-scient words Schiller stated that antagonism between organic freedom and mechanical organizations which has been ignored in the political development of modern Europe with results that we see all round us now.

Anarchism is the final and most urgent protest against this fate: a recall to those principles which alone can guarantee the harmony of man's being and the creative evolution of his genius.

[1] *Letters upon the Aesthetical Education of Man,* VI.

EXISTENTIALISM, MARXISM AND
ANARCHISM

EXISTENTIALISM, MARXISM AND ANARCHISM

The origins of the existentialist movement are usually traced back to Kierkegaard, whose main philosophical works appeared between 1838 and 1855. As these were written in Danish, they did not immediately get into general circulation. Various selections made by Bärthold were published in Germany between 1873 and the end of the nineteenth century, but the first complete German translation of his works only appeared between 1909 and 1923, and the Anglo-American translation began as late as 1936. However, there is no excuse for making Kierkegaard the founder of existentialism. It is true that he gave the movement a specifically Christian twist, but all the main ideas were already present in the philosophy of Schelling, and one should remember that Kierkegaard, however much he may have criticized Schelling, was nevertheless at first profoundly influenced by this great German philosopher, and in 1841 made a special voyage to Berlin in order to sit at his feet.

Incidentally, long before Kierkegaard our own Coleridge had been reading Schelling's early works, and we find in Coleridge's lesser-known writings a good deal of existentialist thought. As I have pointed out elsewhere,[1] all the main concepts of modern existentialism—*Angst*, the abyss, immediacy, the priority of existence to essence—are to be found in Coleridge, and most of these concepts Coleridge no doubt got from Schelling.

It is necessary for my present purpose to give some general description of the existentialist attitude in philosophy, but I am not a professional philosopher and I do not intend to use the technical terminology in which quite obvious facts or ideas are often clothed. It would seem that the philosopher who calls himself an existentialist begins with an acute attack of self-con-

[1] *Coleridge as Critic* (Faber, 1949), pp. 29–30.

sciousness, or *inwardness*, as he prefers to call it. He is suddenly aware of his separate lonely individuality, and he contrasts this, not only with the rest of the human species, but with the whole goings-on of the universe, as they have been revealed by scientific investigation. There he is, a finite and insignificant speck of protoplasm pitched against the infinite extent of the universe. It is true that modern physicists may have succeeded in proving that the universe itself is also finite, but that only makes matters worse, for now the universe shrinks to littleness and is pitched against the still more mysterious concept of *Nothingness*. This is not merely something infinite; it is something humanly inconceivable. Heidegger has devoted one of his most intriguing essays to an attempt—not to define the indefinable—but to define the negation of Being, Non-Being, or Nothingness.

So there we have the Little Man gaping into the abyss, and feeling—for he still retains an infinite capacity for sensation—not only very small, but terrified. That feeling is the original *Angst*, the dread or anguish, and if you do not feel *Angst* you cannot be an existentialist. I am going to suggest presently that we need not necessarily feel *Angst*, but all existentialists do, and their philosophy begins in that fact.

There are two fundamental reactions to *Angst*: we can say that the realization of man's insignificance in the universe can be met by a kind of despairful defiance. I may be insignificant, and my life a useless passion, but at least I can cock a snook at the whole show and prove the independence of my mind, my consciousness. Life obviously has no meaning, but let us pretend that it has. This pretence will at any rate give the individual a sense of responsibility: he can prove that he is a law unto himself, and he can even enter into agreement with his fellow-men about certain lines of conduct which, in this situation, they should all adopt. He is free to do this, and his freedom thus grows into a sense of responsibility. This is Sartre's doctrine, but he does not make very clear what would happen supposing he could not persuade his fellow-men to agree on certain lines of conduct, or certain values. I think he would probably say that a measure of agreement is ensured by our human predicament: that being what we are, when our existential situation is made clear, we are bound to act freely in a certain way. Our necessity becomes our freedom. But I am not sure about this. The characters in Sartre's novels and plays tend to act absurdly, or according to their psychological dispositions, and are not noticeably responsible to any ideal of social progress.

This aspect of existentialism seems to me to have a good deal in common with Vaihinger's philosophy of 'as if'. We cannot be sure that we are free, or that we are responsible for our own destiny, but we behave 'as if' we were. And by a natural extension existentialism establishes a relationship with pragmatism—it is significant that many of Sartre's literary enthusiasms are American, and America is the home of pragmatism. But, from Sartre's point of view, pragmatism of any kind is too superficial: it is based on day-to-day procedures, a sort of balance-sheet of success and failure, whereas the existentialist must for ever keep in view the terrifying nature of our human predicament. To that extent, perhaps, existentialism represents an advance in philosophical rectitude.

More profoundly still, the existentialists object to pragmatism and other such practical philosophies (including, as we shall see presently, marxism) on the ground that they are materialistic. Any form of materialism, by making human values dependent on economic or social conditions, deprives man of his freedom. Freedom is the capacity to rise above one's material environment. 'The possibility of detaching oneself from a situation in order to take a point of view concerning it (says Sartre) is precisely what we call freedom. No sort of materialism will ever explain this transcendence of a situation, followed by a turning back to it. A chain of causes and effects may well impel me to an action, or an attitude, which will itself be an effect and will modify the state of the world: it cannot cause me to turn back to my situation to apprehend it in its totality.'[1]

That turning-back to a situation is the metaphysical act: there is nothing in our environment to compel us to adopt a metaphysical attitude. That is a process of rising superior to our environment, of seeing things, of seeing all nature, from a point of view external to nature. The marxist may protest that that is all poppy-cock—there is no possibility of lifting ourselves outside nature by our own shoe-straps. But that is the crux of the

[1] Trans. *Partisan Review*.

whole question. The existentialist, it seems to me, is bound to assert that mankind has developed a special faculty, consciousness, or intellectual self-awareness, which enables him to do precisely that trick. In this matter I am inclined to be on the side of the existentialist. The higher forms of animal consciousness are connected with this impulse to detachment—detachment from the herd, from society, from any situation including the situation of man *vis à vis* the universe. It can be argued with force that precisely such capacity for detachment is the cause of our social disease, our disunity, and aggressiveness; but it must also be admitted that our major advances in scientific thought are also due to the development and use of this same faculty.

But there is a danger inherent in detachment which the existentialist fully realizes. It is the danger of idealism. In detachment we elaborate a philosophy, a social utopia, which has no relevance to the conditions we are at any moment living through. The existentialist therefore says that man, having experienced his sense of detachment or freedom, must throw himself back into the social context with the intention of changing those conditions. Hence the doctrine of *engagement*. To quote Sartre again: 'Revolutionary man must be a contingent being, unjustifiable but free, entirely immersed in the society that oppresses him, but capable of transcending this society by his effort to change it. Idealism mystifies him in that it binds him by rights and values that are already given; it conceals from him his power to devise roads of his own. But materialism also mystifies him, by depriving him of his freedom. The revolutionary philosophy must be a philosophy of transcendence.'[1]

Before examining this doctrine from the point of view of marxism and anarchism, let us pause for a moment to examine the other typical reaction to *Angst*, the religious reaction, for that is an idealist attitude to which Sartre is also objecting. I am not sure that I can do justice to this attitude, but as it takes shape in the thought of Schelling, Coleridge, and Kierkegaard (and earlier still, in Saint Augustine), it seems to amount to this: We have the existential position—man confronted by the abyss of nothingness. It just does not make sense. Why am I here? Why all this complex structure, of which I am a part, a part be-

[1] Trans. *Partisan Review*.

come aware of itself? It is complete nonsense, but a simple hypothesis will make sense of it all—the prior existence of God. A transcendent creator responsible for the whole phantasmagoria of existence, responsible for me too, and my consciousness —how logical it all becomes! There may be difficult snags left over—the problems of evil and pain, for example—but a little ingenuity will soon get over them. We can't expect even a celestial omnibus to work without a little friction. And so we get, immensely elaborated, the mystical Christian existentialism of Kierkegaard and Gabriel Marcel. I am not suggesting that this is the point of view of the average Christian, or the average theist of any kind; they usually rely on revelation, on sacred scriptures and ecstatic illumination; but in so far as the religious point of view competes in the philosophical field, it is independent of these special pleas, and relies on logical argument. It is another philosophy of 'as if'; it might be called the philosophy of 'only thus'—only thus does our existence make sense.

The sense, in such a case, is identical with what these philosophers call 'essence', and Sartre, if not Heidegger before him, has said that the fundamental thesis of existentialism is that existence precedes essence. Professor Ayer has attacked this proposition on logical grounds,[1] and it is indeed difficult to give it any precise meaning. 'Essence' has a confusing history as a philosophical term. It usually means what we can assert about anything apart from the mere fact of its existence (i.e. subsistence): the possibilities inherent in a thing: the Platonic 'Idea'. Santayana, whose use of the term is a little peculiar, but nevertheless valuable in being what an avowed materialist can admit, defines the difference between existence and essence as that between what is always identical with itself and immutable and what, on the contrary, is in flux and indefinable. This agrees with Sartre's notion of contingency; it is essence which allows for the possibility of change in the world. Santayana has a pretty little myth to describe the relationship: 'Becoming, we might say, in the fierce struggle to generate he knew not what, begat Difference; and Difference, once born, astonished its parent by growing into a great swarm of Differences, until it exhibited all possible Differences, that is to say, until it exhibited the

[1] *Horizon*, July and August 1945. *Rationalist Annual*, 1948.

whole realm of essence. Up to that time Becoming, who was a brisk bold lusty Daemon, had thought himself the cock of the walk; but now, painful as it was for him to see any truth whatever, he couldn't help suspecting that he lived and moved only through ignorance, not being able to maintain the limitations of any moment nor to escape the limitations of the next, like a dancing Dervish that must lift one foot and then the other from the burning coals.'[1]

That is by the way, but Santayana does bring out more clearly than any other philosopher I know the fact that it is by its very ideality, its non-existence, that essence is inwardly linked with existence—it is not a mere extension or part of that which exists. I do not think Professor Ayer appreciates this point, but I would not like to argue it out with him, because it is not my point, nor one to which I attach particular importance. But it does explain why Sartre can support a notion like freedom without being committed to that kind of idealism which involves a whole system of absolute values. I do not think it would make much difference to Sartre's philosophy if for *freedom* we substituted the word *flux*. What we apprehend of the nature of things is subject to constant change, and the change is not so much inherent in the thing itself—in matter—as in our consciousness or apprehension of these essences. According to this view essences do not change, neither do they subsist in space or time. They are merely there when we perceive them. They belong to the object, but can exist without its material presence, like the grin of the Cheshire cat in *Alice in Wonderland*.

Rousseau's mistake was to treat freedom as an essence, as an eternally subsisting value in mankind. Man is not in this sense 'born free'. He is born a mere bundle of flesh and bones, with freedom as one of the possibilities of his existence. The onus is on man to create the conditions of freedom.

Now all this may seem to be of merely theoretical interest, but on the contrary this is where existentialism is making its greatest contribution to philosophy. It is eliminating all systems of idealism, all theories of life or being that subordinate man to an idea, to an abstraction of some sort. It is also eliminating all systems of materialism that subordinate man to the operation of physical

[1] 'Apologia pro mente sua.' *The Philosophy of Santayana*. Ed. Paul Arthur Schilpp (North Western University, Evanston, 1940), p. 526.

and economic laws. It is saying that man is the reality—not even man in the abstract, but the human person, you and I; and that everything else—freedom, love, reason, God—is a contingency depending on the will of the individual. In this respect existentialism has much in common with Max Stirner's egoism. An existentialist like Sartre differs from Stirner in that he is willing to engage the ego in certain super-egoistic or idealistic aims. He has less in common with dialectical materialism which requires him to subordinate his personal freedom to political necessity; less still with Catholicism which requires him to subordinate his personal freedom to God. He seeks alliance with a militant humanism which by political and cultural means will in some unspecified way guarantee his personal freedom.

Let me admit at this stage of the argument that I find it possible to accept some of the fundamental principles of Sartre's existentialism. I believe, for example, that all philosophy must begin in subjectivity. There are certain concrete bases of experience—the so-called scientific facts—to which we can give an existential reality, but though philosophy may use them as a jumping-off ground, they do not in themselves involve the acceptance of a particular philosophy. If they did, we should find all scientists professing the same philosophy, which is very far from being the case. Philosophy begins when we depart from existential facts and flounder about in the realm of essences. In that realm our subjective faculties—intuition, aesthetic sensibility, the esemplastic power (as Coleridge called it) of subsuming the many under the one—with all these personal and uncertain means we begin to construct a philosophy. We should still be guided by practical reason, scientific method, and logic; but these are the methods and not the substance of our discourse (a fact often forgotten by the logical positivists). By virtue of this subjective activity, we reduce irrational essences into some kind of order, the order of a carefully constructed myth or fairy-tale (as in religion) or the order of a coherent utopia (as in political idealism).[1]

---

[1] The Marxists pretend that their Utopia is scientific, but it is just as idealistic as any other projection of our constructive faculties into an unpredictable future; and by their day-to-day modifications of their plans, Marxists as a matter of fact admit how idealistic their original conceptions must have been.

The rationalist and materialist may protest that we are merely trying to reduce everything to the terms of our romantic idealism, but we can turn on him and prove that his philosophical structure, in spite of the pseudo-scientific jargon in which it is expressed, is in no way different. It is a structure of reason, and it is idealistic in that it depends on *faith*—faith that tomorrow will be the same as today, faith that human beings will behave in a way he can calculate beforehand, faith in reason itself, which is, after all, only the means by which the scientist kids himself that he understands existence. Scientific method may be one thing, and productive of separately ascertained truths between which there can only be relative discontinuity, a chaos of atomized facts; or scientific method may be something quite different and move towards some ideal of harmony, of wholeness and order. But such harmony (the ideal of a Marx no less than of a Plato) is a subjective perception. The communist in this respect does not differ from the royalist or the anarchist; we are all idealists, and I do not see how we can be anything else so long as we believe that man is what he makes of himself. The difference is between those who believe that a particular ideal should predetermine man's existence (which is the official communist line) and those who believe (as the existentialists and anarchists do) that the personality of man, that is to say, his own subjectivity, is the existing reality and that the ideal is an essence towards which he projects himself, which he hopes to realize in the future, not by rational planning, but by inner subjective development. The essence can only be grasped from the particular stage of existence which you and I have at any particular moment reached. Hence the folly of all so-called 'blue-prints for the future'; the future will make its own prints, and they won't necessarily be blue.

To most people all this involves a sense of insecurity, as though they were sailing strange seas without a chart, perhaps even without a compass. But that, as Sartre has pointed out, is the whole point. He quotes Dostoevsky—'if God did not exist, all would be permissible'. 'In fact,' admits Sartre, 'everything is permissible if God does not exist, and consequently man is adrift, because he cannot find, either within himself or without, anything to cling to. At first he is without excuses. If in fact existence precedes essence, one cannot explain things in terms of a given and fixed human nature; in other words, there is no determinism, man is free, man is freedom. On the other hand, if God does not exist, we do not find ready at hand values or formulas which will justify our conduct. Thus, neither in front of us nor behind us can we find, in the realm of values, justification or excuse. We are alone, without excuse.'[1] Which is what Sartre means when he says that man is condemned to be free. In my metaphor, he is condemned to be adrift, and he has to invent the instruments by means of which he can steer a course; having invented these instruments, he has to set out on a voyage of discovery. He has no idea of where he will get to, where he will land himself. His life, his existence, is the voyage: his reality is the fact that he is moving in a direction which he himself has freely determined.

For the moment I want to leave on one side the problem of agreement; for after all, we can't move about an ocean in separate boats; we are passengers on ships which contain many other people, and we have to reconcile our freedom of movement with theirs. We shall be in a better position to consider this problem when we have confronted existentialism and marxism.

The marxists have already taken up a position of uncompromising opposition to existentialism. In view of the association of the French existentialist writers with the resistance movement during the occupation, it is a little difficult to follow the usual practice and label existentialism as a philosophy of fascism, so it seems to have been agreed to damn it as Trotskyism. Anyone less of an existentialist than Trotsky it would be difficult to conceive, so it is equally difficult to see how an existentialist can be a Trotskyite: it is merely, of course, a convenient term of abuse. But the examination of existentialism made by George Lukacs, whom I regard as the most intelligent marxist critic of our time, is more serious than such tactics would suggest.[2] It is, of course, comparatively simple to establish a connection between fascist imperialism and the philosophy of Heidegger—the connection was historical and actual during the Nazi régime. But such an association might have been fortuitous—it is difficult for a

[1] *L'existentialisme est un humanisme* (1946), p.p. 36–7
[2] *Existentialisme ou marxisme?* (Nagel, Paris, 1948).

philosopher to resist the flattery which a totalitarian State seems willing to bestow on him. For philosophical purposes we must seek for some more fundamental connection, and this undoubtedly lies in the nihilism which is the philosophical disease of our time. Now nihilism is merely that condition of despair which I have already described, a despair that overcomes man whenever he looks into the abyss of nothingness and realizes his own insignificance. It is a condition from which you can react in various ways: you can, of course, affirm its fundamental reality —you can remain a nihilist and refuse to believe in anything but your own selfish interests. You can react as Dostoevsky did, and become a pessimistic Christian, or you can react as the Nazis did and become a 'realistic' power politician. Heidegger (and Sartre when it comes to his turn) reacts far more metaphysically: he constructs an elaborate fire-escape, a life-saving apparatus by means of which man can escape from nihilism, though not denying that it still remains the fundamental nature of reality. Now that is precisely what the marxist cannot accept. To begin with, what is this pessimistic nihilism but a reflection of the bankruptcy of the capitalist system? It has no reality: the Nothingness which Heidegger and Sartre write about is a subjective state of mind. Lukacs calls it a typical fetish of bourgeois psychology, a myth created by a society condemned to death. Its existence is only made possible by an abandonment of reason, and this is a characteristic trend of modern philosophy, a trend that includes, not only Heidegger and Husserl, but also Dilthey and Bergson.

The marxist is really more existentialist than the existentialists. In theory (but not always in practice) he does not admit the existence of essences. There is only one reality, and it is historical, temporal. Man is an animal who has evolved in historic time. At a certain stage in his evolution he developed the faculty of consciousness, but there is nothing mysterious about it, and its nature and scope will no doubt change again in the future. 'Man', says Lukacs, 'has created himself by his work. When man finally winds up his pre-history and establishes socialism in a complete and definite form, then we shall see a fundamental transformation of the nature of man . . . Creating himself historically, transforming himself historically, man is naturally (*également*) attached to the world by certain constant factors (work and certain fixed relationships which arise out of it). But that does not in any way effect a compromise between such an objective dialectic of history and the timeless ontology of subjectivity. No compromise is possible between these two conceptions: it is necessary to make a choice. Nor is any compromise possible between the existentialist conception of freedom and the historical and dialectical unity of freedom and necessity established by marxism.'[1]

Lukacs seems above all concerned to disallow the possibility of a third way in philosophy and politics. There is idealism and there is dialectical materialism; if you are not a dialectical materialist, you must be an idealist of some sort; if you are a dialectical materialist, you must be a marxist. I think this is playing with words. There is a fundamental opposition between a purely mechanistic materialism and all forms of idealism, but Lukacs, like most modern marxists, is very careful to dissociate himself from the mechanistic school. But as soon as materialism becomes dialectical, it associates itself with contradictions, and the contradictions of matter are essences. You cannot be dialectical in thought or anything else unless you posit a realm of essence over against the realm of matter. But as soon as you admit a realm of essences, you give substantial existence to a state of subjectivity, for it is only in a state of subjectivity that we become aware of essences. If man had created himself merely by his work, he would have remained within a sensational and instinctual world, like the ant. The development of consciousness, which I agree with marxists in treating as an existential, historic event, means that subjective factors, essences, entered into the dialectical process; and only that fact can explain the evolution of man to his present moral and intellectual stature. And, of course, it is quite ridiculous to confine the evolutionary factors to work. The struggle for existence, especially in unfavourable climatic conditions, has always been a grim business. But the higher faculties of man, such as ethical consciousness, probably developed in temperate zones—in Egypt and the Mediterranean basin—and it was *play* rather than *work* which enabled man to evolve his higher faculties—everything we mean by the

[1] Op. cit., p. 203.

word 'culture'. Anyone who doubts this should read Huizinga's *Homo Ludens*.[1] There is no aspect of culture—language, war, science, art, or philosophy, not even religion—in whose evolution play does not enter as the creative factor. Play is freedom, is disinterestedness, and it is only by virtue of disinterested free activity that man has created his cultural values. Perhaps it is this theory of all work and no play that has made the marxist such a very dull boy.

An animal at play—animals do play and man is only an animal that has learned to play more elaborately—an animal at play is not very conscious of *Angst*, of the existentialist's abyss of nothingness. The existentialist and the marxist may retort that only a despicable character like Nero fiddles while Rome is burning, but considering the corruption of Rome at that time, there was perhaps something to be said for Nero's playful disinterestedness. Nero, however, is really beside the point, which is the relevance of *Angst*. To the marxist the whole business—*Angst*, shipwreck, nothingness—is merely another myth, like the myth of the End of the World, or the Last Judgement. But the point of view I now want to bring forward, and recommend as the true one, admits the facts upon which the existentialist bases his *Angst*, but draws a different conclusion from them. There is no generally accepted name for this other fellow standing by the side of the existentialist on the edge of the abyss, but he has some resemblance to Aristotle. He surveys the scene, the little speck of protoplasm which is man, the universe, finite or infinite, on which he finds himself, and, if he thinks of the universe as finite, the dreaded gulf of nothingness beyond. His feelings are feelings of profound interest, excitement, wonder. He sees Fire and Air, Earth and Water, elementary qualities giving birth to all sorts of contrarieties—hot-cold, dry-moist, heavy-light, hard-soft, viscous-brittle, rough-smooth, coarse-fine—sees these combining and inter-acting and producing worlds and life upon these worlds, and he is lost in wonder. His greatest wonder is reserved for the fact that he, man, stands on the apex of this complex structure, its crown of perfection, alone conscious of the coherence of the Whole.

I recommend, as an antidote to the existentialists, a reading

[1] Routledge & Kegan Paul, London, 1949.

not only of Aristotle, but also of Lucretius—particularly those passages where he breaks off from his description of the nature of things to praise Epicurus, the father of his philosophy, the discoverer of truth, who had parted the walls of the world asunder, so that we might see all things moving on through the void: 'The quarters of Acheron are nowhere to be seen, nor yet is earth a barrier to prevent all things being descried, which are carried on underneath through the void below our feet. At these things, as it were, some godlike pleasure and thrill of awe seizes on me, to think that thus by thy power nature is made so clear and manifest, laid bare on every side.' What Lucretius called 'the fear of Acheron . . . clouding all things with the blackness of death, and suffering no pleasure to be pure and unalloyed' is our familiar bogy *Angst*, and Lucretius's great poem was written to dispel *Angst*. 'For often ere now', he says, 'men have betrayed country and beloved parents, seeking to shun the realms of Acheron. For even as children tremble and fear everything in blinding darkness, so we sometimes dread in the light things that are no whit more to be feared than what children shudder at in the dark, and imagine will come to pass. This terror, then, this darkness of the mind, must needs be scattered, not by the rays of the sun and the gleaming shafts of day, but by the outer view and the inner law of nature.'[1]

Aristotle and Lucretius are not exceptions; there is throughout the history of philosophy a tradition that, while taking its origin in the same full look into the nature of things as the existentialists affect, is based on the completely contrary reaction—a reaction of curiosity rather than of shipwreck.

It cannot be said that this positive reaction (or *resonance* as Woltereck has called it[2]) is any more unjustified, any less profound than the negative reaction of the existentialist. It is a question of what Santayana has called 'animal faith', 'an atheoretical force which, torn from the data of experience, constructs and guarantees and extends the world of man'—or as Sanatayana puts it, 'the life of reason'.[3]

[1] Trans. by Cyril Bailey (Oxford, 1910).
[2] *Ontologie des Lebendigen* (Stuttgart, 1940). The translations of passages from this book which follow have been kindly supplied by Mr. R. F. C. Hull.
[3] Antonio Banfi, 'Crisis of Contemporary Philosophy', *The Philosophy of George Santayana* (Evanston, 1940), p. 482.

Animal *faith*, faith in nature—I do not think the marxist likes the word faith—he is afraid of being committed to a god. I agree that it would be better to avoid the word God. As Santayana again has said: 'If by calling nature God or the work of God, or the language in which God speaks to us, nothing is meant except that nature is wonderful, unfathomed, alive, the course of our being, the sanction of morality, and the dispenser of happiness and misery—there can be no objection to such alternative terms in the mouth of poets; but I think a philosopher should avoid the ambiguities which a too poetical term often comports. The word nature is poetical enough: it suggests sufficiently the generative and controlling function, the endless vitality and the changeful order of the world in which I live.'[1]

The philosophy which I am trying to present—a philosophy based on a positive reaction to cosmic experience—might well be called humanism—it is an affirmation of the significance of our human destiny. Humanism is a term which Sartre has adopted and which even an intransigent marxist like Lukacs does not disdain—he calls the Leninist theory of knowledge a militant humanism (*un humanisme combatif*), but he qualifies this acceptance of the term by pointing out that the notion is inseparable from practical action and work. This brings me to the anarchist position, which only now, at the end of this long disquisition, can be revealed in all its logical clarity. Like the marxist—or should we say the leninist—the anarchist rejects the philosophical nihilism of the existentialist. He just doesn't feel that *Angst*, that dreadful shipwreck on the confines of the universe, from which the existentialist reacts with despairful energy. He agrees with the marxist that it is merely a modern myth. He draws in his metaphysical horns and explores the world of nature. He again finds himself agreeing with the leninist that life is a dialectical process, the end of which is the conquest of what Lukacs calls '*la totalité humaine*', which presumably means a world dominated by human values. But whereas the leninist conceives of this conquest in terms of a consciously directed struggle—practical action and work—the anarchist sees it in terms of mutual aid, of symbiosis. Marxism is based on economics; anarchism on biology. Marxism still clings to an

[1] *Scepticism and Animal Faith* (1923), pp. 237–8.

antiquated darwinism, and sees history and politics as illustrations of a struggle for existence between social classes. Anarchism does not deny the importance of such economic forces, but it insists that there is something still more important, the consciousness of an overriding human solidarity. 'It is' says Kropotkin, 'the unconscious recognition of the force that is borrowed by each man from the practice of mutual aid; of the close dependency of everyone's happiness upon the happiness of all; and of the sense of justice, or equity, which brings the individual to consider the rights of every other individual as equal to his own. Upon this broad and necessary foundation the still higher moral feelings are developed.'[1]

There is no need to repeat here the evidence from biology, anthropology, and social history which Kropotkin brought to the support of his thesis. Even the existentialist Sartre recognizes that the liberty he desires for himself implies that he must desire liberty for others. Even the marxist talks of human solidarity, to which capitalism is the only obstacle. But biology is not enough: we are self-conscious animals, animals conscious of 'being', and we need a science of such consciousness: it is called ontology.

There is, that is to say, a science of existence which we call *biology*; there is a science of essence which we call *ontology*. The purpose of these two sciences is to determine the nature of the process of life and the place of our human existence in that total process. There are people who say that this cannot be done with the instruments of reason; that there is a Ground of Being only accessible to super-rational intuition, and not understandable in the terms of rational thought. Some people regard that Ground of Being as transcendent, as more or less actively intervening in the development of existence, particularly in the unfolding of our human destiny; others treat it as merely an unknown quantity; still others, the materialists among us, deny its existence altogether.

The point of view I have adopted myself is not dualistic; I do not recognize two orders of reality, known or unknown. Nor is my point of view materialistic in the marxist sense. I believe, in the words of Woltereck, that '*one* stream of events embraces

[1] *Mutual Aid*, Introduction.

everything that can in any way be experienced as real: whether the events be material or non-material, a-biotic, organic, psychic, conscious or unconscious . . . The psychic or spiritual life of man is also part of this *one stream of events* we call "Nature", even though under special names and with special contents: science, technics, civilization, politics, history and art. The organism "Man" produces these things—in the last analysis no differently from the bird its song and its building of its nest, the tree its blossom and fruit. Also the dawning of consciousness, conscious acting and conscious thinking, are natural processes just like the reactions, instinctive acts and affects in the animal kingdom.' The biologist does not make a distinction between physical events (Nature), and non-physical events (Spirit): there is but one stream of events with as it were a visible (material) surface and a fluid (immaterial) depth, and this distinction between visible surface and fluid depth is, for me, the same distinction that Santayana makes between material existence and fluid essence. Santayana also says that essence is not an extension or a portion of that which exists, but that it is intimately interwoven with existence; meaning, I think, that there is this flexible Inside and Outside division, but no merging across this division. There is always a division between the gas inside a balloon and the atmosphere outside: they cannot mix, but they are intimately related as pressures, as specific gravities, and react in correspondence one with the other. Essence and existence are in this manner interwoven throughout the whole evolution of life.

What is important to emphasize in all this is the presence, throughout the one life-process, of *freedom*. The presence of this element is indicated by the process of evolution itself, which is an *upward* process, 'leading from the elementary physical states of the cosmic nebulæ to a-biotic differentiation. then to simple and increasingly differentiated life, and finally to spiritual events, spiritual creativity and spiritual freedom'.[1] There has existed throughout the whole process of evolution an ability to move on to new planes of existence, to create novelty. Freedom is not an essence only available to the sensibility of man; it is germinatively *at work* in all living things as spontaneity and autoplasticity.

[1] Woltereck, op. cit.

'This "biological" freedom and what becomes of it,' (I am again quoting Woltereck) 'has an ontic significance quite different from the "existential" compulsion of free decision. The latter *cripples* our sense of vitality and consequently the advancing life of man. The freedom of spontaneous events born of the ontic centre and the freedom to mould things in such and such a way enhances our sense of vitality and makes life *more intense*. The joy of creating things of value, self-conquest (freeing the self from selfishness and its instincts), rising above the world, and finally the spontaneous creation of new forms, new norms, new ideas in the minds of individuals—all that is the possible result of man's *positive freedom*.'

Freedom, says the marxist, is the knowledge of necessity. Freedom, says Engels, 'consists in the control over ourselves and over external nature which is founded on knowledge of natural necessity: it is therefore necessarily a product of historical development'. The only thing wrong with this definition is that it is too narrow. The chick that is pecking its way out of its shell has no *knowledge* of natural necessity: only a spontaneous instinct to behave in a way that will secure it freedom. It is an important distinction because it is the distinction underlying the marxist and the anarchist philosophies. From the anarchist point of view it is not sufficient to *control* ourselves and external nature; we must allow for *spontaneous* developments. Such opportunities occur only in an open society; they cannot develop in a closed society such as the marxists have established in Russia. There is also to be observed in Engels and Marx an essential confusion between freedom and liberty: what they mean by freedom is political liberty, man's relations to his economic environment; freedom is the relation of man to the total life process.[1]

I am afraid that these observations will seem somewhat irrelevant to the practical problems of life, but that is a dangerous assumption. Marxism as militant politics throughout the world today had its origins in such philosophical distinctions, and still today rests unshaken on such a philosophical basis. We cannot meet marxism and expect to overcome it unless we have a

[1] See pp. 161–72, below.

philosophy of equal force. I do not believe that any of the prevailing idealistic systems of philosophy will serve our purpose: the marxists have proved that they have weapons powerful enough to demolish that kind of structure. They have now shown that in their opinion existentialism does not constitute a danger to their philosophical position. I believe that another philosophical attitude is possible, and that it preserves the concept of freedom without which life becomes brutish. It is a materialistic philosophy, but it is also an idealist philosophy; a philosophy that combines existence and essence in dialectical counterplay.

If finally you ask me whether there is any necessary connection between this philosophy and anarchism, I would reply that in my opinion anarchism is the *only* political theory that combines an essentially revolutionary and contingent attitude with a philosophy of freedom. It is the only militant libertarian doctrine left in the world, and on its diffusion depends the progressive evolution of human consciousness and of humanity itself.

CHAINS OF FREEDOM

CHAINS OF FREEDOM

1

Under this title I have gathered a few stray notes—ideas, criticisms, quotations—which may serve as tentative prolegomena to a philosophy of freedom. For many years now I have let such thoughts slip by unrecorded, and though they have served *my* purpose, leaving my mind richer, my convictions stronger, they are like the steps of a ladder which I have kicked away.

I do not proceed on any plan. The form is that of a commonplace book, a *cahier*, and though I do not date my entries, they follow more or less the course of my reading, or are inspired by passing events.

2

At the outset, there are a few definitions or axioms which I ought to write down as a guide to those who will follow me, or as a warning to those who might be misguided by me. There is the word *freedom* itself, so often and so glibly used by every interested person or party. The 'freedom' of the Press, the 'freedom' of association, the 'freedom' of trade—all such uses of the word seem to me wrong, for freedom is an abstract concept, a philosophical word. What these people mean by their 'freedoms' is really a negative condition—the absence of control, the liberty of unlicensed conduct (it is significant that a complete ambiguity or equivocation has also overtaken the word 'licence'). Freedom, in this sense, always implies freedom *from*—freedom from some kind of control. But freedom in the sense I shall use the word is a positive condition—specifically, freedom to create, freedom to become what one *is*. The word implies an obligation.

Freedom is not a state of rest, of least resistance. It is a state of action, of projection, of self-realization. I shall discuss some time during the course of these notes whether freedom is essentially personal, egoistic, individualistic; or whether it implies a social setting. We speak of a 'free' wheel on a bicycle, but its freedom has no sense except in relation to the complex function of the machine as a whole, and its use by a human being.

3

A man *is* free: he is given his liberty.

Freedom is a personal attribute; liberty is a civil right.

This distinction is nicely illustrated in the following usages: The *liberty* of a city is a definite area of ground within which the municipal *authority* extends.

The *freedom* of a city is a quality (privilege) conferred on a person.

There are endless nuances of difference between these two words—freedom and liberty, and the fact that we have two words in English, and have developed different meanings for them, is of profound significance. He who does not feel a difference between them does not really possess freedom, however much he may be at liberty.

And what of nations that do not possess two words to distinguish these nuances? At present a long obscure discussion is taking place in France on the meaning of *liberté*. The existentialists have invented 'a new doctrine of liberty'. I, as an Englishman, see nothing new in it: Sartre and his disciples are merely trying to distinguish a state of being which we should call freedom; but since the French have only one word, 'liberté', it has to be given a special definition, a further nuance. The French pride themselves on the 'clarté' of their language, but their philosophers and psychologists are always getting into difficulties simply because they lack alternative words to distinguish nearly related concepts. This word-poverty, which has always been evident in their poetry, afflicts their philosophy with similar limitations. How a Pascal and a Bergson struggle against these limitations!

(Admittedly, both the poetry and the philosophy gain something from the struggle: not *clarté*, but *netteté*; and the ingenuity that is required forces the magnificent imagery of Pascal and Bergson. Since Plato, these two are the most poetical of all philosophers.)

4

The Germans have *Freiheit*, but no word corresponding to liberty. But they are aware of the distinction and have to some extent acclimatized the French *liberté*. It is significant, again, that they have a native word for the personal attribute, but none for the civil right. Hitler often claimed that he had not interfered with the 'freedom' of the people; he did not mean that he had no intention of taking away their liberty.[1]

5

Liberty is concrete: existential.

Freedom is abstract: essential.

Sartre's doctrine of liberty—'une liberté qui n'est limitée que par elle-même'; in one word, *freedom*.

(Significance of the abstract suffix: Free*dom*, Frei*heit*, etc. Existentialist philosophy, which is of German origin, translates with such confusion into French because the French cannot manipulate abstract affixes and suffixes with the prodigious ease of a Husserl or a Heidegger.)

6

'Liberty is not a value but the ground of value.'—W. H. Auden. Introduction to Henry James's *American Scene* (Scribner,

[1] A passage from the recent translation of Martin Buber's *Between Man and Man* reveals the inadequacy of the one word *Freiheit* in German. 'It is the nature of freedom to provide the place, but not the foundation as well, on which true life is raised. That is true both of inner 'moral' freedom and of outer freedom (which consists in not being hindered or limited). As the higher freedom, the soul's freedom of decision, signifies perhaps our highest moments but not a fraction of our substance, so the lower freedom, the freedom of development, signifies our capacity for growth but by no means our growth itself.' Trans. by Ronald Gregor Smith (Kegan Paul, London, 1947).

This need to distinguish between a higher and a lower freedom, between a moral and an outer freedom, is expressed by our separate words, freedom and liberty.

New York, 1946). A perfect statement: but freedom *is* a value, and indeed, the value of all values.

7

The problem of 'free' will, which now exercises the existentialists as much as it once did the scholastics and the calvinists, is again complicated for the French by their poverty of terms. Man, says Sartre, is a product of his free will; he is what he is in virtue of 'un libre choix'. We would say, man is free to become what he is, and that does not seem a complicated statement. But if we were compelled to say that man is 'at liberty' to become what he is, the statement would seem absurd, for it leaves out the activating element of will. However we play with the word 'liberty', we are always compelled to use a phrase which suggests a relationship, either between man and man, or between man and society. A concrete situation is implied. But no such 'concretization' arises from the use of the word 'free'. If a man is 'free', he is free both existentially and essentially. 'Existence precedes essence', Sartre's famous slogan, does not make sense in the state of freedom: in freedom existence is essence, essence existence.

Heidegger writes: 'Das Wesen der Wahrheit ist die Freiheit.' The French translates: 'L'éssence de la verité est la liberté.' I would say: 'The essence of truth is freedom', not liberty.

I read in a French article: 'Si je suis libre de renoncer à ma liberté, il faut bien qu'il y ait un cas au moins où cette liberté est effectivement exercée,' and I instinctively begin to translate: If I am free to renounce my liberty, it would seem that there is one case at least where this . . . (I hesitate) *freedom* is effectively exercised. But this makes nonsense of the French writer's point. Indeed, the whole article, 'Remarques sur une nouvelle doctrine de la liberté', by Aimé Patri (*Deucalion*, No. 1, 1946) is full of pseudo-clarity which becomes ambiguity once we try to translate it into English.

8

Query: in the history of existentialism, where does Max Stirner come in? I have the impression that his name is never mentioned in the popular accounts of existentialism. Sartre may never have read him, but Husserl? The existentialists speak often of Nietzsche's influence on Husserl, and Stirner is recognized as one of the precursors of Nietzsche. But I suspect a more direct liaison. Stirner is one of the most existentialist of all past philosophers, and whole pages of *The Ego and His Own* read like anticipations of Sartre. Buber recognizes his place in the evolution of the existentialist philosophy.

9

A *philosophy* of freedom: a *doctrine* of liberty.

10

A final etymological note. *Free* is derived from OE *fréon*, to love (Sanskrit root, *pri* to love) and is therefore related to friend. Liberty is derived from the Latin legal phrase, used to describe emancipation from the *master-slave* bond. Query: connected with *libra* scales? In any case, there is the implication all through its history, of a legalistic background. But obviously, in French, the word has acquired all the emotional overtones which we attach to the word freedom. Cf. Eluard's poem.

11

Acton's definition of *liberty* brings out its contractual basis: 'By liberty I mean the assurance that every man shall be protected in doing what he believes his duty against the influence of authority and majorities, custom and opinion.' 'Liberty . . . is not a means to a higher political end . . . A generous spirit prefers that his country should be poor, and weak, and of no account, but free, rather than powerful, prosperous and enslaved. It is better to be the citizen of a humble commonwealth in the Alps than a subject of the superb autocracy that overshadows half of Asia and Europe.' (*Letters of Lord Acton to Mary, daughter of the Rt. Hon. W. E. Gladstone.* Ed. by Herbert Paul (London, 1904), p. lvii.)

12

Compare Tocqueville: 'Liberty may be conceived, by those who enjoy it, under two different forms: as the exercise of a universal right, or as the enjoyment of a privilege. In the Middle Ages, those who possessed any liberty of action, viz. the feudal aristocracy, figured to themselves their liberty under the latter type. They desired it, not because it was what all were entitled to, but because each considered himself as possessing, in his own person, a peculiar right to it. And thus has liberty almost always been understood in aristocratic societies, where conditions are very unequal, and where the human mind, having once contracted the thirst for privileges, ends by ranking among privileges all the good things of this world.

'This notion of liberty as a personal right of the individual who so conceives it, or at most of the class to which he belongs, may subsist in a nation where general liberty does not exist. It even sometimes happens that, in a certain small number of persons, the love of liberty is all the stronger in proportion to the deficiency of the securities necessary for the liberties of all. The exception is the more precious in proportion as it is more rare.

'This aristocratic notion of liberty produces, among those who have imbibed it, an exalted idea of their own individual value, and a passionate love of independence; it gives extraordinary energy and ardour to their pursuit of their own interests and passions. Entertained by individuals, it has often led them to the most extraordinary actions—adopted by an entire people, it has created the most energetic nations that have ever existed.

'The Romans believed that they alone of the human race were fitted to enjoy independence; and it was much less from nature than from Rome that they thought they derived their right to be free.

'According to the modern, the democratic, and, we venture to say the only just notion of liberty, every man, being presumed to have received from nature the intelligence necessary for his own general guidance, is inherently entitled to be uncontrolled by his fellows in all that only concerns himself, and to regulate at his own will his own destiny.

'From the moment when this notion of liberty has penetrated deeply into the minds of a people, and has solidly established itself there, absolute and arbitrary power is thenceforth but a usurpation, or an accident; for, if no one is under any moral obligation to submit to another, it follows that the sovereign will can rightfully emanate only from the union of the wills of the whole. From that time passive obedience loses its character of morality, and there is no longer a medium between the bold and manly virtues of the citizen and the compliances of the slave.

'In proportion as ranks become equalized, this notion of liberty tends naturally to prevail.' (*Memoir, Letters and Remains* (London, 1861), Vol. I, pp. 255–7.)

This distinction between aristocratic liberty as a privilege and democratic liberty as a universal right remains within the realm of politics. Equality of wealth, the right to elect representatives, etc., all the devices of the democratic State, do not touch the problem of freedom. The most mentally enslaved people in the world today are the *uniform* citizens of a democratic republic like America. They have retained their liberty but lost their essential freedom. They speak proudly of the American *pattern* of behaviour. Eccentricity is bad taste. The matter is even worse in the U.S.S.R. where the concept of freedom, in our sense of the word, does not seem to exist. We assume too readily that concepts are universal, that 'ideas' exist by some principle of spontaneous origin in every mind. But thirty years of 'collective teaching' can eradicate an idea, destroy a concept. The Russians know the difference between a prison and a factory, between rations and luxuries: they have what they might call 'freedom of choice'. But freedom as a state of being, as a mental climate—that is beyond their present comprehension.

One might compare the historical changes in the concept of freedom with the historical changes in the concept of love, as traced by Denis de Rougemont (in *Passion and Society*) and C. S. Lewis (in *The Allegory of Love*). It is not that a Platonist would have despised the passionate heterosexual love which began in Europe as a reaction to Christianity (which is de Rougemont's thesis): he would have been incapable of conceiving such an emotion, or even the idea of such an emotion; in the same way, the younger citizens of the U.S.S.R. seem incapable now of conceiving the notion of freedom.

13

A profound understanding of the nature of freedom is found in the works of Martin Buber, the Jewish philosopher. But again, as in the writings of Heidegger and Sartre, it is extremely difficult to disentangle the ambiguities which proceed from the use of a single word—in Buber's case, the word 'freedom'. I have already quoted (§4) a passage from Buber which shows that he is aware of an inherent difference of meaning. But when he goes on to distinguish between 'freedom' and 'compulsion', we seem to lose sight of the two meanings of freedom. There is a tendency, says Buber, to regard freedom (in the sense of liberty) as the opposite pole from compulsion. But 'at the opposite pole from compulsion there stands, not freedom, but *communion*. Compulsion is a negative reality, communion is the positive reality; freedom is a possibility, possibility regained. At the opposite pole of being compelled by destiny or nature or man there does not stand being free of destiny or nature or men, but to commune and to covenant with them. To do this, it is true that one must first have become independent; but this independence is a footbridge, not a dwelling place. Freedom is the vibrating needle, the fruitful zero.'

Is it likely that the distinction between freedom and liberty is retained by the reader of this passage? Buber uses three terms —compulsion, freedom, communion. If we use our fourth term, liberty, then the over-paradoxical element in Buber's statement disappears. If we are 'under compulsion', we are not 'at liberty' to commune with one another. In these words, the statement becomes, not a paradox, but a platitude. But 'to become free'— that, as Buber rightly insists, is something quite different: 'Life lived in freedom is personal responsibility or it is a pathetic farce.' In communion, we are responsible for one another and (though this is adding a gloss to Buber) the whole idea of justice arises from that personal responsibility.

Buber says: 'I love freedom, but I do not believe in it', and he adds that we must not make freedom into a theorem or a programme. But here clearly he is using freedom in our sense of liberty; and in that sense I agree with him. But obviously Buber believes in moral freedom, 'in the soul's freedom of decision', and has made freedom in that sense the main feature of his philosophy.

14

The social aspect of communion is community, and 'the commune' is the social unit that preserves the freedom of the person. But here again Buber has made a distinction of the utmost importance to our philosophy—the distinction between 'community' and 'collectivity':

'Collectivity is not a binding but a bundling together: individuals packed together, armed and equipped in common, with only as much life from man to man as will inflame the marching step. But community, growing community (which is all we have known so far) is the being no longer side by side but *with* one another of a multitude of persons . . . Community is where community happens. Collectivity is based on an organized atrophy of personal existence, community on its increase and confirmation in life lived towards one another. The modern zeal for collectivity is a flight from community's testing and consecration of the person, a flight from the vital dialogic, demanding the staking of the self, which is the heart of the world.'

What a light this throws, not only on the development of collectivism in Russia, but on the equally fatal development within many of the co-operative communities of the past. Why have so many of these communities failed? There is a general agreement that *the causes of failure were rarely economic*. Lack of planning, lack of experience in agriculture—these, as Infield points out in his historical review of co-operative communities,[1] contribute to the process of dissolution. But the main cause is psychological, expressed in 'the quarrels among the settlers, as well as between them and the management'. Significantly, the co-operatives with the longest record of success and survival, are religious communities like the Hutterites. And they have survived for centuries, not because of their superior skill in agriculture or their genius for planning, but simply because their members

[1] *Co-operative Communism at Work* (Kegan Paul, London, 1947).

have been *with* one another, in real communion. When the Hutterites presented a petition to President Wilson in 1918, they gave as the fundamental principles of their faith, as concerns practical life, 'community of goods and non-resistance'. 'Our community life is founded on the principle "What is mine is thine", or, in other words, on brotherly love and humble Christian service according to Acts II, 44, 45: "And all that believeth were together, and had all things in common and sold their possessions and goods, and parted them to all men as every man had need."'

Among the 'advantages' of the Hutterite community Infield gives the following psychological factors: permanent security, freedom from individual economic worries, very high 'work satisfaction, with pride in one's unhurried efforts—no competition, but instead friendly co-operation in the common interest. Mental and emotion health are maintained, with no quarrelling, no crime or suicides. A sense of security encourages self-confidence, directness and dignity.' 'The "we-feeling" is strongly developed, for the centuries-old behaviour patterns call on each member to participate in the common effort, and important decisions are made by direct vote in the General Assembly. The colony is restricted as to size, thus keeping all relationships on a face-to-face level of intimacy. From his schooling the child learns to fit into the community. Adults easily readjust themselves to changing conditions, for they can choose from among numerous kinds of work.'

All this might have been written with Buber's philosophy in mind, and will be worth elaborating in relation to that philosophy; but for the moment I am only concerned to emphasize that on the basis of his study of the Hutterite community, and of a similar study of non-religious co-operative settlements in Palestine, the conclusion emerges, in all its clarity, 'that some central emotional impulse, comparable to the religious motive, is important to the success of comprehensive co-operation'.

15

We must remember that in a certain sense all *metaphysics* is a retreat from reality. It is far from the purpose of these notes to elaborate a philosophy of freedom that is a compensation for *lack of liberty*. The philosophy of freedom is an *activist* philosophy —the philosophy of those who create—whether as artists, as co-operators, or as personalities. In the philosophy of existentialism there is an element of *compensation*: there are too many disillusioned communists in its ranks to give one confidence in its disinterestedness. Metaphysics is the opium of the isolated individual: a community seeks, not so much a religion, as the concreteness of a ritual.

Hegelian dialectics, Marxism in its ideological aspects—all this metaphysical opium was manufactured by people without a living experience of communion: the philosophy of authoritarians and exiles.

16

The bankruptcy of historical materialism as a social philosophy is paralleled by the bankruptcy of logical positivism as a general philosophy. The two movements are, of course, closely related expressions of the *Zeitgeist*: they both proceed from unwarranted assumptions about the nature of reason. The Marxist deduces all social phenomena from economic calculations (figures): the logical positivist would prove everything by mathematical processes. Both in the end (which we have now reached) find themselves in a state of arid logomachy without parallel in the history of thought. They are slaves of their formulae—hard, intolerant, and sadistic. The poverty of both historical materialism and logical positivism is explained by their denial of instinctive modes of thought, of super-rational intuitions, of the aesthetic nature of perception—in a word, by their surrender of existential freedom. They are like snails with one antenna, gyrating either inwards to a point of negation (logical positivists) or outwards, towards limitless affirmations of the commonplace (historical materialists).

Wisdom, as I have insisted ever since I became intellectually conscious, is the needle which comes to rest between reason and romanticism (a word which comprises instinct, intuition, imagination, and fantasy). Buber (see §13) uses this metaphor to describe freedom, but he is thinking of the tremors of the needle: wisdom is the direction in which it points.

17

'Equality', wrote Nietzsche, 'as an actual approximation to similarity, of which the theory of equal rights is but the expression, belongs essentially to decadence. The gap between man and man, between class and class, the multiplicity of types, the will to assert the self, to stand out in contrast, that which I call the *pathos of distance*, belongs to every vigorous period.'

There is, of course, an inescapable truth in such criticism: equality, in democratic theory and practice, has too often been identified with a policy of *levelling*. The natural diversity of needs, of merits, of capabilities, has been ignored, and men have been forced into common moulds, fixed routines, standard patterns of all kinds. Not only their bodies, but the minds and sensibilities of men, have been *conscripted* by the State, and all in the name of democratic justice. This democratic tendency, as Nietzsche perceived, conflicts with the essential nature of freedom, and Nietzsche could not see how freedom was to be reconciled with equality in the democratic State. Nor can I. But freedom is another concept which had to be redefined by Nietzsche, and the more he considered it, the more clearly he realized that freedom is not something which one has by natural endowment, or by social contract: it is something which one wins by conquest, by a discipline of the spirit. *Freedom is the will to be responsible for one's self.*

18

Freedom can be defined logically, psychologically, even metaphysically, but equality can be defined only in a sociological sense. Even if we fall back on the equivocal formula of the Christians and say that we are all equal in the sight of God, we are still defining a social relationship with reference to a point outside society—erecting a triangle on a social basis. But the base of the triangle is *level*: and the Christian, in politics, must inevitably be a Leveller.

19

But let us look a little closer at this equivocation—in Kierkegaard, for example: 'The neighbour is your equal. The neighbour is not your beloved for whom you have a passionate partiality, not your friend for whom you have a passionate partiality. Nor, if you are an educated man, is your neighbour the one who is educated, with whom you are equal in education—for with your neighbour you have human equality before God. Nor is the neighbour the one who is more distinguished than yourself, that is, he is not your neighbour just because he is more distinguished than yourself, for loving him because he is more distinguished than yourself, can easily become partiality, and in so far selfishness. Nor is your neighbour one who is inferior to you, that is, in so far as he is humbler than yourself he is not your neighbour, for to love one because he is inferior to yourself can readily become the condescension of partiality, and in so far selfishness. No, loving your neighbour is a matter of equality. It is encouraging in your relation to a distinguished man, that in him you *must love* your neighbour; it is humbling in relation to the inferior, that you do not have to love the inferior in him, but *must* love your neighbour; it is a saving grace if you do it, for you *must* do it. The neighbour is every man; for he is not your neighbour through the difference, or through the equality with you as in your difference from other men. He is your neighbour through equality with you before God, but every man unconditionally has this equality, and has it unconditionally.' (*Works of Love*, II B, trans. D. F. and L. M. Swenson (Oxford, 1946).)

20

This argument seems to imply double-dealing on the part of God. Equality before God apparently does not guarantee equality with your neighbour, and the notion, which Nietzsche and Burckhardt held, that the democratic movement is the inheritance of the Christian movement, is therefore based on a false interpretation of Christ's second commandment. For Kierkegaard, as for Nietzsche, 'differences' are inborn. 'As little as the Christian lives or can live without a physical body, just as little can he live outside the differences of earthly life to which every individual by birth, by condition, by circumstances, by education, etc., belongs . . . These differences must continue as long as the temporal existence continues, and must continue to

173

tempt every man who comes into the world.' *Innerlichkeit*, whether of the Kierkegaardian pattern, or of the Californian Yogi pattern, offers a complete escape from social responsibility.

21

In a society where the preservation *of the community* is the first consideration, love of one's neighbour, as Nietzsche once again pointed out, is a secondary matter. 'A sympathetic action, for instance, is called neither good nor bad, moral nor immoral, in the best period of the Romans; and should it be praised, a sort of resentful disdain is compatible with this praise, even at the best, directly the sympathetic action is compared with one which contributes to the welfare of the whole, to the *res publica*.' (*Beyond Good and Evil*, s 201.)

22

Nietzsche makes no distinction between a totalitarian society (which is welded together by external bonds) and a communal society which coheres by virtue of its internal morale, by instinctive mutual aid. The possibility of such an instinct as mutual aid is foreign to his false darwinism, His conception of evolution as a blind struggle for existence, a manifestation of some universal 'will to power'. Obviously, if evolution is nothing but such a struggle, we must *fear* our neighbour rather than love him, and as a matter of fact Nietzsche had no difficulty in pointing out that fear is the mother of bourgeois morality. 'It is by the loftiest and strongest instincts, when they break out passionately and carry the individual far above and beyond the average, and the low level of the gregarious conscience, that the self-reliance of the community is destroyed; its belief in itself, its backbone, as it were, breaks; consequently these very instincts will be most branded and defamed. The lofty independent spirituality, the will to stand alone, and even the cogent reason, are felt to be dangers; everything that elevates the individual above the herd, and is a source of fear to the neighbour, is henceforth called evil; the tolerant, unassuming, self-adapting, self-equalizing disposition, the *mediocrity* of desires, attains to moral distinction and honour.' (Loc. cit.)

23

It is useless to pretend that a dilemma does not exist here. The growth of democracy and of egalitarian socialism has led to the prevalence and predominance of mediocre men in public life. Our present House of Commons descends below mediocrity to some absolute zero of vulgarity and ineptitude. The House of Commonness, it might be called. I say this remembering all that Bagehot said in defence of stupidity in high places. But the modern politician is not stupid: he is a grotesque figure who seems to have escaped from some circus, and has the sinister quality of the clown. It is not fair to see in this type a final product of the movement that produced Saint Augustine, Pascal, and Kierkegaard.

24

It is obvious that Kierkegaard and Nietzsche could be reconciled, for both believe in an inward relationship to transcendental values in which the individual is oblivious to the social situation. They differ profoundly in how they interpret this relationship, but they were both personalists, and not, in the literal sense of the word, socialists. It is not without significance that some of Nietzsche's best commentators have been Christians (Figgis, Maulnier, Thibon, Copleston, etc.).

25

Equality is a very ambiguous word. There are at least three distinct contexts in which it can be used: the economic, the functional, the intellectual—and four if we include the spiritual (and I think we should, in the sense implied by Bagehot in the quotation I will give in the next paragraph). We cannot legislate for spiritual and intellectual equality, though we might increase the ratio of these qualities in a community by controlled mating. Functional inequality is inevitable in any but the most primitive nomadic communities, but function need not confer differential status—the Elders in a Hutterite community have no special privileges, though the Preacher, who is head of the community, may have the right to the greater degree of seclusion which his duties require. Inequality of intellect or function cannot be avoided, and they only become vicious when allied to economic inequality. And this is the crux of the whole matter, the crossroads where socalism in general takes the wrong turning. For the essential thing is not to make all incomes equal—the ideal of the average democratic socialist—but to abolish all incomes and *hold all things in common*. This principle was the foundation of the early Christian communities. 'The multitude of them that believed were of one heart and of one soul: neither said any of them that aught of the things which he possessed was his own; but they had all things in common . . . Neither was there any among them that lacked: for as many as were possessors of lands or houses sold them, and brought the prices of the things that were sold, and laid them down at the apostles' feet: and distribution was made unto every man according as he had need.'

It is essential to stress the radical nature of this distinction between equal partition, and community of ownership. It is the distinction between false communism and true communism, between the totalitarian conception of the State as a controlled herd, and the libertarian conception of society as a brotherhood. Once this conception is fully realized, the ambiguities of the doctrine of equality disappear: the concept of equality is dissolved in the concept of community.

It will, of course, be said that such a conception of brotherhood is superhuman—that it could never be realized in this imperfect world. The first Hutterite colonies were founded in 1526, and in spite of four centuries of persecution and enforced migration, *they still exist*. Indeed, we might claim that they have proved themselves to be the most stable forms of social organization ever devised by man. No other social system can boast such an undeviating record of stability and self-sufficiency—certainly not our modern democratic systems. But the conception must be *fully realized*: there are no degrees of communal living.

26

Bagehot wrote (in his essay on 'The First Edinburgh Reviewers'): 'A clear, precise, discriminating intellect shrinks at once from the symbolic, the unbounded, the indefinite. The misfortune is that mysticism is true. There certainly are kinds of truth, borne in as it were instinctively on the human intellect, most influential on the character and the heart, yet hardly capable of stringent statement, difficult to limit by an elaborate definition. Their course is shadowy; the mind seems rather to have seen than to see them, more to feel after than definitely apprehend them. They commonly involve an infinite element, which of course cannot be stated precisely, or else a first principle—an original tendency—of our intellectual constitution, which it is impossible not to feel, and yet which it is hard to extricate in terms and words. Of this latter kind is what has been called the religion of nature, or more exactly, perhaps, the religion of the imagination.'

27

Ni dieu ni maître, cries the doctrinaire socialist. The mind which rejects the notion of a social hierarchy tends at the same time to reject the notion of a spiritual hierarchy, and therefore to deny, not only the existence of God, but even a religion of the imagination. This can be excused in a thorough-going Marxian materialist, but it is difficult to see where the Christian democrat, finds his logical footing. A Christian anarchist, like Eric Gill, is conceivable, as is a Christian royalist like T. S. Eliot. One derives from Saint Peter, the other from Saint Paul. The Christian democrat, however, is among those who 'tithe mint and rue and all manner of herbs, and pass over judgement and the love of God', who 'love the uppermost seats in the synagogues, and greetings in the markets', who 'are as graves which appear not, and the men that walk over them are not aware of them'.

28

Equality in its democratic usage is partitive, and a denial of brotherhood, of communion, of true communism. The democratic State is a house divided (though equally) against itself. It is impossible to divide what is held in common.

Equality is a materialistic measure—a balance of weights.

Nature knows symmetry, but not equality—the equal parts in nature are always joined together.

29

The sociologists are slowly beginning to distinguish between two types of co-operation, one which they call 'segmental' or 'partial', the other 'comprehensive' or 'integral'. 'In segmental co-operation the members associate to satisfy *like* interests. This is the type found in consumers', producers', marketing and processing co-operatives, all organized for the better attainment of specified economic ends. Comprehensive co-operation is based upon *common* interests . . . Comprehensive co-operation is practised in a community when all the essential interests of life are satisfied in a co-operative way.' (H. F. Infield, *Co-operative Living in Palestine* (Kegan Paul, London, 1946), p. 3.)

30

We should not be afraid to use the word 'brotherhood' (instead of pseudo-scientific terms like 'integral co-operation') simply because it has sentimental associations. It indicates the necessary physical (sensational) basis of the relationship in co-operative living. Brotherhood is a concrete existential bond; alternative words are conceptual and evasive. Trigant Burrow has something difficult but pertinent to say on this subject: 'The originally total, organic sense of wholeness, co-ordination and fitness, or the basic rightness that is common and consistent throughout all organisms of the species, has been shifted to a mere social image of wholeness or rightness. This shift has been accompanied by a phenomenon of behaviour whereby the isolated, separated individual has been vested with a pseudo-authority or proprietary "right". Right is *his* right. It is his private possession. Inevitably this over-accentuation of the symbol or the outer appearance of right has ultimated in conflicts and disorder within the individual that have their reaction-counterpart in mere peripheral, symbolic representations of unity, harmony, or wholeness in the social community.'

'Under these conditions it is not surprising that there exists socially the hodge-podge of inter-individual relationships, of misunderstandings, of contradictory feelings and impressions, of love in the form of mere ownership, of jealousies, petty competitions, proprietary affections and equally proprietary aversions. It is not surprising that there are the constant incentives at one time to dictatorship, at another to servility, with all the irritation and disaffection which we not only see but which we ourselves feel subjectively both as individuals and as nations. With this basic miscarriage of function within the primary organism it becomes clear why we have such monstrous disfigurements of feeling and thinking as exist in our various social and political dogmas and creeds. It becomes clear why there lurks beneath our programmes of socialism and a wider brotherhood a secret assertion of the self that is in no sense different from the self-assertion that characterizes the most blatant of our monarchial or oligarchical régimes. Nor is it surprising that, as a result of this primary dissociation, we have in the community widely disseminated and rapidly growing principles of communism which, though dynamically active, belong to a purely verbal, symbolic system of behaviour, and that upon analysis these principles indicate as violent an intolerance towards a physiological basis of community feeling and accord as may be found in the most enthusiastic advocates of our prevailing capitalistic systems.' (*The Biology of Human Conflict* (Macmillan, New York, 1937), pp. 93–4.)

31

In this same context Burrow makes an acute criticism of Kropotkin. After pointing out that the first portion of *Mutual Aid* 'gives an excellent account of the principle of organic consisteney uniting and motivating the individuals of an animal species into an integral, organismic whole', he expresses the opinion that the second half of Kropotkin's book 'distinctly falls away in its artificial attempt to relate this biological principle of unity evidenced in animals to the quite sentimental and self-conscfous expressions of "unity" that characterize civilized communities of man. In the author's effort to affiliate our widely systematized charities or the helpful community services of the social worker with the manifestations of this biological principle of mutual aid, his thesis is largely vitiated.' (Op. cit., p. 64.)

I agree that many of the examples of 'mutual aid among ourselves' which Kropotkin gives in his last two chapters are examples of partial sympathy rather than of biological unity, but Kropotkin nevertheless was on the right track, as Dr. Burrow would have discovered had he pursued his researches into the 'little known work' of this author a little further. For example, in his *Ethics* he makes it quite clear that mutual aid, which is the biological principle of unity, precedes and conditions all further stages of group organization—that without this basic, organismic wholeness, concepts like justice and morality are worthless superstructures. For example: '*Mutual Aid—Justice—Morality* are thus the consecutive steps of an ascending series, revealed to us by the study of the animal world and man. They constitute an *organic necessity* which carries in itself its own justification, confirmed by the whole of the evolution of the animal kingdom, beginning with its earliest stages (in the form of colonies of the most primitive organisms), and gradually rising to our civilized human communities. Figuratively speaking, it is a *universal law of organic evolution*, and this is why the sense of Mutual Aid, Justice, and Morality are rooted in man's mind with all the force of an inborn instinct—the first instinct, that of Mutual Aid, being evidently the strongest, while the third, developed later than the others, is an unstable feeling and the least imperative of the three.'

32

'It is not correct to say that the whole of Nature is ruled exclusively by the deterministic force of necessity. No doubt we are obliged to conceive the run of events in general as a causally determined process, but the ontological investigation of life will show that even in the behaviour of simple organisms there is a germ of *freedom* (spontaneity and autoplasticity), which subsequently develops in man into genuine freedom.'

Here, in Woltereck's *Ontologie des Lebendigen*, is the scientific basis for our philosophy. Woltereck was a scientist, one of the most distinguished biologists of his time (1877–1942), fully aware of the metaphysical implications of his empirical analysis of life-processes. His work constitutes the first acceptable alternative to existentialism.

33

'It is of the essence of man to live in the midst of various polar tensions, between the "upper" and the "lower", between spirit and instinct, joy and fear, rapture and triviality. Polar tension is also bound up with the ontically very significant fact of *freedom*. On free-will conceived as "compulsion to personal decision" there rests in part . . . man's "existential dread", and on freedom of decision there certainly rests guilt and the crippling sense of guilt.

'This, however, is offset by a totally different aspect of the fact of freedom. We have been told, without agreeing with such a division, that subjective "spirit" because of its freedom marks itself off from Nature, which is thought of as exclusively filled with necessity, causality and mindless repetitions. To this we opposed the view, and shall later substantiate it, that although freedom only develops in the spirit of man it is germinatively *at work* in all living things as spontaneity and autoplasticity.' (Woltereck, trans. R. F. C. Hull.)

34

Against this confident claim we must set Bergson's warning: 'Our freedom, in the very movements by which it is affirmed, creates the growing habits that will stifle it if it fails to renew itself by a constant effort: it is dogged by automatism. The most living thought becomes frigid in the formula that expresses it. The word turns against the idea. The letter kills the spirit.'

But in the next paragraph Bergson returns to the essential fact —particular manifestations of life are relatively stable 'and counterfeit immobility so well that we treat each of them as a *thing* rather than as a *progress*, forgetting that the very permanence of their form is only the outline of their movement. At times, however, in a fleeting vision, the invisible breath that bears them is materialized before our eyes. We have this sudden illumination before certain forms of maternal love, so striking and in most animals so touching, observable even in the solicitude of the plant for its seed. This love, in which some have seen the great mystery of life, may possibly deliver us life's secret. It shows each generation leaning over the generation that shall follow. It allows us a glimpse of the fact that the living being is above all a thoroughfare, and that the essence of life is in the movement by which life is transmitted.' (*Creative Evolution*, trans. Arthur Mitchell (London, 1914), pp. 134–5.)

35

Everywhere (in nature) we encounter what Bergson calls 'irremediable difference of rhythm'. This biological fact has its social or political implications. 'Natural' inequalities are part of the pattern of life. To what extent should they be reflected in human institutions?

I have insisted elsewhere that equality is a *mystique*—it has never existed in fact, and it is difficult to see how in practice it can be reconciled with differential endowments of skill, strength, health, and temperament. These differential endowments lead to functional differentiations in the economy of society—lead to these by free choice as well as by economic necessity.

There would seem, therefore, to be a double requirement—equality and inequality. Gustave Thibon finds a parallel in melody. 'Each note in a melody occupies a different place in the scale, and all the different contributing factors (including the very silences) are unequal; and if it were not for this inequality, there would be no melody. But neither would there be any melody if you abolished that deep kind of equality among the different factors which results from their communion, or fusion, in the unity of the whole: all you would have would be a chaos of sound.

'This double requirement, equality and inequality, is to be found throughout the scale of human society. It is of the greatest importance to substitute the profound idea of harmony for the two-dimensional idea of equality. The only true and desirable equality among men can reside neither in their nature nor in their function; for it can only be an *equality by convergence*. It reposes upon communion, and communion dispenses with differences . . . In all harmony, inequality is corrected and completed by interdependence.' (*What Ails Mankind?* Trans. Willard Hill (New York, 1947), p. 57.)

But for the too passive notion of 'interdependence' let us substitute the active notion of 'mutual aid'. Thibon tries to draw a contrast between an unhealthy 'atheistical equalitarianism' which 'pares human differences down to the ground', and a healthy Christian equalitarianism which is based on the *surpassing*, and not upon the *extinction*, of these differences—'it carries them back to their common origin, and forward to their common end, in eternal love. And thus it is that the synthesis between equality and inequality is accomplished in the unity of that love.' But this is the *mystique* of equality that has never had any existence in fact. When it comes to the practice, not of equality, but of social harmony, the Christians have nothing to offer us by way of example. They are split into a thousand antagonistic sects, and their history is written in the blood of martyrs (for the heretic of one sect is the martyr of another).

36

Contrast the notions of 'unity' and 'harmony'.

Unity is apt to be the name we give to a foreshortening of our retrospective vision: even parallel lines *seem* to unite if we prolong them far enough away from our point of view.

The question of social harmony should be argued on its immediate or practical merits, or as an abstract question, but not used as a plea for the recovery or renaissance of a defunct ideal.

There can be no doubt that cultural values have always arisen under conditions of strife, rivalry, or emulation. Even within the individual, as within the community. Feeling intensely, grasping intensely, 'realizing' intensely: form struggling to master content; material subdued to spirit; 'a chaos grinding itself into compatibility' (Coleridge)—such is the essential nature of the cultural process. There is no reason to suppose that culture is favoured by unity; there is every reason to suppose that it is stimulated by differences and inequalities. But it is important to distinguish between biological or 'natural' differences, and economic or social differences, which are artificial and maintained by power.

The real drive in culture is teleological, as Woltereck has argued. Culture is intimately related to the process of evolution. Consciousness itself is a 'cultural' development.

The process is retarded by war and tyranny; it is promoted by mutual aid.

37

In a certain sense one can welcome the breaking of the pattern of European history. The State and all its works, banks and their strangulating currency, the international money market, the tariff system and the artificial distribution of industry which shelters behind it, nationalized systems of secular education, of military service, of taxation and amortization—it may all perish. The Black Market has many ugly features, but at least it does represent a certain human vitality—a determination to escape from the artificial bonds of the State. From a cultural point of view, I am somewhat envious of this vitality. What we need is a Black Market in culture, a determination to avoid the bankrupt academic institutions, the fixed values and standardized products of current art and literature; not to trade our spiritual goods through the recognized channels of Church, or State, or Press; rather, to pass them 'under the counter'.

But let me hasten to redress the balance of such a nihilistic utterance! I do believe that a collapse of central government, a relapse to local autonomy is a better condition of life, and offers better prospect of a cultural revival, than any too conscious attempt to preserve existing institutions. But I do not deny the necessity of institutions if we are to elevate a new culture above the primitive level. My point is that we have to begin from some basis of social health and social simplicity which might, in any historical perspective, be called Homeric. I use this word in its concrete sense. When Vico revalued Homer, and placed his poetic worth high above that of Virgil, he was recalling us to cultural realities. That was more than two centuries ago, and his voice has gone unheeded, until, recently, we heard it again.

'In spite of the brief intoxication induced at the time of the Renaissance by the discovery of Greek literature, there has been, during the course of twenty centuries, no revival of the Greek genius. Something of it was seen in Villon, in Shakespeare, Cervantes, Molière, and—just once—in Racine. The bones of human suffering are exposed in *L'Ecole des Femmes* and in *Phèdre*, love being the context—a strange century indeed, which took the opposite view from that of the epic period, and would only acknowledge human suffering in the context of love, while it insisted on swathing with glory the effects of force in war and in politics. To the list of writers given above, a few other names might be added. But nothing the peoples of Europe have produced is worth the first-known poem that appeared among them. Perhaps they will yet rediscover the epic genius, when they learn that there is no refuge from fate, learn not to admire force, not to hate the enemy, nor to scorn the unfortunate.'[1]

39

As Simone Weil says elsewhere in the essay from which I am quoting, 'the spirit that was transmitted from the *Iliad* to the Gospels by way of the tragic poets never jumped the borders of Greek civilization; once Greece was destroyed, nothing remained of this spirit but pale reflections'. But now the mirror is broken, the defences are destroyed; and I hazard a guess that this spirit will reappear where we least expect a revival of culture, among the ruins of that country which has already produced, in Hölderlin, the most Hellenic of modern poets. But, admittedly, that is a speculative opinion for which I have found no support in Germany itself.

Somewhere in its meandering history, Christianity lost the tragic sense of life which the Gospels illustrate. My own difficulty has always been to trace any essential connection between the Gospels and the Christian Church as we know it—as we have known it in European history. There are Christian apologists (Mr. Middleton Murry and Professor Hodges, for example) who agree with me in this—they ask for a new essence, for a revitaliza-

[1] Simone Weil, 'The Iliad, or, The Poem of Force'. *Politics* (New York, November 1945). This posthumously published essay is, in my opinion, one of the most remarkable pieces of criticism to appear in our time. It was originally published in *Cahiers du Sud* (Marseilles, December 1940 and January 1941).

tion. But it does not seem to me that they speak plainly enough. They imply that the Church can in some miraculous way both reform itself and become an agent of social and cultural renaissance. But they must know that religion in the elemental sense, like poetry in the elemental sense, can only come out of a certain way of life, out of a specific economy and social structure. And all that is sour and rotten in Europe today. It is only where the destruction is complete enough, the communication disrupted enough, and where life is consequently on a primitive level, that not only Christian humanism, but the whole complex of Western civilization, can 'die to live'.

40

The first essential institutions will be educational institutions. By 'educational institutions' I do not necessarily mean 'schools', certainly not the abattoirs of sensibility which go by that name today. To achieve 'the greatest lucidity, purity, and simplicity' —that should be the aim of education. Such an achievement is likelier to come from the workshop and the playing field than from the academy or grammar school—in the context of work, in the context of play, of work-play.

41

The modern world has obstinately resisted the great teachers —Plato, Schiller, Pestalozzi, Herbart—being bound to divisive, competitive, vocational ideas of education, and never for a moment contemplating the possibility that education might be directed towards ideals of brotherhood, mutual aid, creative expression. The whole aim of modern education can be summed up in one word—'cleverness'. The whole aim of the opposed ideal of education can be summed up in another word—'wisdom'. Until the world recognizes the incompatibility of these two aims and accepts the revolutionary changes that would be necessary before wisdom could be substituted for cleverness, all hope of a solution of our crisis is vain.

But by wisdom we do not mean solemnity. Man's life, as Plato said, is a business which does not deserve to be taken too seriously—and that is where our communist friends make such a mistake.

42

Greek education, or Plato's conception of it, was directed towards the establishment in the human mind of four cardinal virtues: courage, purity, justice, and wisdom. It does not seem to me that our modern education encourages the development of any of these virtues, and it does little for that characteristically Christian virtue which we should add to the Greek four—charity. But how do we begin to build up a new Europe on the ruins of the old until we have a firm conception of virtue, and direct all our endeavours towards implanting it in the minds of our children? This, I would suggest, is a problem far more urgent, far more actual, than any attempt to save 'the traditional culture of Europe', or even Christianity as part of that tradition. Communism and Christian humanism might be reconciled in some common conception of virtue, which is pragmatic; never in any vision of God, which is transcendental. They might, as Plato recommends, join together in sacrifice, song and dance, and share Heaven's grace.

ON JUSTICE

43

Justice is blind in her ancient personification (popular even in Christian iconography), and is represented as holding, as well as a sword, a pair of scales. She stands impartially between conflicting claims, sees nothing, but weighs everything.

This concept assumes that conflicting claims arise only between persons. The symbol does not fit the complexities of modern civilization, where, more often than not, the person is in conflict with the State. There then enters into the idea of Justice, even to the point of replacing it, the idea of Retribution, originally the punishment inflicted by a revengeful God, in whose place the State now reigns supreme. The scales are no longer appropriate, and all that remains of the symbols of justice is the sword; and it is the sword which, in fact, is suspended above the judge's head at the Old Bailey.

Nevertheless in its evolution, European jurisprudence has been conscious of this anomaly and we have evolved, especially here in England, not merely separate concepts of law, which we call Common Law on the one hand, and the Civil or State Law on the other hand, but also the very precious independence of the judiciary. That independence may by now be more in name than in substance, but at any rate it is a recognition of distinct values.

44

Most people go through life without coming into immediate contact with the judicial system. The greater part of those who do have a direct experience of its workings are only concerned in minor misdemeanours which do not raise any questions of principle. For the most part, unless we are directly implicated, for all we know of it, the legal system might operate in another planet. A case has to be sordid, sexual, or sadistic before the popular Press will consider it worth while to report. To serve on a jury is an initiation into the system, but it falls to the lot of few of us, and one service seems to ensure almost a life-time's exemption. Still fewer people, unless they are implicated, attend the Courts as disinterested observers, and nothing is done by the ushers and other court officials to encourage the public to attend. Indeed, judging by my own experience, there is a deliberate attempt to keep people out of the Courts.

The independence of the judiciary is symbolized in various ways. By means of wigs and gowns, the participants are dehumanized to an astonishing degree. If by chance, in the course of pleading, a hot and flustered barrister lifts his wig to mop his brow, an entirely different individual is revealed. It is as if a tortoise had suddenly dispensed with its shell. The whole business is carapaceous: a shell of custom and formality against which life, plastic and throbbing, beats in an effort to reach the light.

In such a system human values are at a discount: in their endless variety they have to be passed through a sieve of predetermined pattern. If they are too large or too shaggy, they get caught in the meshes.

45

The jury system is an attempt to admit human values: it is a safety-valve for emotional forces. To all rationalists and planners, it is an intolerable anomaly, and should be abolished. But before we abolish it, it would be well to recall to mind the reasons which Henry Fielding advanced in its favour.[1] A jury may be stupid, prejudiced, sentimental, but its main effect is to temper justice with mercy. The only occasion on which I myself served on a jury, I was outraged by the purely sentimental considerations which swayed my companions. I tried to stand out against them, to reason from the evidence (as the judge had done in his direction). But I was in a minority of one: I was overwhelmed. The miscreant got off free. I have lived to rejoice in my defeat, because I now realize that the values which swayed the jury (appeal of youth, force of personality, sympathy for human weaknesses) were greater than the letter and the logic of the law. Only a jury has a right to assert such values. For the system of law to take them into account would negate that system. A system must be rigid. It is our peculiar wisdom in England to create a system as exact as the symbolical scales, and at the same time to throw a little sand into the bearings.

46

So long as Justice mediates between persons, the independence and integrity of the judicial machinery make for a judgement based on natural law. Common law is essentially the common feeling of what is right and just, as between the members of a community. Values (i.e., the common feelings in question) may change more rapidly than the laws which express them: but this is the fault of the community itself, which is not quick enough to ensure that its laws express its will. In morals and in property rights, the law tends to express the will of the conservative mass, the mere inertia of the unaffected and the indifferent. The laws against sexual perversion, for example, are

[1] A charge delivered to the Grand Jury, Westminster, 1794.

harsh and unjust, because they do not recognize natural facts scientifically established. Since the majority of people are not homosexual, they find it difficult to legislate for a minority which is physiologically or psychologically distinct.

These are the inevitable complexities of any social group, and can be removed by patient analysis and publicity. The real danger in our judicial machinery comes when the cause lies between an individual and the State. Then the law which in the other case was based on a sense of values (natural rights) suddenly changes and becomes a code of implacable edicts. Statutory law may need clarification and interpretation, but in intention it is absolute—an exact rack upon which individuals, in all their variety, must be stretched.

Watch the conduct of a public prosecution. The whole procedure and atmosphere of the court has changed. The accused stands in the dock, no longer to be judged as a man who may have wronged another member of the community, but as an individual who, perhaps all unconsciously, may have broken a rule or regulation. His intention or motive does not weigh a feather's weight in the symbolic scales of Justice. Facts, and facts only, deflect the needle. The gowns are ruffled, the wigs are scratched, only to make a point in logic or in exegesis. The man in the dock sits helpless, and the endeavour of his counsel is often to keep him out of the witness-box for fear the truth might complicate the issue. It is not that he wishes to deceive the judge or the jury: the game must be played according to the rules, with white pawns on one side, black on the other. A green pawn, an unaccountable fragment of life or emotion, is out of place on the checkered board.

47

Take a simple case, which happens to be a true case and a recent one. In the state of emergency which arose at the beginning of the last war, certain Defence Regulations were rushed through Parliament and thus became part of the law. They were deemed necessary at that time and in the desperate circumstances of war and imminent invasion. But once in force, those Regulations, perhaps hastily drawn up and certainly ill-considered, had to be administered *to the letter*: as rigid edicts. One of the Regulations made it an offence to attempt to disaffect from their duties any members of the Armed Forces. In other words, in a state of national emergency, it is not permissible to persuade soldiers or sailors to desert their posts.

We all know what was the intention of such a regulation, but there it stands, No. 39A in a printed code, to be administered by the judicial system.

A group of men and women believe that war is an evil thing which must be eliminated from our civilization if we are not all to perish. They realize that war is not something which can be abolished by Act of Parliament, or even by International Agreement. It is a deep-seated disease of civilization itself, the product of frustration and mass-neurosis. The cure is drastic—it is revolutionary. In order, therefore, that the world may be saved for their children, that it may have a fair chance of progressing towards peaceable and creative activity, this group of men and women advocate a drastic change in our society—in the terrorist cliché of the Press, they 'preach revolution'. They preach it openly, to every comer, at all street corners and in such journals and pamphlets as they can print. Some of these publications reach members of the Armed Forces—actually, for the most part, members of the Non-Combatant Corps, which is not armed. The person has no privacy in the Forces: he is subject to periodic searches or inspections, and in the course of these, some of the pamphlets in question are discovered. A lever is pulled, the machine begins to move, and in due course delivers the aforesaid group of men and women into the dock of the Central Criminal Court.

They are skilful and diligent citizens, all of them—that is irrelevant. In their daily avocations they do good and useful actions —tend the sick and wounded, build roads and railways—all that is irrelevant. There is a Code, and it has a clause, 39A. That clause says plainly that no one (at any time, during the legal existence of that clause) may preach any doctrine which *might* cause any member of H.M. Armed Forces to think twice about his duty to die. It is not necessary that one such disaffected person should be produced—all that the State need prove is that action was taken which might have led to one such case of disaffection.

Away with motives and intentions, away with every human feeling and idealist hope. We are in a court of law and a man is being measured against a code. It does not matter what kind of man he is—a Messiah or a Thief: for the moment he is a piece of evidence, a neat bundle of ascertained *facts*, and these only will be measured against the inflexible code. Thus Christ went to the Cross, and Martyrs to the Stake: thus millions were packed like cattle into trucks and sent to Siberia or Poland. It is always the same pattern—human values against the edicts of Authority, of the State. And once the machine begins to move, it is difficult to stop it. All the engineers and technicians disclaim responsibility. They are busy oiling their little wheel and are proud when it runs smoothly. What ghastly grist is in the mill is no concern of theirs—literally, NO CONCERN.

48

In the Central Criminal Court the case is over. The wigs change places. The prisoners leave the dock. A new defendant takes their place—a negro who is to be tried for manslaughter. It is all in a day's work—thieves and messiahs, murders and prostitutes, embezzlers and aborters. A cynic might describe it as society with the lid off, the whole seething cauldron of man's good and evil impulses. But here in the court we are present rather at a vast attempt to put the lid *on*—all these sinister figures in black and crimson robes being so many presiding witches. And that is, of course, the exact and the melancholy truth. Here in this immense centralized cauldron 'the officers of the Crown' are attempting, brutally if necessary, to *suppress* the horrid mass of pullulating sinners, and are only dimly aware that the scene is so horrid, precisely because it is so concentrated—that if the writhing mass were to be *dispersed* and given space and light, it might be reanimated, rectified, by the agencies of human love and divine grace, which operate where two or three are gathered together, but not in a crowd. Justice, like everything else, is suffering from concentration and suffocation.

This concentration is in correspondence with the whole social structure—a parallel development—but it gets its peculiar quality from that very independence of the judiciary which is its redeeming feature. The legal profession is a closed society, a securely protected and clearly differentiated guild within the greater society of the nation. It is invested with ranks and dignities, customs and precedents, robes and rituals. As a result, there grows up within this closed society a feeling of solidarity and mutual understanding which makes of their social function a highly skilled game which only the qualified can play. In any case, as between the counsels for prosecution and for defence, there is never more than an artificial war. If emotion is betrayed on either side, it is immediately disengaged, pilloried, petrified, and becomes one more counter in the game. The judge sits up above, a referee in this match of wits: the defendant, whose innocence or liberty is the gauge, is often reduced to insignificance: *he* does not matter: the point of law is the reality.

The judge is independent: the Attorney-General who is prosecuting and the defending counsel are playing the game, according to the complicated rules. But they and their kind made the rules, for the kind of world they know and experience—a world of property and finance, of universities and clubs, of dinner-parties and fox-hunts. According to their experience, they made the rules with fairness, with honest intentions. They want to be just to the working classes, to the negro, and the prostitute. But it is very difficult to legislate for a world you only know at second hand. A brilliant barrister may be able to project himself into the mind of his client—a feat of empathy rather than of sympathy —but that is the exception, and is not even then all-embracing. There are heights and depths of experience which are simply beyond the average upper-middle-class barrister's conception: worlds of spiritual exaltation and self-sacrifice: worlds of poverty and suffering, worlds of self-abasement and despair. Before the exponents of such experience, the average judge and barrister can but follow the example of Pilate and *wash his hands.*

50

There is justice in the underworld: read a book like *Street Corner Society* and see how it is organized, how it works. Men are naturally just when they form spontaneous groups—to play, to explore, to debate, even to steal. How beautiful is the justice which spontaneously emerges in a boatful of shipwrecked mariners! There is justice in prison camps and in any community of slaves. Man in society is naturally just, because society, if it is real, is a bond of mutual consideration. It is man reduced to a unit, a cipher, who no longer has a sense of justice. He is anonymous, independent, indifferent. He does not feel even the cohesive emotion of a wolf-pack. He is alone, and against him is the State: that complex of laws, rules, and regulations which have no reality for this cipher-individual, in whose making he did not participate, whose meaning he may not understand. 'Thou shalt not kill'—that is a commandment which any man can understand: it is a crime against another man, and a sin against God. But 'Thou shalt not speak of universal peace and brotherhood' —that is a commandment which no man can understand unless he has a black heart. That is a commandment which cannot pass between one person and another, but only between the State and its anonymous citizens.

ON VIRTUE

51

Certain discussions which are proceeding at present, notably the major one concerned with power politics, have shown that there is little hope of social stability or individual happiness in the world unless some universal standard of conduct can be discovered and accepted. There are many competing ethical systems but one cannot expect the world in general, or people in the mass, to make a critical estimate of them and agree to accept the best one. An ethical standard, or moral code, will only be accepted by the world at large under emotional stress. I do not think it follows that the emotive pressure need be specifically religious, in the sense that such pressure would take the form of divine revelation or supernatural sanction. But there are many powerful forces active in mankind as a whole which might assume, under certain conditions, an ethically good or 'virtuous' tendency. War itself, our greatest ethical problem, is a problem of collective psychology. However much cogency we allow to materialistic or economic explanations of the origins of war, no mountains of such historical facts can explain the acceptance of, or indifference to, the actual monstrosities of war. It is not the causes of war that call for some more satisfactory explanation, but its conduct. There are people who consider that the press-button butchery which in a few minutes can dispatch more inno-cents than Herod in his lifetime is in some way 'more humane' than the face-to-face clash of swords or bayonets. That only shows the depths to which the moral aspects of war have been consigned, and consigned by precisely the kind of 'collective agreement' I am referring to. If mankind can accept (or ignore—i.e., unconsciously accept) the horrors of modern war, it is for emotional reasons of a collective nature.

These unconscious mechanisms have been studied by psycho-logists, and there is a growing measure of agreement on what is known as the frustration-aggression hypothesis, which seeks to explain all forms of aggressive behaviour, including war, in terms of prior frustrations. Frustration is, of course, primarily an individual process; but when a number of individuals are all frustrated by the same forces, their aggressiveness takes the same form and coalesces into class-war and imperialistic war.

Ethics is a subject which bristles with philosophical problems, and it is far from my intention to embark on any discussion of them here. I am going to assume (1) that 'good' and other ethi-cal value-terms have only an emotive meaning; and (2) that this very fact suggests the possibility that a universal moral stan-dard could be established by practical means. If goodness can be made a matter of feeling or sensation, then duty or obligation can become a habit. There will be nothing original in such a conclusion: it will be merely a return to the teaching and prac-tice of the Greeks.

52

Certain concepts round which the societies of the Ancient World and the Middle Ages were built and from which they derived their strength and stability were gradually debased after the Renaissance and by now have lost all their original meaning. I have already dealt with Justice, but *Virtue* is the most impor-that of these. It is not yet altogether a dead word: we often hear that virtue is its own reward, and we still make a virtue of neces-sity. A woman of virtue has a very concrete meaning, and can be made the subject of a medical certificate. But what has all this to do with the Greek *arete* or the Latin *virtus*? Even the Latin word from which we drive our own word, represents a particulariza-tion of the Greek concept—the root-word *vir* has the implication of masculinity, or virility, which is not present in the Greek *arete*. What we find rather difficult to realize, after centuries of mora-lizing, is that originally virtue was not an abstract concept of any kind: it was rather, like Tao, a way of life, a form of beha-viour, an activity rather than a characteristic or condition. The quality could only be perceived in deeds: it could not be gene-ralized and codified. Probably our nearest approach to its mean-ing is in the word *grace*, which according to the Shorter O.E.D., now usually means 'the charm belonging to elegance of propor-tions, or (esp.) ease and refinement of movement, action, or expression'. Disraeli, according to the same authority, defined it as 'beauty in action', and that is near to the meaning of *arete* in Greek philosophy.

But already in Greek philosophy virtue was found to be too indefinite as a concept. Analysis broke it into two distinct kinds —*moral* and *intellectual* virtue, and what I have to say in this note is merely a comment on that distinction, which I believe to be of fundamental importance. I believe that the loss of this distinction is the cause of our present moral confusion.

54

The difference between the moral and intellectual aspects of virtue is that while the latter can be made the subject of general agreement (what might be called a science of living), moral virtue is expressed through the temperament or disposition of the individual. Intellectual virtue is a system of accepted beliefs and customs, and a man can be virtuous in this sense without involving his personal conduct. But moral virtue is the interior function of each man's physiological and nervous make-up and involves positive action, even creative effort. Since a man deficient in moral virtue cannot be expected to appreciate properly the values of intellectual virtue (which are always social or collective values, and involve the subordination, or sublimation, of individual values), it follows that moral virtue, as the Greeks taught, should have a fundamental priority in education. To make the distinction still clearer, we might say that whilst intellectual virtue is achieved by the pursuit of truth, moral virtue implies the possession of goodness.

55

If we have not altogether lost the sense of this distinction between moral and intellectual virtue, it is at least certain that moral virtue has relinquished its claim to priority. How this came about is a very interesting question, and not one to which I have found any very satisfactory answer in my limited reading of history. The process of partition occurred during the Renaissance. In the Middle Ages, as in the Ancient World, education had been integral—both moral and intellectual virtue had been the unchallenged responsibility either of the Church or of the State. But at some time during the early Renaissance, at the very beginning of our modern system of education, the responsibility became divided—moral education being entrusted to the Church, intellectual education being left to private enterprise or the State. It was a fatal division of responsibility, as any Greek philosopher would have foreseen. Now we can contemplate the whole melancholy result of this schism. For as the Church gradually lost its power and authority over men, the moral education which had been entrusted to its care was first neglected, and then largely abandoned, until we reach the paradoxical situation of our own time, when moral education is no longer considered even necessary, except by a religious minority.

The problem now is how, by what methods and what agencies,

can we re-establish the teaching of moral virtue. I leave on one side, as not immediately realistic, the possibility that the Church might once again command such universal allegiance that it could be given the sole responsibility for an integrated system of education, and I suggest that we return to Plato and Aristotle, who have a solution to offer which involves only practical considerations.

56

The Greek solution is an appeal to natural law. But it is important to realize that in this connection the Greeks were physicists rather than what we should now call biologists. It is possible for the modern scientist to go to nature for an ethical code, and to find something there which was not in the Greek mind at all. Once the theory of evolution had been accepted, and more particularly the hypothesis of natural selection, it seemed obvious to a philosopher like Herbert Spencer that here was the scientific foundation for a *science* of ethics. The good was identified with whatever was consonant with the inherent tendency of life to develop towards 'higher' forms—ethics became an affirmation of the evolutionary process. That is still substantially the theory of ethics put forward by a contemporary scientist like Dr. Waddington.[1]

For Plato and Aristotle nature was not so purposive and teleological. I agree with Mr. Alfred Cobban, to whom I shall refer again presently, that the Greeks did not conceive nature as a fixed, unchanging framework—that they conceived it in terms of life rather than of law. But when he says that 'they were able to conceive Natural Law on the analogy of biological law rather than positive law, or the laws of mathematics or of the physical sciences', I can only agree with half of his statement. It seems to me that the emphasis, in Plato and Aristotle at any rate, is on the laws of mathematics and of the physical sciences rather

---

[1] 'In the world as a whole, the real good cannot be other than that which has been effective, namely that which is exemplified in the course of evolution . . . And the nature of science's contribution is also clear; it is the revelation of the nature of the character and direction of the evolutionary process as a whole, and the elucidation of the consequences, in relation to that direction, of various courses of human action.' C. H. Waddington, *Nature* (6 September 1941).

198

than on biological law. (I am assuming, perhaps rashly, that the Greeks would have seen an essential difference between, say, the two laws of thermodynamics and the principle of natural selection.) For Plato and Aristotle nature was fixed to the extent that it exhibited its physical structure, and in its dynamism, a certain harmony, a rhythmical inevitability, an aesthetic norm of proportions. The whole art of life was to discover these harmonies and rhythms, and to attune the human body and mind to their pattern. The man who succeeded in doing this would be not only graceful in his actions and behaviour, but also noble in his soul. The whole purport of Plato's theory of education is to devise methods by means of which the harmony of nature could be revealed and imitated. Hence the overwhelming importance which he attached to aesthetic education—to music, dance, and all those concrete and plastic arts which involve the cultivation of bodily grace and muscular skill.

The education we need is primarily an education of moral virtue, intended as a preparation for the education of intellectual virtue. I am not suggesting that certain schools should be set aside for the inculcation of moral virtue, others for the inculcation of intellectual virtue—that would lead to a perpetuation of the post-Renaissance schism. Education must be integral, for only an integral system of education can effect the necessary integration of the personality in Jung's sense of the phrase. One system of education will provide for both aspects of virtue, but it will recognize, for reasons already given, the *genetic* priority of moral virtue, and will not attempt to inculcate intellectual virtue until the mind of the child is prepared to receive it.

That this preparation is largely physical will shock people who are accustomed to a Sunday School conception of virtue, but I am sure that the Greeks were wise in this respect. Man, as Aristotle pointed out, is essentially a habit-forming animal; and if Aristotle's name does not carry conviction to the modern scientist, let him substitute Pavlov's, for the fashionable theory of conditioned reflexes is but another way of expressing the same fact. What is proposed, in this theory of education, is that the physiological reflexes of the child should be conditioned to harmonious patterns of sound, harmonious shapes and colours, until that harmony penetrates and takes hold of the whole disposition of the child; and it is proposed that we should seek that harmony where it immutably exists—in the morphology of the natural world.

57

Let us now examine one or two consequences of such a theory. We may note in the first place that it involves a return to the principles of Natural Law and Natural Rights which the eighteenth century Enlightenment aimed to establish on the basis of Greek thought and which were then abandoned in favour of the theory of popular sovereignty, with melancholy consequences for the whole of our civilization. This historical process has been brilliantly illuminated in a book which has not received the attention it deserves: *The Crisis of Civilization*, by Alfred Cobban (Cape, 1941). I cannot review here all the aspects of this historical disaster which Mr. Cobban discusses, but for our immediate context it should be noted that, to quote Mr. Cobban, 'the ultimate result of the theory of popular sovereignty was . . . the substitution of history for ethics. This tendency is present in the contemporary thought of all countries. It has only achieved a complete triumph in Germany. The distinguishing mark of modern German thought is the dissolution of ethics in the *Volksgeist*; its practical conclusion is that the State is the source of all morality, and the individual must accept the laws and actions of his own State as having ultimate ethical validity.' (Incidentally I should have thought that the tendency had achieved an even completer triumph in Russia.) The association of this principle with nationalism is disastrous enough, but it is even more disturbing to see it associated with movements which would normally be opposed to nationalism in any form. But as Mr. Cobban says, sovereignty is the political religion of today. 'It has won widespread and implicit belief, regardless of party or country, and the most apparently opposed régimes are built upon it. Many of its strongest supporters are ignorant of what they are supporting, for those who most strongly denounce the principle of national sovereignty, scorning inconsistency, uphold the sovereign rights of the people's will; and those who are the bitterest critics of the people's sovereignty when it means socialism, will uphold it to the death in the form of nationalism.'

Under the influence of this doctrine, the tendency of all forms of democratic socialism is to drift inevitably towards totalitarianism. The modern socialist or reformer is usually an intellectualist. He is often a nationalist and he is manifestly virtuous, basing his actions on consciously held ideals of justice, equality, the greatest good of the greatest number, etc. His rational outlook may be coloured by emotional sympathy for the poor and oppressed; and it may be animated by envy and the lust for power. But the modern socialist (democratic or Stalinist) has rarely any sense of *moral* virtue. He associates it with the supernatural religion he has discarded, or with the moral conventions of the ruling classes whom he hopes to overthrow. The socialist, alas, is usually a philistine, and if he ever becomes aware of this fact, he will rationalize his incapacity and attempt to dismiss moral virtue as so much formalism in art or absolutism in ethics. The singular failure of socialist régimes to establish a socialist style in architecture, poetry, or any of the arts is an indication of the poverty of their emotional life and of the fallacy of their arguments on this subject.

58

I am not asking the socialist to accept any transcendental values, or anything more mystical than the physical structure of the universe and the natural processes of his own mind. But I am asking him to discipline his emotions, to educate his sensibility (or the sensibility of his children, for it is probably too late in his own case), and to acknowledge that actions possessing grace are more conducive to the efficiency and happiness of society than actions without grace. The pattern is in nature. Pleasure is simply the reaction of our senses to the perception of such patterns. By the repeated perception and imitation of such patterns, the senses themselves become imbued with grace, the emotions are tempered, the mind is enabled spontaneously to discriminate between good and evil. That, at any rate, is the state or condition of moral virtue which the Greeks regarded as the foundation of happiness, and happiness was the condition towards which they thought a society should aspire.

THE NATURE OF CRISIS

59

There is a general agreement among philsophers that conflict underlies the whole process of life and evolution: the nature of existence, as some of them say, is dialectical. Proceeding from such a very general description of our universe, it has been easy to draw into this natural order of things the very anomalous phenomenon of war. This human institution, which now threatens to destroy the human race, is said to be an inescapable outcome of 'the struggle for existence'. Even humanist philosophers like William James, when they come to deal with this problem, do not seek to deny the premise: they seek a substitute, a 'moral equivalent' for war. What is more remarkable is that they tend to seek it on the same physical or materialistic level, and lead us to suppose that a mass indulgence in international football, mountaineering, or polar exploration, would divert these natural energies into relatively harmless channels.

I would like to suggest that this solution of the problem of war rests on a confusion between two kinds of war: that one kind of war is quite unnatural, and can be eliminated without any danger to the continued vitality of the human race; and that the other kind cannot be eliminated and does not need to be in any way sublimated. If once the distinction between these two kinds of war was generally recognized, the first kind of war would be discontinued because it would be regarded as obsolete and as confusing the issues of the real war.

60

Jakob Burckhardt, in a passage in his *Reflections on History*,[1] deplores the fact that while modern wars are aspects of a great general crisis, they lack individually the significance and effect of genuine crises. In words which seem singularly untrue today, he points out that 'civilian life remains in the rut in spite of them'. Writing in 1871, he complains that wars are too short to

[1] *Weltgeschichtliche Betrachtung.* English translation: *Reflections on History* London, (Allen & Unwin), 1943.

have any value as crises; they merely bequeath the main crisis to the future. Only when this final crisis is allowed to engulf us all, so that the full forces of despair come into play, can a regeneration of life be expected; only with the triumph of such forces will the old order be supplanted by a really vital new one.

We who now, seventy or eighty years later, are suffering the impact of these forces, may perhaps take some comfort from Burckhardt's words. But only if we still seek to distinguish the general crisis from its particular aspects. That is not so easy to do as it was in 1871. Then 'war' and 'crisis' stood against each other as quite distinct concepts. Now war and crisis are simultaneous, and it needs a considerable effort to discern that they are not also homogeneous. Modern warfare is not free from a certain duplicity of character—an ambiguity reflected in the propaganda which, from both sides, is apt to invoke the same spiritual values.

61

Modern wars are fought on two planes, which we might call the 'local' and the 'universal'. On both planes, consciously or unconsciously, it is possible either to participate or not to participate. The local war is the actual war, the war which is being waged at a particular moment, in the Mediterranean, in Russia, in China, or Africa; the war which breaks suddenly from the sky, over a peaceful village, a busy port, a crowded industrial town; over Amsterdam, Bristol, or Tokyo. Comparatively few of us are engaged in that kind of war—millions, but still comparatively few. There is also the war of forced work and skilled research: of watching and guarding—the kind of war in which most of us are in some degree implicated, even if we happen to live in a so-called neutral country. But that is still the local war, fixed in time and place, of definite historical duration.

The same war is also universal, or rather, part of a universal war, a phase in the unfolding of a more indefinite historical process. But because this universal war is more indefinite, it is not therefore less actual, and we who are fated to take part in it cannot escape our responsibility—as Tolstoy showed in those chapters of *War and Peace* which are skipped by most readers of that profound book. But nevertheless we can move in and out

203

of this universal war. Just as in a physical sense we move in and out of the front line or a bombed area in the local war, so mentally we can disengage ourselves from the universal war.

On both sides of the conflict, we are encouraged to disengage ourselves from the universal war because it is not a war fought with the lethal weapons which are most effective in local war. In fighting the universal war we do not seem to be contributing any share to the local war. The weapons will not serve a double purpose. Even if we use verbal weapons in local war, they cannot be snatched from the armoury of universal war, for the words stored there are not barbed with the hate and exaggeration needed in local war. In the midst of local war, this universal war is therefore waged silently, in the imagination; and like all true imaginative activity, it is intermittent. But nevertheless it goes on, even in the din of local war.

62

The universal war is a war between the forces of change and the state of inertia. World historians like Burckhardt and Spengler, recognizing the inevitability of this struggle, have tended to give it the status of a natural law; and since Darwin's day, though not with the complete assent of the scientific world, this struggle among men has been regarded as an aspect of 'the struggle for existence'. If human history and human destiny are to be explained in purely materialistic terms, then there is little to say against such a view of the universal war. But though political leaders are inspired by such motives, and often call upon their followers to fight for 'Lebensraum', or for a higher standard of living, in actual fact these motives have never inspired any large proportion of the people. It may be doubted whether fighting motives have often been positive, in the sense of a calculation of gain. Left to themselves, men fight instinctively, but usually defensively. They may sometimes fight adventurously, and a few fight professionally. But even when they advance beyond their own borders, it is generally to ward off a danger which threatens them, or a fear which obsesses them. For the most part fighting men are not exercising their free will;

they are in the grip of anonymous forces, those historical forces of which Tolstoy wrote.

War has been held to be inevitable because of the anonymity of these historical forces. Obviously if men recognized the collective nature of their hysteria, and understood its causes; if, further, they understood the nature of the historical trend in which they were caught, like dead leaves falling on a stream, they would not struggle against it, but would acquiesce, and, indeed, strive to hasten the process. They would give up wasting their lives in internecine strife: they would draw together to save the world from the catastrophe which threatens it.

63

In its widest aspects the crisis which the world is now experiencing is evolutionary. I know no better description of its real nature than the one given by a contemporary Indian philosopher Sri Aurobindo, in these words:

'At present mankind is undergoing an evolutionary crisis in which is concealed a choice of its destiny; for a stage has been reached in which the human mind has achieved in certain directions an enormous development, while in others it stands arrested and bewildered and can no longer find its way. A structure of the external life has been raised up by man's ever-active mind and life-will, a structure of an unmanageable hugeness and complexity, for the service of his mental, vital, physical claims and urges, a complex political, social, administrative, economic, cultural machinery, an organized collective means for his intellectual, sensational, aesthetic, and material satisfaction. Man has created a system of civilization which has become too big for his limited mental capacity and understanding and his still more limited spiritual and moral capacity to utilize and manage, a too dangerous servant of his blundering ego and its appetites. For no greater seeing mind, no intuitive soul of knowledge has yet come to his surface of consciousness which could make this basic fullness of life a condition for the free growth of something that exceeded it . . . At the same time Science has put at his disposal many potencies of the universal Force and has made the life of humanity materially one; but what uses this universal Force is a

205

little human individual or communal ego with nothing universal
in its light of knowledge or its movements, no inner sense or
power which would create in this physical drawing-together of
the human world a true life unity, a mental unity, or a spiritual
oneness.'[1]

64

We find the actual symptoms of this evolutionary crisis revealing themselves as the greatest sociological transformation that
has taken place since the feudal system gave way to the mercan-
tile or capitalist system. Now in its turn that capitalist system is
disintegrating. Its break-up may be delayed by a decade or two,
perhaps in some parts of the world by a century or so. We may,
that is to say, prolong in some way or other, and *always by means
of local wars*, the period of transition. We do this because we do
not yet visualize clearly enough the goal towards which we are
moving—because we disagree, not about the necessity of moving,
but rather about the speed at which we should move. Some
people would like more time to consider such remote goals. The
world is moving towards greater integration (the close knitting
of swift systems of communication), towards greater stabiliza-
tion of production (due to the international control of shrinking
markets and the gradual exhaustion of the scope of those inven-
tions which made the mechanization of industry possible). As a
consequence of these inevitable forces, we may also say that the
world is moving towards a complete communization of the means
of production and distribution. What we still dispute is merely
the form of communization—or, more precisely, the distribution
of power within the constituent communes (industrial collectives, cartels, or whatever form this system of power may take).

65

There are groups which have inherited a system of power from
the past—these naturally wish to preserve their status in the
future. There are other groups to whom power has in the past
been delegated—administrators, scientists, and managers: they

[1] *The Life Divine* (Arya Publishing House, Calcutta, 2nd ed. 1944),
vol. ii, Part II, pp. 925–6.

wish to assume completely the powers they have hitherto exercised vicariously. Beyond these groups are the dispossessed who aspire to power. All these forces are active in the world, disrupting the peace of the world because they seize the control of national armed forces, and in the name of a nation, seek to establish the power of a class.

66

In the modern world, the concept of the nation has been so strong that those interests which in reality cross from nation to nation and obliterate their frontiers have not been able to establish their separate identity. Every attempt to unite the workers of the world, the Christians of the world, even the business-men of the world, the bankers and munition-makers, has failed before the barriers of an armed and always irrational ideology of nationalism. This ideology has triumphed over the selfish interests of social groups no less than over the disinterested motives of men of good will.

67

Wars between nations are always 'local' wars, in the sense already defined; but the crisis of which they are the symptoms is universal. The paradox of the present situation is that universal motives determine wars which are then waged locally, between geographical entities. The causes of modern wars are social and economic: but these common causes are dressed up in the military uniforms of various nations, and war is conducted in a confusion as complete as any blind-men's buff.

Some day we may discard our uniforms and then 'the full forces of despair' will come into play. War will then be waged openly, not between groups of nations, but simply between the protagonists of the old order and the new. It may be that in its first stages this war too will be waged with lethal weapons, and then it would be the bitterest and bloodiest of all wars. But perhaps men who have thrown off their national disguises will recognize for the first time in history their common manhood. Already in the last war the deepest emotions were stirred, not by purely military operations, but by the bombing of open towns, by the massacre of women and children, by the enslavement of whole races: in short, by the *social* impact of war. A bond of sympathy, stronger than any bond of nationalism, was forged between the dazed and decimated citizens of Rotterdam and Hull, Cologne and Coventry, Sebastopol and Saint Nazaire. Since then war politicians and experts have tried to plan a new world, but they have not so far succeeded because they have not gathered into a common fund the emotions and aspirations of these bruised and bewildered people.

68

There exists at this moment of history a common experience of mutual aid round which we could build a world community. And if this is at present too vast a conception, then there is a European tradition which has not been altogether obscured by recent history. England has never been separated from this tradition; certainly not in the Middle Ages, not in the Renaissance or the Enlightenment, not in the modern period. From the beginning of the nineteenth century, when the English, German, French, and Russian strands in the Romantic Movement were so inextricably interwoven, down to the modern poetic renaissance which begins with Baudelaire and Rimbaud (French), continues with Apollinaire (a Greek), Yeats (an Irishman), Valéry (French again), Rilke (a German-speaking Czech), Eliot (an Anglo-American), Lorca (a Spaniard), and Pasternak (a Russian), there is no separate cultural strand of any significance. Even French impressionism is unthinkable without Constable and Turner; and more recent trends in modern art are of Spanish inspiration (Picasso, Miró): England, Germany, Italy, France, Norway, Russia, Spain—all the nations of Europe have contributed to a common European culture.

69

Against the unity and integrity of this cultural expansion, nationalist wars are futile anachronisms, filling all reasonable minds with nothing but anger and despair. But the secret and universal war of which I have spoken moves these same minds to partisanship. They realize that a true culture demands, not the petrifaction of dead social forms, but dynamic change: and that the impact of this change must be felt by mankind in its spiritual oneness, rather than in the artificial categories of divided nations. The artist, moreover, has never been inspired by these artificial categories: he feels and expresses the human, social forces of his time, simply because they are real and near to him. The great art of the Classical Age was fostered by civic pride, and not by military power; the great art of the Middle Ages was fostered by small coherent communities, to the glory of a universal God; the great art of the Renaissance was again of civic origin, sometimes created to the glory of God and sometimes in celebration of intellectual virtue: all these arts, in every age, were in lieu of war. War interrupted, and was woven into the fabric of man's creative activity, but always as a broken thread.

70

The common tradition is creative, demanding respect for personal values, the preservation of human life, but continual rivalry in social relations. It was the failure of philosophical historians like Nietzsche and Burckhardt to distinguish between dialectical strife (which is always universal, even when most local) and lethal strife (which is local even when, as in our time, most universal), which led them to accept the inevitability of war. We must now work for a world whose organic articulation will encourage the growth of the dialectical war, but will for ever exclude lethal wars. The energies which are manifested in biological and cultural growth will always have a militant aspect: in the recognition of this inevitable war, which is fought with dialectical weapons, and fought most fiercely when most intimately, rather than in any supposed sublimation of the lethal, local war, lies all hope for the future unity of our civilization.

THE ETHICS OF POWER

71

It will be found that those who defend the exercise of power always assume that power is some sort of abstract energy, equivalent to energy in the physical world. They are therefore willing to delegate the right to exercise power to a particular person or body of persons on the assumption that this is merely an effective way of getting things done, and perhaps the only effective way. My own point of view is very different. I believe that power is not an abstract energy when vested in persons, but a corroding essence; that it always entails more evil than good; and that another method of achieving good does exist and should always be preferred to the use of power.

72

From the ethical point of view the problem of power is fundamental, and has been recognized as such by all the great ethical teachers. I will not dilate on the condemnation of the use of power which we find in early Oriental philosophy—in Lao-tze and Chuang-tzu—and in certain Greek philosophers, because these doctrines are embodied in the gospel of Jesus Christ, which is much nearer to our hearts and understandings. What Jesus said on this subject is not, in my opinion, at all ambiguous. His ethic of power is not only expressed negatively in one of the beatitudes ('Blessed are the meek, for they shall inherit the earth'), but it is most beautifully, and most dramatically, illustrated in a decisive moment during the Temptation in the Wilderness. When the Devil took Christ to the top of a high mountain and showed him 'all the kingdoms of the world and the glory of them' and proposed that He should fall down and worship him, the inspired conscience of Christ resisted that temptation—rejected the use of worldly sovereignty for the attainment of his moral kingdom.

I know that Christians have found it possible to get round this lesson of the Master, and I remember in particular a broadcast given by Reinhold Niebuhr some years ago. Niebuhr, a professor of Christian theology, argued that the organization of power is the basis of order and peace, and I, who do not claim to be either a theologian or a Christian, was profoundly shocked by what seemed to be a betrayal of Christ's essential message. It is not merely that Reinhold Niebuhr, and many of his fellow-Christians, deny the teaching of Christ on this subject: they also fly in the face of all the historical evidence. Order and peace never have been established by power and never will be, for the simple reason that power always corrupts the authority—pope, king, dictator, or parliamentary majority—which exercises it. Lord Acton's dictum has been quoted rather too often of late, usually by people who are not aware of its context. I quote it again, to give it in full, and in its context. Acton was not only a great historian—one of the greatest of modern times—but he was also a very sincere and consistent Christian. The famous sentence occurs in a letter he wrote to Bishop Creighton about the latter's *History of the Papacy*, which Acton had reviewed in a periodical edited by Creighton. Acton had found in Creighton's history what he called 'a spirit of retrospective indulgence and reverence for the operation of authority', and he insisted that historians 'maintain morality as the sole impartial criterion of men and things, and the only one on which honest minds can be made to agree'. In his letter to Creighton, Acton was more explicit. He said, 'I cannot accept your canon that we are to judge Pope and King unlike other men, with a favourable presumption that they did no wrong. If there is any presumption it is the other way, against the holders of power, increasing as the power increases. Historic responsibility has to make up for the want of legal responsibility. Power tends to corrupt, and absolute power corrupts absolutely. Great men are almost always bad men, even when they exercise influence and not authority, still more when you superadd the tendency or the certainty of corruption by authority. There is no worse heresy than that the office sanctifies the holder of it.'

74

If we can accept the evidence of history as established by Acton—and I do not think anyone can question Acton's unrivalled learning and scientific integrity—then power as a means of attaining moral ends stands condemned, without any possibility of doubt or remission. And Acton does not stand alone in his condemnation of power. Some twenty years before Acton wrote the article from which I have quoted, another great historian, Jakob Burckhardt, was giving a course of lectures at Basle entitled 'Introduction to the Study of History', and in one of these lectures he condemned power in words which anticipate Acton's. 'Power', Burckhardt said, 'is of its nature evil, whoever wields it. It is not stability, but a lust, and *ipso facto* insatiable; therefore unhappy in itself and doomed to make others unhappy.'

Burckhardt and Acton do not qualify their statements. They deduce a universal law from the evidence of history: power is evil, power corrupts, always and absolutely. Now a universal law such as this must rest on some inherent human weakness, and I think we can say that the historical evidence is fully supported by the psychological probabilities. The aggressive instinct, the will to assert the self against others, against society, if it is not born in us, is certainly developed in the earliest days of infancy.

75

The frustration of this instinct by social codes of behaviour, by traditional concepts of right and wrong, tends to separate the personality from its loyalty to the family, the clan, the social body. But normally we would be ashamed to confess to such instincts, and so that feeling of separateness is pushed away into the unconscious, only to reappear in times of civil strife or international war when aggressiveness is socially approved. But this aggressive instinct, which is the basis of the will to power, can, if its existence is openly recognized, be transformed. I do not think that any psychologist would claim that it can be exorcised —or should be; but it can be turned into creative instead of destructive channels: it can be deployed against the hostile

forces of nature, to conquer disease or reconstruct our social
environment, in all the arts of peace; it can become the very
essence of mutual love, of charity, of communion. When social
cohesiveness exists, then morality takes on a different form: it is
no longer a brake on aggressive impulses, but a transformed
energy which maintains social integrity.

76

A moral code is not only possible but acceptable so long as we
are members of one another, so long as we have a collective personality, a spiritual cohesion. If we are divided, either into
masters and slaves, or into upper and lower classes, or into
governors and governed, then this collective integrity no longer
exists. There is one law for the rich and another for the poor,
one for the 'haves' and one for the 'have-nots', and the dreary
scene of tyranny or oppression is once more re-enacted in history.
I do not think the position would be altered by giving power to
the scientists—a corrupt scientist is much more dangerous than
a corrupt politician.

77

I have admitted that the will to power is a biological factor.
It is one aspect of the struggle for survival. But there is no
reason at all why this biological factor should be erected into a
moral principle. There is nothing absolute about it; and there is
evidence which points to the existence of another and very different biological factor. This factor allows us to believe that the
social integrity we seek has already made sporadic appearances
within the process of evolution. This factor we call mutual aid.

78

A philosophy of power may be based on what is called political realism—by which is meant the cynical opportunism of
philosophers like Machiavelli or Hobbes. But that is the philosophy of absolutism, of tyranny and totalitarian dictatorship—a
philosophy I need not demolish because no one will be found to
defend it. But there is a subtler philosophy of power, or rather

of 'the will to power', which was developed by Nietzsche, and which claims to be more than opportunism—to be a philosophy with a scientific foundation. But this philosophy is obviously based on a misunderstanding of Darwin, and Darwin himself insisted that his conception of the struggle for existence, of the survival of the fittest, must be taken in what he called a 'large and metaphorical sense, including dependence of one being on another'.

79

In *The Descent of Man* Darwin pointed out how in numberless animal societies the struggle between separate individuals for the means of existence disappears, how struggle is replaced by co-operation, and how that substitution—that replacement of struggle by co-operation—develops intellectual and moral faculties which secure the species the best conditions for survival. But this important aspect of Darwin's theory has been generally neglected, and it was left for Prince Kropotkin to explore the biological, sociological, and ethical implications of this factor in evolution, which he did in his great book *Mutual Aid*, written about fifty years ago. I cannot now summarize the mass of facts which Kropotkin brought forward in support of his thesis—of this phase of biological and social evolution—but his book is strictly scientific; Kropotkin had a thorough scientific training, and he sticks to the facts. But he also draws the obvious conclusions. For example, from the study of the inner life of the medieval city and the ancient Greek cities, he concludes that 'the combination of mutual aid, as it was practised within the guild and the Greek clan, with a large initiative which was left to the individual and the group by means of the federative principle, gave to mankind the two greatest periods in its history— the ancient Greek city and the medieval city periods; while the ruin of these institutions during the state periods of history, which followed, corresponded in both cases to a rapid decay'. But what concerns me more here are the ethical conclusions which he drew from his study of mutual aid: again I will quote from his own words:

'Love, sympathy, and self-sacrifice certainly play an immense part in the progressive development of our moral feelings. But it is not love and not even sympathy upon which Society is based in mankind. It is the conscience—the unconscious recognition of the force that is borrowed by each man from the practice of mutual aid; of the close dependence of every one's happiness upon the happiness of all; and of the sense of justice, or equity, which brings the individual to consider the rights of every other individual as equal to his own. Upon this broad and necessary foundation the still higher moral feelings are developed.'

Many people are ready to admit the truth of these observations of Kropotkin's, and would welcome a society based, not on power but on mutual aid, but they cannot see how it is to be brought about. Power is a present fact: it is an ugly fact, both in international politics and in commerce. We say that trade follows the flag (by which we mean the guns under the flag), and there are all sorts of undesirable elements—not only dictators and agitators, but criminals and gangsters—that must be kept down by the armed forces of the State. We do not approve of power as a moral principle, such people say, but it is necessary as a final sanction for legality.

80

Against this point of view one can only repeat that power corrupts, and that the evil its use entails is always greater than the evil it would repress. Can anyone, surveying the condition of the world today, reasonably maintain that the exercise of power has secured any permanent good, any sense of stability or social ease? Power was ranged against power in the First World War, and a tyranny was destroyed by means of power; but from the battlefields of Europe a thousand new evils sprang from the soil and menaced our peace, until power again was invoked to suppress these evils. Again a tyranny has been eliminated, but again evils have multiplied in the wake of war, and our condition relative to any epoch within the memory of man is now infinitely worse. Power has eliminated this evil or that evil, but it has not reached the evil at the heart of things: it has achieved nothing positive, nothing creative, nothing which contributes to the well-being of mankind. Must we not therefore conclude, in all soberness and humility, that evil is not overcome by power?

Must we not rather turn to that other principle which is embodied in the command: Resist not evil? The doctrine of non-resistance to evil may be hard to understand and difficult to practise, but its effectiveness has been demonstrated again and again in the course of history.

81

The outstanding application of this principle in our time has been the various campaigns conducted by Gandhi in South Africa and India. Leave on one side the political aspects of his campaign for the independence of India: consider only its tactics, and we must then admit that the whole conception of power—imperial power, military power, economic power—has been defeated by a man in a loincloth. preaching a gospel of meekness, of non-resistance.

82

I do not pretend that the alternative to power is easy: it demands immense sacrifice and angelic discipline. But that very sacrifice and discipline will create the ethical atmosphere which excludes the impulse to exercise power. Instead of a multitude of restless individuals, each seeking separately to gain some advantage over his fellows, we become part of something greater than individuality, something wider than a pious sect or an exclusive élite: we become part of one another, in work and in play a co-operative community, in aspiration an indivisible brotherhood.

THE ETHICS OF COMFORT

83

The Samoans, according to Margaret Mead,[1] are that rare cultural phenomenon—a happy, integrated social community. 'The Samoan adult sex adjustment may be said to be one of the

[1] *Male and Female: a Study of the Sexes in a Changing World* (Gollancz, London, 1950).

smoothest in the world. Passion and responsibility are so blended that children are loved and cared for and reared in large stable families that do not rely on some slender tenuous tie between two parents for their only security. The adult personality is stable enough to resist extraordinary pressures from the outside world and keep its serenity and sureness.' But alas! 'the price they pay for their smooth, even, generously gratifying system is the failure to use special gifts, special intelligence, special intensity. There is no place in Samoa for the man or woman capable of a great passion, of complicated aesthetic feeling, of deep religious devotion.' It is true they have a religion—English Congregationalism—but they have gently remoulded some of its sterner tenets. 'Why repent so bitterly', says the Samoan preacher, 'when God is just waiting to forgive you all the time?'

84

Samoa contradicts some of the most cherished notions of the philosopher of history, for it proves that it is perfectly possible to have all the social virtues without the coercion of a supernatural religion. The worst that can be said about the Samoans is that they gossip too much! It cannot be said that they are a decadent race, for they are physically very healthy and have the highest rate of population increase in the world. But they have no complexes, no intense emotions. They produce no saints or heroes, no tortured geniuses, no Kierkegaards and Dostoevskys, no Ibsens and Kafkas!

85

Samoa, it will be said, proves nothing of value to Western civilization—the climate is so different, and it has an unorthodox economy of plenty. We may feel this way about it in Western Europe, faced as we are by the evils which accompany an economy of scarcity. But across the Atlantic there is another civilization, dynamic, expansive, seeking a basis for its civilization, a principle of social unity. Is there any particular reason why it should accept the supernatural authority of the Church—in other words, be coerced into a system of inhibitions and repressions which make for a moral order and a high degree of culture at the cost of personal happiness? The philsopher of history may protest, if he is a Christian, that there is no guarantee of happiness in the application of Samoan techniques to modern industrial communities. But for Samoan techniques the anthropologist substitutes psychoanalytical techniques, and the evidence amassed by the anthropologists in support of the main Freudian hypotheses is indeed impressive. It is enough to convince Margaret Mead 'that increased knowledge can indeed make men free, that one can fashion one's culture closer to the image of all human hearts, however different, without manipulation, without the power that kills, without the loss of innocence that deprives us of spontaneity'. Finally, she believes that 'enough of the American people are committed to the importance of freedom that comes by knowledge and understanding rather than from coercion, fixed authority, or final revelation'. From my own observations of the American people I believe that this is true, and it explains the contempt for culture that is characteristic of the typical American citizen. He would rather be a Samoan than a poet or a mystic, and his choice is based on a knowledge and understanding of the alternatives.

86

I suspect that the valid criticism of this social philosophy is not theological, but teleological. Mankind has not suffered passion and intensity and tragedy for any immediate gain but because such suffering has developed his powers of apprehension and comprehension—his consciousness, in short. Christopher Dawson, whose social philosophy is very different from Margaret Mead's, makes an admission of this kind. 'All the importance of these centuries . . . is not to be found in the external order they created or attempted to create, but in the internal change they brought about in the soul of Western man—a change which can never be entirely undone except by the total negation or destruction of Western man himself.'[1] He is not at all explicit about the nature of this 'internal change'. In earlier books, particularly in *The Age of the Gods*, he has shown how the great stages

[1] *Religion and the Rise of Western Culture* (Sheed & Ward, London, 1950).

of world-culture are linked with changes in man's vision of Reality. These latter changes are the essential steps in human evolution; if they had not occurred we should still be anthropoid apes. According to the Christian religion man has to suffer to gain the kingdom of Heaven; in a similar and very physical sense, man has to suffer to gain extension of sensibility, refinement of consciousness, intelligence itself. It is the same nervous system that suffers deeply and enjoys intensely.

87

To return to the questions with which these notes began: Liberty is one of the *conscious* values of a civilization. It is conceived and cultivated, defined and protected: it can also be abrogated, denied, perverted.

But freedom is the *unconscious* creation of a culture. It cannot be abstracted or defined, it cannot be cultivated and protected. It is a pulse, a living breath of which we are scarcely aware until it ceases. It sinks low when the body is sick or kept in restraint.

88

Freedom and liberty, culture and civilization—such words enable us to distinguish between two categories of being: between growths which are organic, and organizations which are artificial. If from this point of view we look at human society, we can then distinguish certain developments which are biological, determined by human needs for which mutual aid is requisite. The general character of such a social development is perhaps best indicated by the word *community*.

But distinct from such social developments are those segregations of human beings into classes determined, not by biological needs, but by political necessity. These classes are economic or military, and their aim is to create areas of absolute power. To these areas we give the name *nation*, or, more concretely, the *state*.

If we bear in mind these distinctions—
    between *freedom* and *liberty*
    between *culture* and *civilization*
    between *community* and *state*

distinctions which are all related to a fundamental distinction between *biological growth* and *intellectual organization*—we shall then be in a better position to discuss the claim we make for the autonomy of art, for the freedom of the artist.

89

Art, in its inmost nature, is biological. It is an expression of spontaneous instincts, and though it may be elaborated in a secondary manner by the intellect, its vitality depends on its freedom to contribute to the evolutionary processes of life itself.

When we speak of the autonomy of art, we do not mean a state of independence, a condition of isolation. We mean the freedom to function organically—we mean exactly the same kind of condition that is implied in phrases like 'the freedom of the limbs', 'the freedom to breathe'. We mean the freedom to perform an organic function within the complex body of a biologically determined community.

Such freedom implies *responsibility*, but not *obligation*. It implies *integration*, but not *subjugation*.

90

Enough of these logical and etymological distinctions. But our confusions, our quarrels, our wars, arise from an incapacity to see logical distinctions of this nature, and that incapacity is not confined to one side of the Iron Curtain. The calculated stupidity of the authoritarian treatment of the artist is only matched by the inept callousness of the democratic treatment of the artist.

91

Democrats agree about the stupidity of the authoritarian 'attempt to transform art into an instrument of state power and to regiment the artist'—I quote a typical formulation of the charge. It would be merely preaching to the converted to discuss that aspect of the question. To those people and states who persist in the regimentation of the artist we need address only one question: *where, then, is your art?*

But let us turn to the beam in our own eyes. Where, after all, is *our* art? Picasso, do you say? Braque, Corbusier, Kokoschka, Moore, Gropius—you can take a dozen or a hundred names and mix them in a salad-bowl with oil and vinegar and then do you think you have a culture? A culture is not expressed in the isolated achievements of a few individuals. A culture is a unity of expression, visible in the tilth of a landscape or the plan of a city, in rituals and ceremonies, in manners and monuments, in colour and in joy. A culture of that kind, with its attendant arts, does not exist anywhere in the world today. Culturally we are dispossessed, or live on the loot of the past. We stagger blindly into a new age of darkness, of vulgar oblivion, of mere utility and ugliness.

92

The decline began long ago, with the growth of capitalism. I concede to the Marxists everything they have to say about the decline of culture under capitalism. To the relationship which the capitalist established with the artist we give the name *patronage*. We now, in our democratic innocence, think we can save art by substituting for *private* patronage *State* patronage. It is an ignorant deception. Apart from the fact that the cold monster of the State can never replace the human contact of the person, it is patronage itself which is wrong—socially wrong, psychologically wrong, morally wrong. We do not safeguard 'the autonomy of the creative imagination' by submitting it to the dictation of an individual patron—and still less by submitting it to the deliberations of a committee. In that way we may save from despair an individual artist, but, as I cannot too often repeat, a culture is not a collection of individual artists. A culture is an organic growth.

93

For the relationship of patronage there must be substituted, by natural growth within the body of the community, a relationship of *incorporation*. The artist must become once more a limb of the communal body. Only in that condition can the artist be nourished by the blood of the community, and live to express its spirit.

94

I do not believe that we can solve this problem directly, by piecemeal action. We cannot create a culture by taking thought about culture. Culture is the spontaneous expression of an integrated community. If I am asked what kind of community is an integrated community, I can only reply that I cannot point to the existence of one anywhere in the world today, for the world is shared between two unintegrated civilizations. Nor do I see much hope of the emergence of such a community, unless it is in Palestine! It is perhaps significant that the integrated communities of the past—Athens, Etruria, the Christian communities of the Middle Ages, Venice in its republican glory—it is perhaps significant that such communities were never large. They were small and democratic, and if sometimes they were careless of civil liberties, they always respected the integrity of the craftsman, and gave him a functional position within the body of the community. They did not patronize their artists— they were not even conscious of the artist as a separate and peculiarly dependent kind of man. They were only conscious of a living community, its members differentiated according to their individual skills, and all contributing to the common glory.

THE DERELICTION OF THE ARTIST

95

In the modern world two distinct views prevail as to the role of the artist in society. One, the Marxist view, is definite and often clearly expressed. The artist is the exponent of the ideology of his time, and in an emergent society, such as the socialist society which is coming into being in Russia, he has the immediate duty of helping to establish the new order: he is a propagandist, and even if his work is of a practical kind, such as that of an architect, it is still his duty to express in his creative activity the ideals which inspire his political leaders and which consolidate the people as a political unit.

The other prevailing view is by no means so precise in its formulation. It makes use of such words as 'freedom' and 'liberty' and it can show, by an appeal to the history of art, that the springs of art are so subtle and imponderable that any conscious interference with their operation is likely to result in frustration and sterility. Even state patronage, which democracies are urged to practise in default of an extinct private patronage, does not seem to inspire any vital movement in the arts, and when directed officially it results in a lifeless academicism.

Such futile attempts at patronage apart, the democratic attitude to the arts is *laissez-faire*. It recognizes the artist as a useful member of the community (since it encourages the profession by the establishment and maintenance of art schools) but it does not venture to define the role of art in society, nor does it exercise any direct control of the artist's activity—indeed, it makes a virtue of this neglect by much talk about the freedom of the artist. That freedom is in effect a dereliction, however. As a consequence of the economic developments of the past two centuries, and equally as a consequence of intellectual developments which can be traced much farther back in history, the artist has been gradually excluded from the normal life of the community, in particular from the prevailing system of production.

96

It is not necessary to idealize ancient Greece or the Middle Ages—the artist in those epochs shared a common fate which was often no better than a slave's, but it was a *common* fate: no distinction was made, either in the quality of the talent involved or in the recognition due to their respective achievements, be tween the artist and the artisan, or any other citizen engaged in a productive activity involving the making of things. There were different kinds of craftsmen, and different skills appropriate to each craft. Degrees of skill were recognized and rewarded, and in this sense there was a distinction between Praxiteles and a stonemason, between Matthew Paris and any competent illuminator. There were hierarchies in every walk of life, but no walks were marked 'private' or 'professional': there was a free circulation of producers, and the interweaving of their activities made for an integrated structure of society.

The Marxists are surely right in connecting the break-up of this structure with the growth of capitalism—capitalism is the economic word: the philosophic word is individualism. It was not merely that the new merchant classes, secure in their possession of a private fortune, wished to give substance to their status by personal commissions to the artist; the artist himself wished to become an independent merchant, selling his wares in an open market, free from the humiliations of ecclesiastical patronage. The change in attitude, the encouragement of acquisitive and possessive instincts, was quite general, and one must not treat the artist in any unique sense as the victim of capitalism. He was merely one of the first to succumb to the nascent ideology of profit.

But he was also one of the first to suffer from the effects of industrialization and mass production to which the development of finance capitalism inevitably led. Of all productive processes, art is the only one which cannot admit the subdivision of labour. It is true that the labour involved in a practical art like architecture can be subdivided, and always was to some extent subdivided; but it has always been recognized that the great building is one which most clearly expresses a personal vision, controlling all particular elements. It is also true that some of the great masters in painting, such as Rubens, delegated some of their work to assistants, but again with doubtful results (now the preoccupation of modern critics). Aesthetic values, the values which constitute the very nature of art, are values determined by individual sensibility, and no factory could have produced the plays of Shakespeare or the paintings of Rembrandt. That is obvious enough, but the fact is often ignored in Marxist doctrine.

So long as the artist could support himself as a capitalist (drastically 'limited') in a society of profiteers, an individualist art could flourish. It has been a great art—the achievements in sculpture, painting, and architecture since the Renaissance cannot be dismissed by labelling them 'capitalist'. But it is absurd to assume that there is any inevitable connection between art and capitalism. Art is an absolute, and absolutely independent, activity of the human spirit, and what it seeks is not any extraneous support, from capital or from the State, but merely a

224

climate in which it can flourish. This 'climate' is always communal—to that extent the Marxists are fundamentally right. A climate is all-environing, pervasive, and generally invisible. The people who live in it are adapted to it and only notice its extreme vagaries.

A social climate is an emanation of mutuality: it exists when a people live in a circumscribed geographical space, rooted in the given soil, engaged in a common enterprise, which is the creation of a 'life', a good system of living. The social climate in such a society is temperate and productive when all the units, inspired by a common purpose, practise mutual aid. I am not speaking of mutual aid in any idealistic sense—rather in the biological sense. Mutual aid existed in feudal society; it existed in fifteenth-century Florence and even in seventeenth-century Holland. It existed in these imperfect communities because there was an integration of social purpose, and though the rewards might be outrageously unjust, and though there was too much scope for personal tyranny, nevertheless the artist *belonged*. He might starve, he might be misunderstood and neglected; but then he felt merely unfortunate. The modern artist, on the other hand, has no 'fortune' to lose, for he has no share in the commonwealth. He is an outcast, a rustic implement for which modern society has no further use.

97

In his dereliction the artist in a democratic State may try to woo the people, though the people no longer belong to him or he to them. If he is a Marxist (and many artists, seduced by the apparent reintegration of art in the U.S.S.R., have adopted the Marxist ideology, without any real understanding of its theoretical basis), then as an artist he will attempt to paint for a popular audience, not realizing that the populace in a modern industrial state is spiritless and vulgar, and quite indifferent to art. He will try to arouse their interest by painting violent scenes of revolution or of the resistance movement, portraits of revolutionary heroes or records of contemporary events. In doing so he debases himself twofold: firstly, he is setting out from the concept or idea and then attempts to illustrate or symbolize it, whereas true art always sets out from the immediate concrete vision and the concept must be read into that vision by the spectator. Secondly, he is acting with more or less conscious hypocrisy, for only in rare instances does the modern artist share the feeling of his proletarian audience: he paints not as he himself feels, but rather to capture what he supposes to be the feelings of his 'comrades' (political allies with whom he does not associate socially, for there is no common language: they speak the language and have the habits of an industrialized proletariat: he still speaks the language and has the habits of a pre-industrial humanist).

There is no escape from this dilemma because the proletariat is the product of a system of mass production (intensified in the so-called communist countries) which has no use for the artist: there is no place for the artist at the conveyor belt. The attempt of certain artists to adapt themselves to the modern industrial system by calling themselves 'design consultants' has had no appreciable effect on the cultural situation—the intervention of such 'fancy boys' in industry is violently resented by the general mass of skilled labourers and technicians.

There is no place for the artist in a modern industrial society— he can only continue to exist in such a society as a parasitic dilettante, or a propagandist. In neither case is he 'integrated'. As a dilettante he may still (if he can manage to support himself economically—and it is in that sense that he is bound to be parasitic) give expression to a private vision, to a subjective poetry (which is what the art of a Picasso or a Klee essentially is); and this private vision may penetrate to some level of the collective unconscious. Picasso's public is wider than the few patrons who can afford to buy his pictures: he is a 'man of our time', and has a certain representative value, if only as a scapegoat for our collective guilt. But he remains outside society, a voice from the waste land, an apocalyptic voice, prophesying doom rather than announcing any brave new world.

The modern artist will remain this derelict outcast just so long as the artist is excluded from direct participation in the processes of economic production. He cannot be introduced into those processes by any conscious act of statesmanship or planning—for the simple reason that there can be no reconciliation of human sensibility and mass production. All attempts by authoritarian régimes to find a place for the artist in the modern industrial system have only turned the artist into a kind of clown, a jester whose role is to amuse the industrial worker in his off time (decorate his canteen, etc.) or keep his mind off disturbing problems—art as a soothing syrup for exasperated Stakhanovites. All the attempts of the State to find a place for the artist—and it makes no difference whether it is the communist State in Russia, the fascist State in Germany or Italy, or the New Deal State in the U.S.A.—have merely created a type of lifeless academicism which has no relevance to the desires and aspirations of the people at large; Hollywood has a better idea of what people really want.

98

This is a pessimistic conclusion, no doubt. It is more than that —it is a tragic conclusion, for the modern artist is worthy of a better fate. On his individualistic level he has shown more evidence of sensibility and creative potentiality than any generation of artists since the Middle Ages. His technical accomplishments and his consciousness of the tasks of art, not to mention his understanding of his own creative processes, are far in advance of any previous epoch. His art will survive as an index to the potentialities of art if for no other reason. The modern artist has an acuteness of perception and a sensibility for form perfected by a century of intense professional experiment. We might claim that he has all the necessary equipment for a new and a greater Renaissance. But 'Uns trägt kein Volk' as Klee said at the conclusion of his great statement of the modern artist's position[1]—*we lack a people!* We are not part of a people, we do not feel at home in the modern world, and it is not our fault. Forces beyond our control have created an immense artless machine, driven by inhuman forces, and in this system there is no place for my sensibility, my creative vision. That is how the modern artist feels about his role in modern society, and to say that it is not the modern artist who feels like this, but only the

[1] *Über die moderne Kunst.* A lecture delivered in Jena, 1924. English trans. by Paul Findlay (Faber, London, 1948).

bourgeois artist, is to ignore the uncreativity of any other kind of contemporary artist.

It is no use calling on the artist to reform himself; art is not a conscious creation of an élite: it cannot be deliberately determined either by academic teaching or by the cultural decrees of politicians. It is the by-product of a complex tradition, into which enter not only the technical 'mysteries' of a craft, but the organized interplay of all crafts, of all forces that promote the growth of a vital community. To expect a popular art to flourish in modern society is to expect steel to bud with roses. There will be no integral style such as prevailed in all civilizations down to the eighteenth century until we advance beyond mechanization, to rediscover the secret of organic living.

The modern artist in his dereliction, his isolation from the economic errors of our time, is, by maintaining his attitude of resentful independence, a tragic survivor from one mode of organic living. He is the only active survivor from the wreck of the humanist tradition; he is by the same token the pioneer of a new humanist tradition.

99

A final quotation—from Gustave Thibon again:

'. . . there is no worse social misdeed than forcing the masses to holiness.

'Placed as we are at the very core of a failure of moral habit such as has never before been known in history, it behoves the thinker to beware more than ever of ideal constructions and universal systems and the intoxication of words and "pipe-dreams". Moral erethism has been cultivated quite long enough: what we need above all now is a propelling, a *motive* morality. After our too numerous, too protracted and sterile intellectual and affective debauches, it is time to teach people to put the ideal they bear in their spirit, and the feeling they bear in their hearts, into their hands and fingers. It is a matter of *incarnating* the human truth humbly and patiently; giving the human truth a body and reality in the life of each and all. The noblest of ideals attains to meaning only in proportion as it gives birth to this simple, lowly, flesh and blood effort. The deepest elementary bases of human nature have been shaken: man has to be rebuilt from the ground up. Nor is it enough to preach to everybody and nobody from the top of the tottering edifice: we must *get down* and repair the threatened foundations stone by stone.' (Op. cit., pp. 134–5.)

100

And, as a twisted tailpiece to these scattered notes, a sentence from a very different source—the Journals of Caesar as imagined by Thornton Wilder:

'At the closer range we say *good* and *evil*, but what the world profits by is intensity.'

INDEX

231